SOLVING IMPØSSIBLE PROBLEMS

Working through Tensions and Paradox in Business

Joe Cheal

GWiz
Publishing

Published in England
by GWiz Publishing
(A division of The GWiz Learning Partnership)
41a Bedford Road, Moggerhanger. Beds. MK44 3RQ
Tel (+44) 1767 640956

info@gwiztraining.com

www.gwiztraining.com

First published 2012.
10 9 8 7 6 5 4 3 2 1

Cover illustration by Rob Banbury
'Pair a Dogs: The Double Bind' © 2007

ISBN: 978-0-9548800-1-9

Contents

Acknowledgements

I'd like to thank the following people for their help and support along the way:

Melody Cheal... For the space and time you graciously gave me for writing this book.

Sam Attenborough... For the elegant feedback you gave me along the way... I am blessed to have found in you a perfectionist with a heart!

Julie Hay... For the wisdom you have shared with me.

JC 2012

Foreword

Welcome to Solving Impossible Problems and thank you for joining me on a journey into the dark, absurd and yet sometimes amusing world of organisational tensions and paradox.

Within this book you will discover my fascination with the bizarre and paradoxical. It seems to me that perfectly reasonable people can get together and with all good intention create absolute chaos. Other people can get together and create something extraordinary and innovative.

I am truly curious about 'impossible problems' and although not always pleasant to experience first hand it is nice to know that there are ways of resolving these problems and making change happen.

When I was about sixteen I read a book called 'Gödel Escher Bach: The Eternal Golden Braid' by Douglas Hofstater. It was a challenging book that rewarded me with talk of 'strange loops' and paradox. Motivated (in part by this love of the inexplicable), I went on to do a degree in Philosophy and Psychology. Although much of those three years escapes me now, I particularly enjoyed the metaphysics section…

> Bertrand Russell entertained me with story of a clean shaven man who was the only barber in the town he lived in. He shaved all the men in the town who didn't shave themselves. Nothing extraordinary here… or is there? Who shaved the barber? No-one else could shave him as *he* shaved all the men who didn't shave themselves. But he couldn't shave himself because if he did, he couldn't have shaved himself. Oh dear!

And the language and logic sections…

> A man tells us: "Don't listen to me, I always lie." If this is a lie, it must be true, but if it is true, it must be a lie… ad infinitum.

The strange and ambiguous is all around us. How about the road sign that says: "Sign not in use"?

The path I have walked career-wise has been in 'learning and organisational development'. Since 1993 I have heard about and seen hundreds and thousands of 'impossible problems' that wouldn't go away. People have found themselves in situations where there seemed to be no answer. All possible solutions were met with the response: "Yes, but…" or "the problem with that is…" or "the difficulty there is…" or "the trouble with that is…" There were dilemmas that went back and forth, situations that went round in circles and issues that came back again and again.

My fascination with paradox as a student had been in what it does to the brain (i.e. creates a sense of confusion) and here I was seeing and hearing about the very same phenomenon (i.e. confusion) in everyday working life. So I began to wonder if these workplace situations were real world paradoxes.

People talk about trying to 'get their head around' a problem but this is challenging with the slippery twisty nature of paradox. As soon as you get your head 'around' a problem driven by paradox, it seems to slide off to one side and remain incomprehensible.

Any problem that seems to have no solution is a challenge to me, both intellectually and emotionally. I want to find a rational answer and I want people to get on with each other! I want to help make people's lives easier. Although this is perhaps not *always* possible, it is very satisfying when it all comes together. I am delighted when, with a little help, someone goes away with a workable solution that they and their colleagues can feel pleased about.

A few years ago I embarked on the adventure of an MSc in Organisational Development and Neuro-Linguistic Technologies and I had the opportunity to research the nature of paradox in organisations. Here was a culmination and synthesis of my love of the absurd, of philosophy and psychology and of the consultancy I had done over the previous fifteen years.

The MSc research led me on a massive reading spree, from books to journal articles... anything that was paradox and business related. From that literature, I have discovered a range of models, tools and techniques that you will find in this book and I have referenced them wherever I can. Having then run a series of Paradox and Tension Management workshops, I then developed a set of new models and tools which you will also find here.

Wherever your path takes you, enjoy the journey. I hope one day that our paths will cross.

Preface

According to some, the nature of genius is being able to take two conflicting positions and hold both as true at the same time. Others suggest that genius is being able to synthesise the two conflicting positions to develop something new.

Paradox management allows you to see the real issue, to see both sides of the equation and handle the *whole thing* rather than just one side or the other. Impossible problems are often a 'mess of paradoxes' where there are, for example, vicious circles within dilemmas that create their own contradictions and no-win situations. Herein you will find methods for recognising, mapping and resolving these multi-layered problems. The main aim of this book is to provide a methodology than can be applied to *any* paradox with a view to moving through it.

Solving Impossible Problems draws from a range of interconnected business disciplines including management and leadership theory, organisational development and change management. These business disciplines interweave with influences from social psychology, neuro-linguistic programming and transactional analysis. You will also find traces of philosophy thrown in for good measure.

Here you will find a book written for managers, management theorists, students, business owners, consultants and OD, HR & L&D practitioners. My goal for you is that in reading this book you will probably, like Charles Handy, see paradoxes everywhere. You will begin to see and feel the movement/dynamics of paradox as people describe situations to you. You will be able to map out the process of the problem and the layers/levels. And then you will see a 'mess of paradoxes' becoming a manageable 'shape'.

For those who wish to explore further, I have referenced other literature and where material has come from. This will be useful for my fellow researchers. To balance this, wherever possible I have given real world examples to demonstrate the concepts, models and tools.

Solving Impossible Problems is 'game of two halves': identifying the problem and then resolving the problem. These halves in turn, break down as follows:

Chs. 1 – 4   Understanding organisational paradox
Chs. 5 – 6   Deeper understanding
Chs. 7 – 12   Approaches to solving and resolving
Chs. 13 – 14   Applications for handling uncertainty and conflict

The Route Planner

Sometimes it is useful to have an overview of where you are going. This book is, in effect, a process... a set of steps with information designed to deepen your understanding and appreciation of the process you are using.

Here is an overview of the process of managing paradox with the associated chapter numbers:

Process	Chapter
Understanding the nature of polarity, tensions and paradox	
• Recognising the dynamics and types of paradox	1 & 2
• Mapping the problem	2

Introduction

What are Impossible Problems?

Impossible problems are those that cannot apparently be resolved. They can appear logically inconsistent, circular, elusive, complex or ambiguous. They may split a group, creating conflicting positions or no-win scenarios where people feel that they will lose out no matter what they do. Perhaps the solutions to a problem are unacceptable or unworkable. More than likely, the problem or solution seems outside the control of those affected.

We might say that problems are impossible when:
- They take us round in circles or cause further splits and divides
- The consequences of the solution are worse than the problem itself
- We don't understand them
- They seem to be outside of our control
- We don't know what we want instead of the problem
- We find the solution(s) unacceptable

When described in an organisational context, 'impossible problems' may bring up phrases like:

❑ Ambiguity
❑ Blame
❑ Competing demands
❑ Conflicting priorities
❑ Contradictory communication
❑ Damned if I do, damned if I don't
❑ Dichotomies
❑ Dilemmas

- ❑ Entrenched positions
- ❑ Groupthink
- ❑ Indecision
- ❑ Interpersonal conflicts
- ❑ Mixed messages
- ❑ Polarised thinking
- ❑ Procrastination
- ❑ Silo mentality
- ❑ Tensions
- ❑ Vicious circles/cycles

Obviously, there are many other phrases that might indicate that there is an 'impossible problem' and some of these are discussed later in Chapter 3.

Researching Impossible Problems: The 'Paradox Study'

Having seen, heard and experienced about twenty years worth of impossible problems and organisational paradox, it seemed an excellent time to take the opportunity to study 'impossible problems' more formally. This book is, in part, a result of my MSc dissertation and I have referred to the research within these pages as the 'Paradox Study'.

After a fascinating journey though the literature about paradox, tensions, dilemmas and polarities within business, I carried out a series of in depth interviews with senior managers and first line managers from the public sector, the charity sector and the private sector. Each person was shown the following words on a sheet and asked if they had experienced any of the items mentioned (and if so, which ones). Without exception, each manager was able to describe at least one 'impossible problem' that they faced in the position they held in their organisation.

Ambiguity	Groupthink
Blame	Indecision
Competing demands	Interpersonal conflicts
Conflicting priorities	Mixed messages
Contradictory communication	Polarised thinking
Damned if I do, damned if I don't	Procrastination
Dilemmas	Tensions
Entrenched positions	Vicious circles/cycles

The examples given in the interviews led to some rich data about more than seventy different 'impossible problems' (which I suspect is just the tiniest tip of the iceberg). One of the most striking things about these problems was that they all appeared to loop back on themselves in some way, sometimes flipping back and forth and sometimes taking the person round in circles. Here are three example scenarios:

Case 1: To act or not to act?
A senior manager (who himself had had no direct manager for over a year) was having to act and make decisions beyond his level of responsibility. There was no-one else in the hierarchy who understood his specialist area. He felt that if he took action and things were to go wrong, his neck would be on the line. However, if he took no action, people would say "you should have done something". Either way, he felt he couldn't win.

Case 2: Input from those with low knowledge levels
In a risk-averse organisation, a frustrated senior manager had group members inputting into his proposals when they had no personal expertise in the area. Because they didn't (and couldn't) understand the proposals, they could not reach consensus and so the conclusion was continually "go back and have another look at it". Democracy was leading to paralysis.

Case 3: The Can of Worms

In an organisational culture of 'shoot the messenger', issues existed but were buried. This defensive behaviour happened at nearly all levels of the organisation. At some point in the future, issues would inevitably become apparent and would probably not surface at a good time. Potentially, they would create more serious problems later. When a junior auditing manager became aware of these issues, she was caught in a psychological trap. If she opened up the 'can of worms' there would be an immediate amount of extra investigative work and a degree of stress. The 'can owner' thought the junior manager was interfering and undermining their authority. However, if she did not open the can, she was not doing her job properly. Whilst she was not directly affected by the issue, the junior manager was aware of the hidden issues and 'time-bombs' that could go off later costing the organisation dearly and causing the can owner to lose their job. The junior manager was either a 'grass' or an 'accomplice' and there was no reward for either.

Exploring Impossible Problems

If you consider a problem that has yet to be resolved (perhaps a personal, interpersonal or organisational issue), in all probability, if it appears unresolvable, it will have some kind of tension in or underneath it that prevents it from being resolved. This tension may be in the form of, for example: conflict, contradiction, opposing positions or dilemma. The point is that as soon as a potential way forward is found, another part of the problem negates this way forward and sucks those involved back into the problem again. Often, in discussion, this comes with the words: "yes, but…"

As soon as we think we have emerged from the murky pool of the impossible, unresolvable problem, we are pulled back under the surface to start the process again. The link between paradox and 'unresolvability' gives us a useful working principle that:

an unresolvable problem will be driven and perpetuated
by at least one paradoxical tension.

This principle helps us to work through an impossible problem by giving us new levels to explore and hence an opportunity for new and innovative solutions. When a problem won't be solved on the surface level, we need tools to understand and manage what lies beneath.

As Albert Einstein is often quoted as saying: "A problem will not be solved by the same kind of thinking that created it in the first place." Within the following chapters, you will find a guide to thinking... and to thinking differently.

Chapter 1

Organisational Paradox

In This Chapter...

In this chapter, you will be introduced to the nature of paradoxical problems, what keeps them going and why dealing with the underlying paradox and tensions is so important. By understanding how paradox works you will begin to see organisational problems in a different light.

We will be exploring the following questions:

- What is paradox?
- Is paradox always negative?
- Can paradox be managed?
- What happens if you hold a paradox open?
- Why understand and manage paradox?

What is Paradox?

Having spoken to many people about paradoxes in business there seems to be a mixed reaction to the word 'paradox'. Some people are immediately fascinated by the idea whilst others seem to switch off. Perhaps the term 'paradox' is a tough concept to start with. For some it seems to conjure up unknown territory, the realm of philosophy and impractical abstract thinking. Some have confessed that they don't really know what paradox is and this is hardly surprising. The definition of paradox is varied and seems rather tricky to grasp. According to Buenger & Daft (1988, p197): "paradox is a slippery concept".

There is stark disagreement in terms and definitions of paradox, ranging from the simple: "an apparent contradiction" (Quinn and Cameron, 1988, p290) to a more hard-line approach where paradox necessarily contains self reference, contradiction and vicious circularity (Hughes and Brecht, 1978). This hard-line approach is known as a 'logical paradox', for example: "This statement is untrue". This, as a statement, is self referential, contradictory and goes round in circles because if it is true, it is false, which means it is true etc. Poole & Van de Ven (1989, p564-5) suggest that "the paradoxes in management are not, strictly speaking, logical paradoxes... Organisational and management theories involve a special type of paradox – social paradoxes" which "tend to be looser: the opposing terms are often somewhat vague, and instead of logical contradictions, tensions and oppositions between incompatible positions must be considered... This opens the possibility of dealing with social paradoxes not only through logical resolutions, but through taking into account the spatial and temporal nature of the social world."

To establish a definition of paradox that can be used within an organisational context, a key component appears to be 'contradiction'. Smith & Berg (1987, p85) add that for "paradox to occur, the contradictions must be linked to each other. It is the connection between two statements, emotions, or reactions that creates the condition of contradiction".

It seems that the defining points of a paradox (particularly a 'social paradox' which is looser than a 'logical paradox') are:
1. A contradiction between two (or more) things,
2. These things are interconnected in some way (often polar opposites),
3. Each of these things are valid, feasible and defendable when viewed on their own,

4. Collectively, they create two or more opposing things that can all be true
5. The problem here is that it would seem logically impossible for something and its opposite to be true at the same time... it has to be one or the other
6. This 'logical impossibility' means that we switch back and forth between one of the two (or more) things, or go round in circles.

To simplify matters, for our purpose here, we might say that paradox is:

a contradiction between interconnected positions or concepts that still holds true.

In an organisational sense, paradox appears to have a number of stages:

1) It begins with a polarity between two things... sometimes expressed as an 'either/or':

2) It continues with the tension(s) that the polarity creates. This acts like an energy, a sparking between the poles:

3) There is then a dynamic movement that occurs when we try to solve it which invariably brings us back to a starting point.

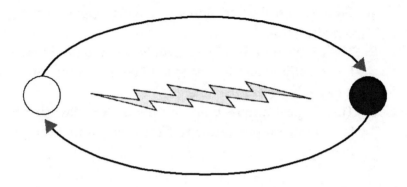

This could be summed up:

Polarity⟶ Tension⟶ Dynamic Movement = Paradox

A metaphor for the polarity/tension/paradox dynamic would be a magnet. The two ends (north and south pole) are the equivalent of the polarity and there is a tension that plays out between them, a game of repulsion and attraction. If we look at the electromagnetic movement between these poles, we see the circular motion.

Three Forms of Paradox

In order to clarify what we are dealing with in this book, paradox could be sorted into three categories:

1) Linguistic
2) Internal
3) Social

1) Linguistic Paradox

Linguistic paradox is the logical paradox, the 'plaything of the philosophers'. It is based around the problems in language where something refers to or describes itself. A sign that says: "Do not read this" would be paradoxical and so is the sign on the motorway that reads: "This sign is not in use". On the subject of such things, how about a sign attached to some railings that reads: "All signs attached to these railings will be removed". It is not just signs that exhibit paradox; a local authority produced an information leaflet that had a 'helpful' piece of information on the back: "If you cannot read this leaflet, please enquire about the audio version."

Hughes and Brecht's (1978) 'tight' or purist definition (above) would apply to the linguistic paradox. In an organisational sense, this form of paradox is usually less of an issue. It might occur here and there in the odd sign, brochure or mission statement but it is usually picked up and seen as a bit of nonsense.

Linguistic paradox might also occur as a tautology where something is defined by referring to itself. For example: "delegating means delegating a task" or "empowerment means empowering people". This is sometimes used when a person is not really able to define what something is. A broader form of a tautology is the 'circular argument', also known as 'bootstrapping' (trying to pull yourself up by your own bootstraps). For example, a manager tells a member of staff that policy says that X is the right way to do things. The member of staff asks: "How do you know it is the right way?" The manager replies "Because the policy says so". Another example might be: "This organisation does not tolerate bullying". When an issue of bullying is raised and not dealt with, the response from the organisation is: "This is not bullying".

Paradox can also appear in policies, procedures, processes and plans particularly when a step (or series of steps) loops back on itself. An example in a procedure might be some guidelines that read: "1) Do 'A', 2) Do 'B', 3) Do 'C', 4) Follow guidelines". This can also be a problem in computer programming where a command tries to reference something that doesn't yet exist or it goes into a recursive loop that will keep running ad infinitum. Again, these are issues that are usually picked up and changed or ignored.

11

2) *Internal Paradox*

An internal paradox will often present itself as a dilemma, for example, should I go for that job or stay where I am? Should I speak up and say something or keep my head down? Should I go for house 'a' or house 'b'?

When expressing dilemmas, people often talk in terms of 'parts'. For example, "part of me wants to exercise but part of me wants to watch television". Paradox occurs when there is a 'parts conflict'. One part says one thing, but another part says another. In addition, we might say we have mixed feelings about something.

In most organisational situations, an external paradox will lead to an internal paradox. We will see later on how people often feel internally conflicted when they are in a paradox. We will also explore how paradox can be perceived at an individual *and* system level.

3) *Social Paradox*

Poole and van de Ven (1989) introduced the notion of 'social paradox' as a broader, looser way of exploring what happens when people get together in a system. Sometimes it is the system itself which causes the problems by blocking productivity or creating additional barriers that people then have to deal with. At other times it is the people *in* the system that create the problems by being inconsistent or antagonistic. Organisations tend to be full of these social paradoxes, particularly conflicts between individuals, teams and departments.

Because of its ironic nature, social paradox is sometimes seen a source of humour and hence humour and irony is often a sign of social paradox. We seem to find nonsensical and/or awkward situations funny. If you read any Dilbert cartoons by Scott Adams, you will see paradoxical problems played out time and again (I would recommend the Dilbert Principle 1996). According to Rhodes (2002), the Simpsons (TV show) is also an example of showing paradox in organisations through humour. Hatch & Ehrlich (1993, p518) suggest that "what makes humour funny is the juxtaposition of incongruities and the recognition of contradiction and incoherence... [and these] can be recovered from discourse involving humour, and when submitted to an interpretive reading are capable of revealing the usually hidden paradoxes and ambiguities of organisational life."

Examples of 'Social Paradox' in Organisations
In terms of interdepartmental struggles, there is often a tension between the sales department and the engineering/production departments. Sales want new things to sell and will often sell prototypical ideas to get ahead of the rest of the field. Production haven't actually developed or produced it yet! In order to get the work, sales will sometimes 'over promise' on deadlines, prices, quantities and/or specifications. Production then go mad trying to sort out the delivery and are then in turn hampered by Quality Control who have a backlog of things they need to test and trial properly.

Some organisations have businesses within the business. A retail company I worked with was in competition with itself on the high street. It had three brands and people could go from one shop to the other haggling best price. Internally, people from one brand were not allowed to talk to people in the other brand. Needless to say, one of the brands was eventually closed down and merged into one of the other brands because it was losing money.

Another organisation had two directors who disliked each other. Each director wanted their own HR (Human Resources) department neither of which was allowed to talk to the other. In the sense that teams and organisations will often become a reflection of the leadership, I wondered what the Group CEO (level above the

---

directors) must have been like to put up with such a schism. It turned out that the Group CEO was seen as a little schizoid himself.

What about the consultant that is called in to 'solve' the impossible problems? Who are they called in by? Usually, consultants will only be able to solve problems below the level they were called in at because initially they will only have as much power as the person who called them in. If they are blocked from going further and the levels above are not supportive (or are not aware of the 'intervention') then the consultant can only work with a part of the system. If the rest of the system resists, any change is likely to fail organisationally and at best succeed in just a small area. The lower in the hierarchy the consultant is brought in, the more restricted they are. This is also true of course for interim managers, called in to rescue a sinking ship where the directors are busy scuttling from the control room. Bailing water ceases to become much fun after a while.

As well as conflict, there are management dichotomies. In order to motivate staff, should we reward at the level of individual or at the level of team? If we use individual reward, we get competitiveness within the team and hence less co-operation and 'team work'. If we reward at a team level then we get some people not 'pulling their weight' (known in sports psychology terms as 'social loafing') and so there is a perceived lack of fairness.

Some people see a contradiction between 'equality' and 'diversity': "So we have to treat everyone the same whilst at the same time treating them differently?"

It is perhaps the puzzling nature of 'logical paradox' that causes people to shy away from understanding paradoxical problems. However, the idea of 'social paradox' frees us up from philosophical constraints and allows us to recognise the absurdities that occur in human interactions and organisations. The nature of social paradox (and its relationship with 'internal paradox') is the focus point for this book. Here we will explore and look at tools to resolve tensions, polarities, contradictions and management dilemmas.

Is Paradox Always Negative?

Most of the examples cited so far have been rather negative. The reason perhaps is that we are looking at 'impossible problems' and problems by definition are generally unwanted and therefore negative. Consultants are rarely called in because things are wonderful!

However, paradoxes can be considered positive, neutral or negative depending on the perception of the person viewing it and/or on the effect that it has on the system or the individuals within the system. In this way, paradox is analogous to 'stress'. Stress itself could be considered neutral; indeed without stress we would be in a coma or suspended animation. The negative of stress is where it goes out of balance and becomes 'distress' (which is where there is an unpleasant emotional experience related to an event or thing). There is also positive stress known as 'eustress', for example excitement about getting a promotion (where the prefix 'eu' means well or good).

A positive paradox might be to take job 'a' or job 'b', both of which are better than your current job. Another positive paradox is 'win/win'... how can both sides win? Charles Handy (1994, p87) talks about the 'Chinese contract': "a good agreement is self enforcing because both parties go away smiling." The art of win/win negotiation is explored further in chapter 14.

It could be argued that most paradoxes are neutral particularly in their 'static' form. For example: team reward versus individual reward is neutral but it could become negative if action is taken that causes unrest in the team. Many neutral paradoxes are simply ironic. Again, Charles Handy (1994, p37) provides us with an interesting ironic paradox: "Every generation perceives itself as justifiably different from its predecessor, but plans as if its successor generation will be the same." In organisational terms, this could translate to succession planning, where new up and coming talent is trained and mentored for the future with the skills and tools of the past. This could be seen as negative paradox in the long run, depending on the consequences.

Cannon (1996, p109-10) suggests: "In business... a paradox that is neither understood nor managed causes confusion and can lead to mixed signals and cues." Perhaps it is not the paradox or tension itself that is positive or negative; it is the management or mismanagement of the paradox that makes the difference. Bateson et al (1978, p34) suggest: "It seems likely that paradox, ambiguity, or the double bind can produce positive or pathological results." This tallies with the idea that well managed paradox can be positive (e.g. leading to innovation) whilst mismanaged paradox can be negative (e.g. leading to stress). The same has been said of conflict (which is an example of paradox), where conflict out of control or mishandled leads to bad feeling, whereas conflict resolution can lead to new and creative ideas and plans.

Here is a simple formula...

Mismanaged paradox → *Stress*

Well managed paradox → *Innovation*

Why understand and manage paradox?

In order to get to the root or underlying dynamic of an impossible problem, it is essential that we are able to get underneath the problem and use it for innovation rather than allow it to fester and manifest as stress.

According to a range of management and organisational development gurus, there are great benefits in studying paradox, particularly in the areas of:

1) organisational effectiveness,
2) leadership and management,
3) change,
4) innovation and problem solving.

1) Organisational Effectiveness

Cameron (1986, p545) suggests that: "To be effective, an organisation must possess attributes that are simultaneously contradictory, even mutually exclusive." Cameron (p549) goes on to add: "It is not just the presence of mutually exclusive opposites that makes for effectiveness, but it is the creative leaps, the flexibility, and the unity made possible by them that leads to excellence." It appears that effective organisations utilise polarity and paradox for new solutions and continuous improvement. Managing paradox becomes part of the organisational learning process and perhaps it could be argued that working with paradox is a fundamental capability of the 'learning organisation'.

2) Leadership and Management

Quinn (1990, p3) states that: "Managers spend much of their time living in the fields of perceived tensions. They are constantly forced to make trade-offs, and they often find that there are no right answers. The higher one goes in an organisation, the more exaggerated this phenomenon becomes." In this type of environment where organisational tensions and paradox proliferate, in order to be effective, the leadership and management need to be capable of working with, managing and utilising paradox. According to Schneider (1990, p160) "the best business people... are able to confront paradox... The poorer business people, by contrast, appear to be intimidated by paradox. They tend to be constrictively or expansively polarized and disabled by the prospect of bridging those poles." Peters (1989, p391) goes as far as to say that: "Today's successful business leaders will be those who are most flexible of mind. An ability to embrace new ideas, routinely challenge old ones, and live with paradox will be the effective leader's premiere trait." Peters (p396) then adds that we should: "Promote those who deal best with paradox..."

3) Change

Change is an inevitable part of organisational life and perhaps change is a result of the dynamic created between tensions in the market place (e.g. competitors forging ahead and developing new services and products) and/or within the organisation itself (e.g. out of date systems). But how does managing paradox sit within or around change management? Quinn & Kimberly (1984, p302) propose that: "Understanding the centrality of opposition, paradox, and transcendence is the key to the effective management of transitions." Cannon (1996, p112) considers not just change but also the speed of change: "The faster the rate of change and the more fundamental and complex the dilemmas, the more important it is for managers to understand and manage paradox."

In seeking the role of paradox management in organisational change, McKenzie (1996, px) asks: "Why should paradox management be effective? Two reasons. It brings the most fundamental prejudices out in the open, and so attacks one of the key change inhibitors and benefit degraders that often remain hidden and unmanaged. Then it puts the argument into a framework designed to stimulate creativity and learning, both of which are necessary to drive the revolution forward. Dilemmas are a way to encapsulate and manage the ever-present value differences in our business world."

4) Innovation and Problem Solving

A significant part of organisational excellence and effective change management is the drive for innovation and ability to solve problems. Bolman & Deal (2003, p69) tell us that: "Managers rarely face well defined problems with clear-cut solutions. Instead, they confront enduring structural dilemmas, tough trade-offs without easy answers." Cannon (1996, p108) adds that: "The most difficult business decisions regularly centre on the management of paradox."

The main benefit of a well managed paradox is in utilising polarities and tensions to generate innovative solutions. Naisbit (1986, p12) agrees that: "At least one purpose of a paradox is to provoke fresh thinking... But more than that, a paradox can be a powerful tool for understanding." Rather than an organisation avoiding its polarities and disagreements, it would seem more useful for that organisation to embrace them. Pascale (1990, p110) suggests that: "Paradoxical qualities within an organisation have value because they force people to *think* outside the box, and to break away from convenient categories and patterns... When we transcend a paradox there is often a quality of obviousness that produces a shock of recognition."

Van de Ven & Poole (1988, p25) take the notion of 'paradox as innovation' further than specific organisations by applying it to organisational theory. They state that "addressing organisational paradoxes is an exciting and challenging effort. It is an issue on the edge of organization and management theory, and one that will spawn new ideas and creative theory. Looking at paradoxes forces us to ask very different questions and to come up with answers that stretch the boundaries of current theories."

Many of the organisational experts acknowledge that paradoxes exist within companies and also that there is a need to manage them effectively. However, not many of them tell us specifically '*how*' we can manage paradox. The purpose of this book is to provide a set of guidelines on the '*how*' as well as the '*what*'.

Chapter 2

The Dynamics and Types of Organisational Paradox

In This Chapter...

In this chapter, you will deepen your understanding of the dynamics that maintain an impossible problem. You will also discover the different types of paradox that appear within organisations. By understanding the components, types and movement of paradox, you will be better equipped to address the problem at its core. In essence this chapter is designed to give you some different aspects and examples in order to establish what could be conceived as an organisational paradox.

We will be exploring the following questions:

- What is the difference between a polarity, a tension and a paradox?
- What are the dynamics that underlie impossible problems?
- How does an organisational paradox work?
- What types of paradox are there in an organisation?
- How might we see paradox running at a system level and an individual level?
- How do we map a paradoxical problem?

From Polarity to Tensions

A paradox begins with a polarity of some kind and in and of itself a polarity is static. However, when the polarity is introduced into a system and made 'live', a tension is created between the poles. For example, a manager asks a member of staff to carry out an action when the member of staff already has a busy to-do list. The polarity of 'conflicting priorities' is always a possibility even when it is not actually happening. In this sense, a polarity is there as potential, always existing in concept form. It takes *action* or *thought* to bring the polarity into our experience and therefore 'manifest'.

So, in order for there to be a tension, there must be some kind of polarity. Sometimes, the polarity equates to two contradictory opposites, *either* X *or* not X. Indeed, organisational paradox is often the result of '*either-or*' style thinking.

For example, the people in one particular organisation I worked with felt that they were limited to having *either* high sales *or* high integrity. They perceived that their competitors were gaining sales by misdirection, so they felt that they would have to either lose out or resort to misdirection too.

Tensions are everywhere, fuelled by any number of differences between, for example, two or more people, points, positions or places. A tension might also occur as a mismatch between what someone says and what they do. Chris Argyris (1994) refers to this 'say/do' mismatch as the difference between *espoused theory* (what people say they would do in a situation) and *theory in use* (what they actually do when in that situation). The 'say/do' mismatch might also manifest as a mixed message of "do as I say, not as I do".

It could be argued that a negotiation starts with a tension between what two (or more) parties want. When those parties are prepared to move and look for ways forward, some kind of outcome is inevitably found. However, if parties are not prepared to move, the negotiation shifts into a conflict situation. This is the point where parties become 'stuck' in positions (also known as 'loggerheads', stalemate, impasse and deadlock). Some useful pointers and processes in negotiating and conflict resolution are explored in chapter 14.

Most people can relate to the notion of 'tensions', either being in or witnessing a tugging match between two or more parties/positions. However, this is not really the full story. Tensions are often problematic because of their shifting and contradictory nature. There is a kind of energy that is created by a tension which generates a set of dynamics. In order to be an effective manager of tensions, we need to understand the basics of what paradox is and how it works. We also need to know how to recognise it, map it and resolve it.

Dynamics of Paradox

In chapter 1 we defined a paradox as: "*a contradiction between interconnected positions or concepts that still holds true.*" However, this still does not give us the full picture as there are different types of paradox with different components.

Having explored hundreds of organisational paradoxes, it seems that there are different things being described; sometimes the paradoxes are about vicious circles or dilemmas and double binds. Other problems are about unintended consequences or people getting the opposite to what they wanted. Alternatively, the paradoxes are about polarity and conflicting positions.

There is an apparent gap in the literature in the form of a 'grand unified theory' of agreed terms and typology of paradoxes and of the relationships between these types. From the varying definitions and conditions of paradox I have encountered to date, here is a summary of the dynamics of paradox:

Poles   Poles are the underlying contradiction of a paradox and are conceptual and inert. They can appear as 'digital' (i.e. mutually exclusive) or 'analogue' (i.e. a continuum)

Splits   Splits are active and cause the 'paradoxee' to feel pulled in two or more directions or decisions. It can also feel that whichever option they take, they lose.

Loops   Loops are active and cause the 'paradoxee' to feel like they are going round in circles, either ending up where they started or perhaps having lost a little or gained a little.

Flips   Flips are active and cause the 'paradoxee' to feel like they ended up with the opposite to or negation of what they actually wanted or intended.

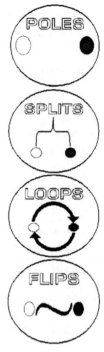

When the pole is made live and a tension is created, the paradox then goes into a dynamic form where it splits, loops and flips. Splits, loops and flips are the active expression of the underlying pole and are how the paradox plays out or is experienced by the 'paradoxee'. In this sense, splits, loops and flips are perceptual as opposed to conceptual. It is also possible that the components will combine, the most common perhaps being a flip-loop, where the 'paradoxee' goes round in circles but keeps getting flipped each time. The classic 'liars' paradox would be an example of this: "I am lying" – if this is true then it must be a lie, but if it is a lie, it must be true, which means it must be a lie etc.

An organisational example of a flip-loop might be where the leadership is driven by the short-termism of the shareholders to initiate 'profit enhancing' change. The change takes place but needs time for the staff to adapt. Because this doesn't happen quickly enough, the business is driven to change again. This loop continues, but with each change the performance (and hence profits) are inadvertently driven down.

The dynamic nature of the splits, loops and flips has a bit of a 'quantum' edge to it where the paradox begins to dance its 'electromagnetic' dance. If you try and solve a paradox by choosing one end of the polarity over the other, it will tend to take you for a ride, up and down, round in circles, upside down and inside-out until confusion reigns.

Someone suggested to me that 'splits, loops and flips' have a gymnastic feel to them. Indeed, they do add a kinaesthetic (physical) element to the problem. Have you ever felt pulled in different directions, felt split between options, gone round in circles, ended up where you started sometimes worse off than when you began? When I'm listening to a problem now, I tend to get a sense of the pulling, pushing and circular forces at work in the background. I can also see by the person's body language and hear through their language as to what the paradox has been doing to them.

Types of Paradox

Building on the dynamics of 'pole, splits, loops and flips', table 2a shows some key types of paradox:

Table 2a: Basic typology of paradox

	Type of Paradox	**Dynamics**
1.	Polarity & Conflicting Positions	Poles
2.	Double Bind	Splits
3.	Dilemma	Splits
4.	Self Reference	Loops
5.	Recursion & Spirals	Loops
6.	Vicious or Virtuous Circles	Loops

7.	Self Fulfilling Prophecy	Loops
8.	Knots	Flips
9.	Unintended Consequences	Flips
10.	Logical Paradox	Flip-loops

These ten types of paradox are explored below with examples given:

1) *Polarity*

Polarity is the conceptual aspect of a paradox, the underlying opposition or contradiction. Most conflicts start with polarity where the people in conflict are 'poles apart' and are taking opposing positions on a subject. This can happen at an individual level, where one person likes the window open and the other likes it closed, or it can happen at a bigger picture level (group, department or organisational).

- In an organisation the quality assurance people want to audit the raw materials being bought in and hence they will recommend the *best* options. The buyers want to get the *cheapest* options as they have targets to achieve. This creates a polarity of *quality* versus *cost*. In the same company, production want to get the end product out of the door, but quality assurance want to take the time to check it all. This creates a polarity of *clear out* versus *delay*. This issue is compounded however as quality control are becoming slower and slower. This is due, in part, to them spending a lot of their time arguing with the buyers about the buying process for the quality raw materials!
- Some service departments (e.g. I.T.) face perpetual competing demands and conflicting priorities. In all likelihood, a service department will also face many ongoing dilemmas and double binds. For example, in the case of I.T.,

26

> everyone who needs their computer fixing considers themselves top priority... so who should be dealt with first?

2) *Double Bind*

In a double bind, the 'choice' (which is really a *limited* choice) is between doing something and not doing it. However, when a double bind is negative, whether they do it or not, the outcome is still 'negative'. This is sometimes known as a 'no win trap'. The person in the double bind has a feeling that they are damned if they do and damned if they don't. Some double binds could be considered neutral, for example, do I employ Fred or not? Obviously this is still a very limited choice and it will depend on the context of the choice as to whether it's positive or negative. Perhaps you don't really want Fred but he is the only candidate.

Gregory Bateson et al (1978) proposed that there are a number of layers to a true double bind and that the double bind is complete when it becomes embedded, normalised and unchallenged in a system. In essence, the layers are:
1) The double bind is set up.
2) The 'victim' cannot go meta (i.e. comment on or talk about the double bind).
3) The 'victim' cannot escape or leave the situation.
Robert Dilts (in Dilts & Smith 1999) then added another layer:
4) The 'victim' has to act immediately and is not given time to think about it.

We will be expanding the concept of 'layers of paradox' further in chapter 4.

> • Bill works for two managers who dislike each other. Both delegate a piece of work that must take 'top' priority. Bill tries to talk about it to each of the managers but both are unresponsive and berate Bill for trying to take sides with the

> other manager. Apart from the two managers not getting on, Bill likes his job and doesn't think he'll get another one like it. He feels he cannot leave. Both managers begin putting pressure on Bill to get their piece of work finished.

3) *Dilemma*

A dilemma is a difficult decision caused by a tension between two positions or options. The person in the dilemma will often feel torn or split between the two 'lemmas' (or horns of the dilemma) and will go backwards and forwards between which one to choose. Usually the person says things like: "I really like the fact that house 'a' has a big kitchen, but it has quite a small garden. House 'b' has a lovely garden but there are only two bedrooms when I really wanted three... House 'a' has three bedrooms which is good but it isn't in such a nice area..." etc. If you encourage them to select one or the other, they begin to take themselves in circles again being pulled towards the advantages and repelled by the disadvantages as they go.

There is a subtle distinction between dilemmas and double binds (as suggested by Dilts & Smith 1999) in that a dilemma will be a choice (albeit limited) between two options: 'a' or 'b' whereas a double bind will be a 'choice' between 'a' or 'not a'. Having said that, there are certain 'choices' which *look* like a dilemma but *feel* like a double bind; for example, a manager might delegate a task saying: "it's up to you... you can do the report tomorrow or before the meeting this afternoon, I don't mind." Whatever the person decides, they will still have to do the report. There is an outdated sales technique called the 'sales close' that works the same way... "Now that I've shown you the product, would you like to pay by cash or by cheque?" Most people see through this now as a cheap trick.

Dilemmas do not have to be limited to an opposition between two points. There are some situations that create a three way dynamic; imagine a triangle where if you change one corner of the triangle, the other two corners change as well. The *time-cost-quality triangle* is an example of a three way tension (or 'trilemma') that is common place in organisational life. Consider the dynamic between time, cost and quality. If you want to cut cost, what impact will that have on time or quality? Usually, bringing the cost down implies a drop in quality or a need for more time. Each of these three areas are related to the others. It is tough to change one without affecting the others. Enhancing quality (which might also mean adding new features) usually means higher costs or more time. Reducing time (e.g. by shortening a deadline) will either reduce the quality or mean extra resources at extra cost.

- Imagine a project meeting. We are part way through the project and there have been a couple of deadlines missed. This means that a milestone may end up being delayed, setting the whole project back. We join the meeting as an argument ensues. Daphne, the project manager, wants to bring the project back on track and is exploring ways to make sure the delivery date does not overrun. One idea is to cut back on the features in the original specifications. Fred wants to maintain the integrity of the project so that it meets the original objective with all the features. A dilemma is now set up in the group, time versus quality. In order to resolve the dilemma, Fred suggests that some additional resources need to be added. However, Bill the finance manager, is reluctant to seek further funding. Now we have a 'trilemma' (time versus quality versus cost) and the meeting goes round in circles!

---

4) *Self Reference*

Self reference equates to circularity caused by something referring to itself, like a tautology or defining something by using itself (rather like this very definition!)

Horn (1983) suggests that organisations themselves are self referential as they are systemic, where every part has a cause and effect relationship with every other part and hence the parts act in a circular fashion. An HR department often governs itself, applying employment law and pay etc. Who quality controls the quality control department? Usually it controls itself. The IT department is self referential too when it comes to fixing its own computer systems. We could have an organisational version of Bertrand Russell's 'barber paradox' here about the IT department that declares that due to shortage of resources they will only fix the computers of people who cannot fix computers for themselves. If this is so, how do the IT department computers stay fixed and what happens if one goes wrong... who will fix it?

- In an organisation that always has 'Monday morning meetings', someone might ask: "why do we have the Monday morning team meeting when there is nothing to discuss?" The reply is: "We have the Monday morning team meeting because we have always had a meeting on Monday morning and since it's now Monday and in the morning, we will be having the meeting."
- In a Scott Adams' 'Dilbert' cartoon a few years ago, Dilbert was asked to lead The 'TTP' Project. When he asked what TTP stood for he was told 'The TTP Project'.
- And now we have PIN numbers when PIN stands for Personal Identity Number. So that means we have 'personal identity number' numbers!
- I remember one person writing on a post-course evaluation form: "Why does no-one ever read these forms?"
- Beliefs can be self referential too. A chief executive might say: "I believe in this approach because it is the right thing to do." When asked: "How do you know?" the reply is: "I just do!" This means the chief executive needs no other evidence than their own belief.
- Whenever we think about ourselves and the way our minds work we are self referencing.

- Might it be that when an organisation refers to itself (for example: "We are the best clothing manufacturer in the world") that this is also self referential? It may not be totally paradoxical but it does lack credibility without any corroboration!

5) *Recursion*

Recursion is a circular movement in a system where you end up back at the start. However, with each loop, the value or movement of the loop may become bigger or smaller each time round. Another version of recursion is a spiral where the loop leads to a higher or lower level each time.

- In many teams, individuals will say before they go home: "I'll just finish this..." or "just one more thing..." and then realise that the 'little things' that they've been adding to their day means they are working longer hours than they are paid to do. This leads to a 'long hours' system level paradox where more people stay longer and so this becomes the norm. The team then self regulates and someone going home on time is labelled a 'light-weight' or 'just doing a half day'.
- Organisations may be cursed by recursion when they attempt to increase the quality of experience for their staff, for example through a pay rise. Most satisfiers or hygiene factors (including money) will soon become expectations and hence lose their motivation power. If a manager introduces 'cakes on Friday' as a way of motivating the team, after about week four, the cakes will become an expectation. If the cakes are taken away, people get grumpy. Biscuits in meetings are another favourite, but when they become expected they tend to lose their value.
- A classic version of 'merry go round' change is where the leadership is driven by short termism of the shareholders to initiate 'profit enhancing' change. The change takes place

but needs time for the staff to adapt. Because this doesn't happen quickly enough, the business is driven to change again. This loop continues, but with each change the performance (and hence profits) are inadvertently driven down.

- Investors and shareholders may also suffer from (and cause) recursion. In the 'investment paradox', investors (e.g. in property development) will sometimes hit the top end of their budget but cannot stop as they would then only have a half-built building. The Scottish Houses of Parliament was a classic case in point, where the budget was estimated at about £10 - £40 Million. The final cost was £414 Million! Any project that is part way through and goes into cost overrun has the potential to fall foul of the investment paradox. The stakeholders and/or investors feel they have no choice but to continue funding the project through to completion.

- Those trading in stocks and shares may face an added 'system level' recursive paradox where selling as the market falls encourages the market to fall.

- There is a similarity here to the 'gambler paradox': "I've already lost hundreds of pounds, so what's another ten?" In poker terms, this is known as 'pot committed' where the player is part way through a round and having put money into the pot realises that they don't have a good hand. They then face a dilemma of whether to pull out (losing what they already put in) or to bluff (with a high risk of losing even more). If they stay in, they are facing an ever more compelling recursive loop of avoiding losses.

- The 'auction paradox' works the same way: "I've already gone up to a hundred pounds so what's another five pounds... I couldn't bear to lose it for the sake of five pounds and so I'll bid again." This could go on ad infinitum if two people share the same philosophy and get caught up in the excitement of the auction.

6) *Vicious or Virtuous Circle*

A vicious or virtuous circle is a series of cause-effect events that loop back to the original cause. Vicious circles are negative and virtuous circles are positive.

- A member of staff may become efficient at what they are doing and so they are given more work to do. When they become efficient again they get given more work. This is a vicious circle for the individual that may end up in a system level 'knot' (where the individual is overloaded until they cannot do their job anymore).
- Another member of staff gets stressed and finds they cannot sleep properly. This stresses them even more which then affects their sleep.
- Some people eat when they are unhappy but overeating makes them unhappy which causes them to overeat.
- A member of staff may be feeling overwhelmed and so goes very quiet. The manager doesn't realise the member of staff is struggling as they are not saying anything, so continues to act as normal, delegating more work to the member of staff.
- A system is updated but people don't perceive that the system has changed so they carry on acting as if they are working to the old system. The new system reverts back to the old system and is then changed again.
- Members of staff see something that is not right in the organisation but they think that if they 'stick their head above the parapet' they may experience retribution so they don't speak up and the situation doesn't change. They are then left staring at something that is not right and wondering whether to say anything.
- Managers are sometimes a little distant from making informed decisions about what their staff are doing so their staff don't ask the manager to get involved and hence the gap remains. Then the staff don't know what the manager is

> thinking so they mind-read and create myths and the gap grows.
> - A manager is seen as unsupportive, so staff don't feedback information or raise issues and this causes the manager to stay distant and not communicate information back to the staff. The staff are then uninformed, time is wasted and people feel demoralised... so the manager stays distant and appears unsupportive.
> - A person feels that his manager is uninformed so he doesn't communicate with the manager and instead 'sits on things'. This means his manager doesn't input, praise or reward, so the person feels demotivated and hence 'sits on things' and so on.
> - Problem behaviour is often perpetuated in organisations (and sometimes even rewarded!) People who are measured by performance alone are often rewarded by results. However, they walk over others and treat colleagues dreadfully in order to achieve those results. This sends a signal that it is okay to behave badly.
> - When people are busy (perhaps 'fire-fighting'), things are less likely to get checked. Quality suffers and more things have to be redone creating more fire-fighting.

7) *Self Fulfilling Prophecy*

The 'self fulfilling prophecy' is a term coined by Robert Merton (see 1996). It is a loop caused by the 'paradoxee' expecting a certain outcome and hence looking for the evidence of it. There is usually a hidden double bind contained in a self fulfilling prophecy where the paradoxee accepts evidence that agrees with expectations and rejects all evidence that does not. Often, a self fulfilling prophecy is a way of maintaining a belief. By filtering out counter evidence, we see only the evidence that supports the belief. Then we get to say: "see I told you so".

- A manager has labelled one of his team members as 'difficult'. Despite the fact that the individual is a high performer and gets on with the rest of the team, the manager only notices when the individual does or says something wrong.
- A lady goes on a presentation skills course believing that she is no good at presenting. When she stands up, she does an okay job but can only see what she did wrong. She focuses on a couple of mistakes she made and decides that her whole presentation was rubbish despite her colleagues' giving her feedback about what she did well.

---

8) Knots

When people experience knots, not only do they feel 'knotted' up, but they also end up with 'not' what they wanted. This type of paradox can range from the simply ironic to potentially dangerous. Knot paradoxes tend to create the opposite to what was intended.

Knots can also be created by trying to hang on to one side of a polarity. Quinn (1990, p66) says: "A manager who pursues the right strategy may nevertheless find that the situation continues to get worse. He or she has unknowingly created a vicious cycle that results in a paradoxical phenomenon. Positive values become negative. For example, innovation, adaptation, and change become premature responsiveness and disastrous experimentation. Stability, control and continuity become habitual perpetuation and ironbound tradition. Good becomes bad."

Trying to hang on to one end of a polarity implies avoidance of the other end. Paul Watzlawick (1993, p60) suggests that avoidance can lead to "the possibility that under certain circumstances it may bring about precisely that which it was meant to prevent and avoid."

- Technology often increases pressure rather than relieving it. One notional benefit of the computer was that it would create a paperless environment. Actually it encouraged more paperwork and more printing.
- A health and safety training initiative increases the apparent amount of accidents instead of reducing them. This is not because of more accidents; it is because more people *report* accidents that were previously ignored (as told to do in the training). Whilst this should have been seen as positive, it is misinterpreted as a failure of the initiative.
- An organisational reward scheme ends up irritating people as the scheme is perceived as unfair and not worth the effort.
- A manager attempts to motivate their demotivated team in such an awkward way that they end up demotivating people further.
- During a period of 'unpleasant' change (i.e. a restructure with redundancies), a manager puts off briefing their team until the last possible moment. The manager is trying to be nice to the team and doesn't want to upset them. However the manager ends up with more aggravation than if they had relayed the message immediately.
- A manager tries to be too friendly with the team, so they end up not giving enough direct leadership or explaining things clearly. Instead of getting to be liked, the manager ends up being disrespected.
- Another manager who is a strong autocratic leader might have been considered a saint when they were called in to rescue a failing organisation. However, now the organisation is back on its feet, they are considered a dictatorial tyrant.

9) *Unintended Consequences*

Robert Merton introduced the concept of the 'Law of Unintended Consequences' in 1936 with an article entitled "The Unanticipated Consequences of Purposive Social Action" (see Merton 1996). The idea of the 'law' is that in addition to the results expected, every action will also tend to lead to a range of unforeseen (often negative) results. It is of course possible to have positive 'lucky' unforeseen consequences (i.e. benefits) too; however, those that get reported are more often than not the negative ones. Unintended consequences are usually the result of decisions and actions that have not been thought through properly.

Some unintended consequences may start with something seemingly innocuous... a new toaster in the staff kitchen for example, that sets off the fire alarm, causing the whole building to evacuate and costing the company thousands of pounds.

- Senior management change a 'customer charter' (i.e. a published promise to the customer) without consulting the front line staff who have to deliver a service to the customer. This creates an increase in customer complaints as the staff are neither resourced nor trained to handle the promise.
- A manager tells his staff: "If you don't hear from me you are doing okay." Although the positive intention of the manager is to leave people alone to get on with their jobs, there are a variety of resulting negative consequences. Firstly, people try and avoid the manager. Secondly, no-one takes the initiative or goes the extra mile as there will be no thanks for a success, only criticism if it goes wrong... so it is better to do the bare minimum! Thirdly, most people prefer something (e.g. feedback) to nothing (e.g. being ignored). If they are ignored for doing things right but get feedback for doing things wrong, guess what happens? More things get done wrong!
- Another aspect of unintended consequences is a phenomenon called 'risk compensation'. In health and safety terms: when things are made safer, people take more risk; when someone feels safe, they adjust their behaviour because the perceived risk seems smaller. For example:
a. People with protective clothing might enter more dangerous environments or stay for longer.

---

b.	Staff with an 'alarm bell' will often stay in an interview room with someone who is becoming violent for longer than those with no bell.
c.	Protective screens in councils and banks often lead to angry behaviour escalating more quickly.

10) *Logical Paradox*

A logical paradox is a statement or event that contains apparently simultaneous contradictory concepts. In order for them to be true they need to be false and in order to be false they need to be true. Although usually referring to problems in the structure of language (and hence the 'philosopher's plaything') there are some 'real world' applications and examples.

• A manager appraises a member of staff saying that they should use their initiative more and be more creative. When the member of staff shows initiative, the manager complains that they only did that because they were told to!
• Someone receives an email that reads: "If you are not the intended recipient of this email, please do not read this." Not only had they already read 'this' and hence contradicted the email, in order for the person to know if the email was for them, they had to read most of the email to see if it was applicable to them or not.
• In a similar vein, someone receives a letter containing software for his PC. On the envelope is the message: "Do not open this envelope until you have read the guidelines enclosed".

Perspectives of Paradox: System and Individual

An impossible problem may need to be looked at from different perspectives, particularly from an objective angle (e.g. the system from an outsider's view) and from a subjective angle (e.g. an individual's view from within the problem). This is a bit like looking at the experience of a cog in a wheel as well as the whole machine. There are two classic paradoxes that help make this point:

<u>Groupthink</u>

Groupthink is a term coined by Irvine Janis (in his book entitled *Groupthink, 1982*) and is also known as 'the problem of agreement', where groups make poor decisions because no-one will disagree. Of course, we usually focus on 'disagreement' being the problem, where people won't agree and so the group cannot make a decision at all. However, when no-one is prepared to challenge a proposal, there is a risk of a poorly thought through decision being made. The paradox here is that people are not disagreeing because no-one else is disagreeing and hence they are conforming to the group's lack of disagreement!

Harvey (1996) wrote about this same phenomenon in a book called *The Abilene Paradox*, where no-one really wanted to go to Abilene but everyone was too polite to say anything, so the group all went and didn't enjoy it!

> **System perspective**: A group of people come together to make a decision. An ineffective proposal is made but no-one disagrees or argues and so the proposal is accepted and passed, to negative effect. This appears as an 'unintended consequences' (flip) type paradox.

> **Individual perspective**: A person is in a group where an ineffective proposal is made. The individual does not agree but notices that no-one else is disagreeing. And so to maintain the harmony of the group, the individual does not speak up. This appears as a double bind (split) type paradox, where the individual risks alienation if he/she speaks up, but becomes party to a bad decision if they do not speak up.

The Peter Principle

Peter and Hull wrote *The Peter Principle* in 1969, and it still remains a significant issue for organisations today. The basic problem is that unless an intervention is put in place, organisations tend to promote people to their level of incompetence.

> **System perspective**: If people are good at what they do and they make the 'right noises', the organisation will seek to promote them. At each level, if a person is good at what they do and this is flagged up, they move to the next level. Where do they stop getting promoted? Often when they are no longer good at what they do. System-wide there may be a lot of people stuck at various levels of the organisation in a state of incompetence. This appears to be an 'unintended consequences' (flip) type paradox because the organisation needs to perform effectively and yet by promoting effective people, it loses the effectiveness!

> **Individual perspective**: For an individual, there appears to be no real problem. They still get paid even if they are less competent. However, they may experience a higher risk of losing their job and a sense of dissatisfaction if they no longer perform. What looks like a motivator ultimately becomes a demotivator which is 'knot' type paradox. Consider the number of people that are high performers in their chosen role who then get promoted to a management grade and then hate it there because it doesn't let them do what they are actually good at.

It is useful to understanding both the system and individual perspectives, to gain further information on where the underlying problem really is and also to acknowledge that the reason a problem seems impossible is because it sits at a number of levels (and is often a dynamic relationship between these levels).

Mapping and Diagnosing Paradox

Because impossible problems are often a mess of paradoxes, it can be helpful to map the problem out. Mapping allows us to see the problem at a system level and see it in 'black and white'. By mapping the paradoxical problem we can gain some distance and explore the problem from the outside.

In order for impossible problems to continue, they will usually have a series of steps that loop round in a circle, running a strategy like a computer program. Even a simple dilemma may have a circular nature to it. For example, to accept a new job or stay with current job:

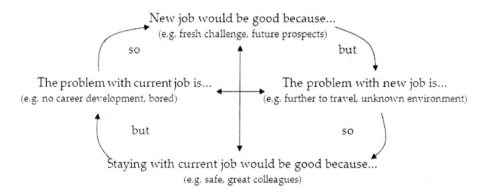

Although a dilemma tends to be a 'split' type paradox, it can also act in a circular nature. Not only might we 'yes but' ourselves round and round in circles, we might flip back and forth between the advantages of each option (trying to select the best option) or possibly the disadvantages (trying to select the 'least worst' option).

Hampden-Turner (1990, p15-16) calls this circular process a "cybernetic loop or recursive system [and that] there is within this circle at least two tensions or dilemmas." It is suggested that the dilemmas in the system need to be related and he goes on to say (p18) that systems "can grow 'virtuously' or they can regress 'viciously'... In a vicious circle the tensions between opposing 'sides' of the circle (horns of the dilemmas) become so severe that 'the rope snaps'... and the system 'runs away'." In the above example, this would probably result in the person beginning to worry about the situation and 'go round in circles' with it. Perhaps 'worry' could be defined (or described) as the point where a tension fires into action, going round in circles without an apparent exit.

Paradoxes can also be mapped out using system diagrams (e.g. Senge 1993), particularly where there is a chain of apparently circular 'cause and effect'. Senge's systems diagrams (or "feedback circle diagrams" p76) demonstrate the problem with paradoxical loops (e.g. vicious circles and self fulfilling prophecies) in that *they seem to have no exit point.*

Consider the following scenario:

> *A bonus scheme is introduced into an organisation in order to increase performance levels. Although morale is okay, senior management perceive that many people have been 'coasting' as they were being paid the same amount whatever they did. The senior management team sets higher targets with a view to financially rewarding those that exceed the targets. Some people see the targets as unachievable so continue to do their 'normal amount'. Others perform but do so at the expense of others and they do just enough to achieve the bonus. Conflict increases along with absenteeism and staff turnover. Senior management decide to try and fix this problem by removing the old bonus scheme and introducing a team bonus scheme. However, the new scheme is seen as unfair as those who perform don't get rewarded for their efforts (particularly when others in the team don't 'pull their weight'). Frustration, aggression and conflict increase and morale drops.*

If we map this:

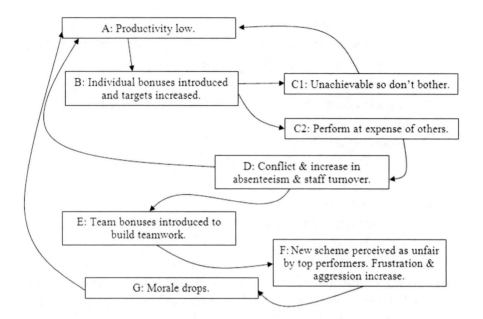

Senge (1993) and O'Connor & McDermott (1997) draw system diagrams without an exit point. Perhaps the exit point is assumed but in visual terms, the cycling never ends. When seeking to resolve an impossible problem we will want to find exit points or generate a 'solution' diagram that has exit points. According to Dilts et al (1980) the fundamental rule of any strategy is having an exit point; otherwise we will be caught in a perpetual loop.

Applying Classic Problem Solving to the Map
When we have a diagram, what can we do with it? What interventions might this diagram suggest? Here are some examples:
a) Seeking exit points.
   e.g. treat bonus as pilot study, evaluate at 3 month stage and exit at initial reaction stage (C1/C2).
b) Breaking a link in the chain (or a connection between links)
   e.g. Stop performers creating conflict with other staff (C2 to D)
c) Removing a link.
   e.g. Resolve the issue of conflict before introducing alternative bonus scheme (E)

d) Interrupting a link.
   e.g. Seek to resolve conflicts by open communication and clamping down on bullying (D & F)

e) Reframing a link.
   e.g. Demonstrate how the team bonus scheme can be done fairly. Give guidelines to staff (F)

f) Changing a link.
   e.g. Make bonuses dependent on behaviour as well as performance (B)

g) Adding a link.
   e.g. Briefings and guidelines given to staff and managers (After B and after E).

An additional approach is to see if it is possible to create a positive feedback loop (a virtuous circle). Sometimes this can be done by reversing the flow of the problematic vicious circle. For example: Use the initial morale and involve staff in ideas for raising productivity (and/or creating a fair bonus scheme). If deciding on a bonus scheme explore a combination of team and individual bonuses and seek methods of preventing conflict by making it achievable. Acknowledge, publicise and celebrate increases in productivity.

Chapter 3

Recognising Impossible Problems: Symptoms and Language

In This Chapter...

In this chapter, you will be exploring a range of organisational, group and personal symptoms that may indicate the existence of underlying tensions and paradox within an organisation (global or local). By developing your ability to notice patterns in individual and group behaviour, you will be able to uncover issues more effectively and efficiently. We will explore symptoms first and then move on to the language section.

We will be exploring the following questions:
- What are the different symptoms (and types of symptoms) of tensions and paradox?
- What is learned helplessness and why is it so detrimental to an organisation?
- How do group mood and behaviour relate to tensions and paradox?
- What are personality clashes really about?
- What is the difference between dysfunctional teams and high performing teams in how they handle difference?
- What language, metaphor and non-verbal behaviour might indicate tensions and paradox?

Symptoms of Impossible Problems

How do we know that we (or others) are experiencing an impossible problem? How do we identify it? What are some of the signals? To simplify things, this chapter begins with a set of 'lists' that could be symptoms of impossible problems. The content of the lists should be self explanatory and are not necessarily exhaustive. They are designed to give you an idea of how impossible problems impact on the organisation and the individuals in the organisation.

If you wander round a company talking to people and watching how they behave, you may begin to notice particular patterns emerging that are signs of organisational tensions. Here are some of the organisational issues that might indicate an underlying organisational tension:

Absenteeism	Contradiction	Procrastination
Anxiety	Denial	Productivity drops
Avoidance	Despair	Silo Behaviour
Change fatigue	Inconsistencies	Staff turnover
Chaos	Inertia	Stress
Conflict	Lack of motivation	Team tensions
Confusion	Overlong meetings	Upset

Ultimately all of these symptoms will have an impact on the bottom line. A company with too many unmanaged paradoxes will likely be a company losing money.

There will also be symptoms on an individual level manifesting in the person's behaviour. These behaviours could be sorted into the categories of fight, flight or fright. The 'fight/ flight/fright' model is based on how people react to a perceived threat. In difficult, 'stressful' circumstances the human body will tend go through a set of survival strategies, including an adrenalin kick and blood being diverted to the major muscles. The body is preparing to stand and fight or to run. There is also a third state that appears to affect people and that is to 'freeze up'. This may be in part because blood is taken away from the brain – this is a time for action not thinking. Nowadays however, because we rarely need to fight or run in a work setting, freezing is a strong contender. Of course, a person's reactions are likely to depend on their personality type and their current mood. Here are some examples:

Fight	Flight	Fright
Aggression	Avoiding	Anxiety
Confronting	Desire to stay away	Delay
Putting in even	Detachment	Indecision
more effort	Keep a distance	Procrastination
Take on more work	Lying	Worry
Taking work home	Retreat	
More urgency		

As well as external behaviours, it might also be useful to note the 'internal' signals of perceived tensions, which are akin to the symptoms of stress, for example:

Physical	Emotional	Mental
Aches and pains	Anger	Forgetfulness
Headache	Anxiety	Hard to concentrate
Indigestion	Bad mood	Indecision
Muscle twitch	Irritability	Lack of clear thinking
Recurrent colds	Mood swings	Negative thinking
Skin irritation	Tiredness	Obsessive thinking
Tension in back	Unexplained sadness	Worrying
and/or neck		

There are also a set of stronger, more embedded symptoms that typically identify an underlying paradox (or set of paradoxes). This could be seen as a second layer of emotional and cognitive responses to not being able to resolve an issue and/or where things have got more serious. Prolonged exposure to these symptoms is detrimental to the health of the individuals and ultimately to the company. If a problem persists over a longer period of time you may see (or experience):

Cynicism	Inertia	Perceived
Defensiveness	Job dissatisfaction	powerlessness
Demotivation	Lack of enthusiasm	Pointlessness
Depression	Loss of confidence	Purposelessness
Drained	Low energy	Sadness
Exhaustion	Low self-esteem	Strong scepticism
Fatalism	No motivation	Taking things
Hopelessness		personally

In the literature around organisational paradox, some of the other negative effects of paradox have been recorded as: severe anxiety (Watzlawick et al 1967), helplessness, fear, exasperation and rage (Bateson 1978), feeling withdrawn, diminished, subdued, trapped, suffocated, constricted, depressed or explosive (Schneider 1990). However, perhaps one of the most insidious symptoms of paradox is something called 'learned helplessness'. Some of the elements above are part of learned helplessness but it is worth exploring this phenomenon further...

Learned Helplessness

Learned helplessness was a term introduced by Seligman (see 1998) whilst conducting some rather barbaric experiments on animals. He noticed that when an animal was not allowed to escape an unpleasant environment, after a series of unsuccessful escape attempts it would simply give up. Then later, even when there was an opportunity to escape, the animal would remain in learned helplessness as if it was still trapped. This phenomenon is obvious in people too. If they feel they are unable to make a difference, they give up. Faced for long enough with a no-win situation they will say things like: "Nothing I do works... it's outside of my control." It is like they have tried everything possible that they can think of but nothing has worked. Because of this, they have shut down, saying: "I can't do anything about this." When this happens and people give up, the paradox is free to remain in the system. However, even if the paradox disappears later on, people *act as if it was still there*. It seems that once a paradox is perceived long enough for people to go into learned helplessness, they stop looking for answers or solutions. From an outsider's view, it is extraordinary to see people acting as if there is a problem that doesn't actually exist anymore!

Learned helplessness is often the result of the double bind, where people feel 'damned if they do, damned if they don't' or 'whatever I do, it doesn't matter' (Seligman 1998). Learned helplessness in organisations has been linked to organisational failure (including inadequate systems, poor communication, unrealistic workloads) (Walshe 2003), disempowerment and feeling a loss of control (Warn 2001), passivity, frustration and powerlessness, people feeling "less than happy with their lot but soldiering on because they felt that they had no alternative" (Hayes 1991).

According to Dilts & Smith (1999), learned helplessness is not the end of the story since there is a level beyond that called 'learned hopelessness'. This might be expressed as: "No-one can do anything about the problem... it's not possible." In this sense, learned hopelessness is a further generalisation of learned helplessness, from "I can't" to "no-one can".

It could be argued (and the work of Seligman supports this), that learned helplessness is akin to a form (or degree) of depression. When someone gets to "I can't" or "no-one can" the next step is likely to be: "What is the point?" This kind of language indicates a loss of purpose and herein lies the state of depression.

Gilbert (1993) also points out the connection between paradox and the kind of thinking that causes and maintains depression, which he calls 'dilemmas', 'traps' and 'snags':

- Dilemmas: polarity/dichotomy 'judgement' thinking (particularly 'good or bad'),
- Traps: negative assumptions which lead to behaviour that leads to consequences that reinforce the negative assumptions (unhelpful self-fulfilling prophecies),
- Snags: 'yes but' thinking to possible solutions

On the last point of what Gilbert calls 'snags', Rowe (1987) suggests that 'yes but' thinking is a defence against new ideas since such new ideas make the world an uncertain place and might also mean that the person has been wrong. This would imply that people will sometimes maintain a paradoxical problem in order not to have to change their belief system/model of the world. Some people wear paradoxical problems like a badge of honour, even though it causes them pain and discomfort. On a deeper level, they are perhaps not willing to resolve the problem as this would threaten their identity. When seeking to deal with paradoxical problems, people may not always thank you as you may be challenging their beliefs and identity.

As well as paradox being apparent through an individual's emotional states, moods and behaviours, there are also potential indicators in group behaviours/dynamics and in the general organisational mood.

Group Behaviours and Organisational Mood

Having run training courses for a range of companies over the last twenty years, I have noticed that when groups come together (particularly from different parts of the business) they are usually keen to speak of the tensions and paradox in the business. There is a particular energy that bursts out and around the room when a paradox is uncovered. A group can happily work through a course (or meeting) agenda until a 'sticking point' is reached and an animated discussion starts up. There is suddenly a higher level of energy/ emotion and the group will often want to keep returning to the point/issue. Even when it is not initially clear what the tension is, a couple of questions nearly always elicit the paradox.

As well as working with groups of individuals from around the organisation, my partner and I are often called in to help with teams that want to develop. Sometimes this a new team coming together, wanting to build rapport and contract with each other. At other times, we are being called in to help a 'dysfunctional team'. From our experience, a dysfunctional team is nearly always the result of a tension of some kind (or series of tensions). This may be, for example, a tension driven by the manager, a personality clash within the team or ongoing dissatisfaction with an organisational issue. Classic symptoms of team 'dysfunction' include: falling out, arguments, complaining/moaning, bitterness, resentment, unwillingness to communicate, alienation, picking on/bullying, cliques/factions, low morale and "it's not fair".

Sometimes the symptoms of a dysfunctional team may appear to be petty. However, it may be that the surface issue is one that is 'socially or culturally acceptable', for example, to moan about or criticise others. It is amazing how many teams present tea-making and washing-up as the presenting problem. When working with these teams, it is often these types of issue that gets talked about first. Although they may each be a legitimate issue unto themselves, they are usually a metaphor or gateway to deeper issues.

Understanding 'personality clashes'
A particular model that we use when working with groups is called 'Working Styles' (Hay 2009). This model comes from the organisational branch of Transactional Analysis and is an adaptation of the therapeutic model known as Drivers (Kahler 1975). Whereas 'drivers' were designed to describe a person's pathology (i.e. what is wrong with them), the 'working styles' model explores both sides of the personality in terms of strengths and weaknesses.

There are five Working Styles: *hurry up, be perfect, please people, try hard* and *be strong* (outlined below) but the important thing to remember is that we all are a blend of styles, not just one of them. What makes each of us different is our combination and hierarchy of styles (for example, someone might have a 'high' level of *hurry up*, an 'average' level of *be perfect* and a 'low' level of *please others*.) For the sake of introduction and simplicity, the five styles are separated out into their key components.

Working Style	Personality Positives	Personality Pitfalls
Hurry Up	❏ Speedy, fast, quick ❏ Focus on quantity, getting things done ❏ Sense of urgency, strive for action ❏ High output & productivity ❏ Efficient ❏ Meet short deadlines	❏ Tendency to rush, prone to mistakes ❏ Quality can suffer ❏ Impatient with self and others if 'too slow' ❏ Doesn't like waiting ❏ Reluctant to plan or explore detail
Be Perfect	❏ Accurate and effective ❏ High quality output ❏ Think things through ❏ Tidy & organised ❏ Professional & smart ❏ Attention to detail	❏ Perfectionist ❏ Slow, can be pedantic ❏ Wants to know in/outs before starting ❏ Wants to be right and can appear patronising ❏ Intolerant of: mistakes, not getting it right, poor presentation and mess
Please People	❏ Empathetic ❏ Kind and caring ❏ Polite and pleasant ❏ Like to find connections with others ❏ Good listeners ❏ Able to see things from others perspective	❏ Can be attention seekers, wanting more time with people ❏ More people focused than task focused, so may chat and 'waste time' ❏ May take on the personal problems of others ❏ Can be self-effacing, perhaps fishing for compliments or validation

		Desire to 'rescue' other people when they are in trouble
Try Hard	❑ Creative and innovative ❑ Enthusiastic ❑ Energetic and passionate ❑ Lateral thinking ❑ Playful ❑ Fun	❑ Easily distracted and tends to digress ❑ May not finish tasks ❑ Doing more than one thing at a time – lack of focus ❑ May get bored if not having fun or kept interested ❑ Doesn't like repetitive tasks
Be Strong	❑ Stays calm in crisis ❑ Reliable and consistent ❑ Methodical ❑ Practical and realistic ❑ Independent ❑ Conscientious	❑ Doesn't like to show any weaknesses ❑ Won't tell you if they are struggling ❑ Won't ask questions ❑ Can appear insensitive, distant and without feeling ❑ Likes to work alone, so can alienate themselves from the team

Within a team, some people will predominate in one or two areas and other people will be a 'bit of everything'. When we have a number of people with different 'predominances' in the team, this is where we may get some clashes. In this sense, a 'personality clash' is really a tension (or set of tensions) caused by the difference between Working Styles.

The examples in the table below are just examples! People will find all sorts of reasons to get irritated and to fall out with each other. It is also possible for similar styles to fall out too (in part because we are a blend of other things), for example two *try hards* might try to outdo each other or two *be perfects* who believe different things may both believe they are right.

Examples of potential 'personality clashes' between working styles:

	Hurry Up Thinks That...	**Be Perfect Thinks That...**	**Please People Thinks That...**	**Try Hard Thinks That...**	**Be Strong Thinks That...**
Hurry Up		HU is 'slapdash' - rushing and making mistakes.	HU is too task-oriented – no time for socialising.	HU is too impatient – not enough time for variation.	HU is too pushy and quick to action.
Be Perfect	BP is too slow and 'pernickety'.		BP is hard to please, too critical, has impossibly high standards.	BP is too rigid, rules driven and single minded on doing 'one thing at a time'.	BP is too focused on perfection and doesn't get when enough is enough.
Please People	PP is too chatty – not enough urgency to action	PP is too interested in people to produce quality outcomes.		PP is too worried about what people think of them.	PP is invasive, nosey and 'fluffy' – wants to know personal details.
Try Hard	TH is too distracting and has a 'butterfly' mind.	TH won't finish things.	TH doesn't consider the impact of their ideas on how people feel.		TH is a joker.
Be Strong	BS is slow and won't respond to urgency.	BS is not interested in getting things absolutely right... they just make do.	BS is uncommunicative and unfeeling.	BS is too serious.	

With team working styles, we might also find a secondary level paradox. Each of the styles has the potential to fall out with each other, but they are all required for an effective team. Consider that a team without *hurry up* has no sense of urgency to get things done. A team without *be perfect* has no quality control. A team without *please others* is not really a team, it is just a group. A team without *try hard* may never change or innovate. A team without *be strong* may have no 'groundedness' or task focus.

The good news is (and this may help to prevent the above paradox) that working styles combined *can* lead to innovation and productivity when managed well. As with all tensions, effective management leads to innovation and mismanagement leads to stress.

Layers of team and relationship dysfunction
In an extraordinary series of studies, John Gottman (1999, 2007), a social psychologist, has been able to consistently predict the long term condition of a couple's relationship. By observing just five minutes of how the couple interact when discussing an issue, Gottman and his team have a 91% success rate at predicting whether the couple will still be together in five years time.

Gottman's work has been primarily about love relationships; however the principles of his work seem to apply very well to team dynamics. It appears that one of the most critical factors in successful relationships is how people handle difference (e.g. of opinion, perspective and/or personality). Gottman (2007) highlights a series of behaviours that appear when a relationship is less likely to succeed in the long term. He calls these the 'Four Horsemen of the Apocalypse' for a relationship: stonewalling, defensiveness, criticism and contempt.

Stonewalling is about *avoidance*; certain topics become off limits so we don't talk about them. Defensiveness is linked to *apprehension*; not taking responsibility and by implication wanting to blame someone else. Criticism is about *antagonism*; attacking the other party overtly. Defensiveness and criticism are usually two sides of the same coin, where one side wants to attack and the other side parries. Contempt is about *aversion* and is considered to be the worst and most poisonous horseman. Here we are in the realms of insults, name-calling, sarcasm, hostility and cynicism; and according to Gottman the body language of contempt includes sneering and eye rolling.

If the four horsemen are in place, there appears to be a degree of 'learned helplessness' that may set in which creates a new level of stonewalling and avoidance. Here, people in the team will tend to avoid issues by shutting down completely or leaving the scene. It is as if they are caught in a double-bind of 'damned if I say anything, damned if I don't'. And so they move from *difference* to *indifference*. Impossible problems can often be recognised indirectly by the *layers* that surround the tensions and paradoxes. These layers and 'defences' include avoiding the subject, resisting solutions, blaming and/or becoming defensive or hostile when the problem is raised. These layers are discussed in the next chapter.

Do successful teams argue? Of course they do, but Gottman also found that successful couples tend to have a ratio of at least five good experiences to one bad and this is also likely to be true for teams. Good experiences might include positive interactions like smiles, helping one another, sharing a laugh, kind words, compliments and talking about joint interests.

Something that Gottman alludes to but does not pull together into a model (like the 'Four Horsemen') is the positive spin. What is the model for successful relationships and how do they handle difference? When working with teams, we have introduced the four *counter-horsemen* of awareness, acceptance, appreciation and admiration. As well as providing a direct counter for each of Gottman's horsemen, these act like levels that people transcend as they face and resolve their differences.

The first level, *awareness* is about acknowledging that there is a difference and being prepared to discuss it rather than avoiding it. The second level, *acceptance* is about staying open to our partner's perspective and knowing that it is more productive to listen than it is to get defensive. The next level, *appreciation* is about valuing the fact that our partner can be and do different things to us and instead of criticising them, we understand that this is useful to the relationship. We may even praise the fact that they do certain things better than we do ourselves. The final level, *admiration,* is where we see our difference as a part of relationship excellence. Gottman (1999) suggests that: "fondness and admiration are antidotes for contempt." Here we seek to find integration between opposing positions and to create synergy rather than contempt.

Responses in the Face of Difference

Levels of Resourceful Responses/States *(Four Horsemen of Affiliation)*		
Admiration	+4
Appreciation	+3
Acceptance	+2
Awareness	+1

Levels of Unresourceful Responses/States *(Four Horsemen of The Apocalypse)*		
Stonewalling (Avoidance)	-1
Defensiveness (Apprehension)	-2
Criticism (Antagonism)	-3
Contempt (Aversion)	-4

Gottman's Horseman	Behaviours		The Counter Horsemen	Behaviours
Contempt *(Aversion)*	• Eye rolling • Sarcasm • Insults		Admiration	• Show interest & respect • Encourage & extol virtues • "Difference is excellence"

Criticism (Antagonism)	• Criticising • Attacking • Generalising (eg. always, never)	Appreciation	• Feedback & praise • Show support • "Difference is useful"
Defensiveness (Apprehension)	• Making excuses • Defending oneself • Countering (yes, but)	Acceptance	• Stay open • Listen • "Difference is okay/good"
Stonewalling (Avoidance)	• Topics become 'off limits' • Changing subject • Withdrawing and ignoring	Awareness	• Engage in dialogue • Acknowledge difference • "There is difference"

Successful teams seek the positive in one other and in each other's positions, perspectives and personality. When faced with difference they seek synthesis and synergy and by doing so spiral upwards through innovation, connectedness and unity. According to Michael Hall (2007), synergy is part of the self-actualisation process which "operates as an integrative process of opposites and polarities." As we self-actualise, distinctions and differences disappear. Relationships become greater than the sum of their parts and together, people can achieve things they could never have achieved independently.

On one level, it is as simple this... when we see the negative/disadvantages of each other's position, we will likely fall into conflict. When we see the positive intentions/advantages, we transcend from (i.e. 'end the trance/illusion of') difference into innovation and connection.

Although originally associated with love relationships, the four horsemen of the apocalypse and the counter horsemen are very relevant within a work environment. Dysfunctional relationships and teams follow the same model through avoidance, apprehension, antagonism and aversion. However, high performing teams seem to work the other way. Team members seek to discuss issues, welcoming difference and diversity as roads to innovation and progress. As they spiral upwards through the levels, they accept, appreciate and then admire differences in the team. When you hear someone from a high performance team talking about a fellow team member it is usually in a respectful and complimentary manner.

The Language of Paradox and Tensions

1) *Linguistic Indicators*

If you want to pick up on impossible problems from what people say, you will find that there are some key terms that give an indication that something paradoxical is going on. During my research, there were certain frequently occurring words and phrases that seemed to be linked to paradox, polarity and tensions.

Aside from the word 'or' which immediately flags up a possible 'either x or y' scenario, the word 'between' is a classic example of an indicator. As a preposition, the word 'between' implies that there are at least two things, one on either side. As you will see from the table below, there are plenty of phrases that include the word 'between'.

Linguistic Indicators	
Explicit Polarity/Tension	**Example/Notes**
o Ambivalence	
o Between	"it's between x and y"
• Balance	"strike a balance between x and y"
• Compromise	"compromise between x and y"

• Conflict	"conflict between x and y"
• Dichotomy	"dichotomy between x and y"
• Difference	"difference between x and y"
• Divide/division	"divide between x and y"
• Happy medium	"happy medium between x and y "
• Juxtaposition	"juxtaposition between x and y"
• Split/torn/caught	"split between x and y"
o Contradiction	
o Contrary	"what you have to do might be contrary to your values"
o Counter	"counter productive", "counter balance"
o Either/or	"either x or y"
o Opposite/opposition	
o Versus	"x versus y"
o Win/lose	"I win, you lose"

Implied Polarity/Tension	Example/Notes
o But	"they will get skills but other people will have to wait"
o Despite	
o Don't	"I don't see it as x"
o However	"x however y"
o Instead	"instead of x, y" (or "if not x, y instead")
o Nevertheless	"x nevertheless y" (acts like 'but')
o Not x	implies polarity between x and not x
o On the other hand	"x, on the other hand, y"
o Otherwise	"x, otherwise y"
o Ought/Should	implies a mismatch between expectation and reality
o Rather than	"x rather than y"
o Right	Implies there's a wrong (works for any truth value)
o So	"x so y" (problem so need/solution)
o Though	"x though y" (acts like 'but')
o Too	Implies being at the end of one

	polarity
o Whereas	"x whereas y"
o Which?	"which one?"
o Whilst	"whilst x, y"
o Without	"talk a lot without any action"

The 'meta model' from neuro-linguistic programming (e.g. Bandler & Grinder 1975) gives us another avenue for language exploration. A by-product of polarity and conflict is where people speak in generalised terms. For example, universal quantifiers are absolute statements *which suggest a polar position is being taken*. Words like 'all', 'always', 'never', 'no-one' are all universal quantifiers: "My manager never listens to me... She's always doing something else... No-one understands a word she says... All managers are the same." A second category of generalisations are modal operators of impossibility (e.g. can't, won't, impossible) and necessity (e.g. should, ought, must). For example: "I can't do presentations" implies a rejection of an alternative, opposing possibility that "I can do presentations". It also precludes any possibility of somewhere between cannot and can... many people can 'sort of' do presentations!

2) *Metaphor*

When you listen to people speaking or read what they have written, you will find a colourful array of metaphors, analogies, similes, hyperbole, metonymy, clichés, allegory, euphemisms, colloquialisms and so on. Although this may make an English language expert cringe, for the sake of convenience I will be referring to all such symbolic oriented language as 'metaphor'.

When we use metaphor, we are using concepts that stand for what we are actually talking about. This makes what we are saying more abstract and sometimes more accessible. It is often easier to talk about a difficult or emotional issue in metaphorical terms. Metaphor creates a broader frame of reference, allowing for flexibility in the interpretation of meaning. This creates a kind of 'safety net', making ideas less threatening.

Here are some examples of metaphors picked up during the research...

o Actions speak louder than words	o Doublethink	o Out of frying pan and into fire
o Banging head against a brick wall	o Entrenched	o Over a barrel
	o Eggs in one basket	o Plate spinning
o Better the devil you know than the devil you don't	o Feeding into itself	o Round in circles and end up at square one
	o Gordian knot	
	o Grass is greener	
o Between a rock and a hard place	o Grey areas	o Running hot and cold
	o Halos and horns	
o Bone of contention	o Heart trying to do the stomach's job	o Running on the spot, moving to stand still
o Brush it under the carpet		
	o In two minds	
o Busy doing nothing	o Juggling	o Self fulfilling prophecy
o Can of worms	o Loggerheads	
o Catch 22	o Many balls in the air at the same time	o Shooting oneself in the foot
o Chasing your tail		
o Clash of Egos	o Merry-go-round, merry dance	o Silk glove with iron fist
o Comparing apples and pears		
	o Mixed messages	o Silo mentality
o Damned if I do, damned if I don't	o Move the goalposts	o Spiralling
	o Old hat on	o Split the pot
o Devil and the deep blue sea	o On different wavelengths	o Square peg in a round hole
	o One step forward & two steps back	o Stalemate
o Different angles		o Sweet and sour messages
o Double edged sword		o Thin end of the wedge
		o Vicious circle/cycle
		o Woolly priorities

Not all of the above metaphors are specific to paradox and tensions but they are usually indicative of a problem. You will see however that some are very clearly referring to a polarity, tension or paradox; for example: between the Devil and deep blue sea, between a rock and a hard place, silo mentality. My absolute favourite was from a young lady who said: "we keep going round in circles and then we end up at square one!"

It is important to note that some people seem to use and understand metaphor more readily than others. It is as if there is a continuum of 'metaphorical' at one end to 'literal' at the other. Some people use very little metaphor and it appears to annoy them when others speak in those terms. Those that are highly 'literal' will challenge metaphor by saying things like: "what are you talking about... that doesn't make any sense" or "that doesn't mean anything". It is important to remember that a metaphor is just a metaphor... it is not meant to be real. A metaphor is not meant to *be* the reality it represents. As Korsybski (1958) pointed out: "the map is not the territory" (and we might also say that a picture is not the same as what is in the picture or a menu is not the food).

As metaphor is meant to be a representation of reality, it allows us some distance from the problem so we can explore options without feeling stuck in it. It is hard to find solutions from the middle of an impossible problem, like 'not seeing the wood for the trees' if you'll pardon the metaphor (or more correctly 'analogy'). It is thinking from that problem place that keeps us stuck there. Metaphor abstracts us from the problem and hence allows us to create solutions.

3) Non Verbal Language

If you watch people's body language as they speak, they will sometimes paint the problem for you with their gestures, for example, running their hand round in a circle to indicate circularity or pointing in two directions to indicate a split. They may hold both hands out as they say "on one hand... but on the other..." Facial expressions can also give clues as to the feeling of the speaker, for example, shaking the head with a look of contempt can indicate 'nonsensical' or shrugging shoulders with a look of bewilderment or confusion as a way of saying: "I don't know what to do". Remember that body language in isolation (i.e. without a context) is meaningless. You need to read the other signals that are going on and if possible check with the person what you think you are seeing.

Another interesting behaviour around dilemmas and polarity is when the person's body language shifts and their voice changes half way through the sentence. For example, they might say: "I'm happy to go to the meeting this afternoon *but*..." (and at this point they shrink down a little and use a slightly higher pitch and slower voice tone) "... I have all this work to do for my manager."

Chapter 4

Layers of Problems

In This Chapter...

In this chapter, you will be exploring the nature of layers that are created around tensions and paradox and hence become part of the 'impossible problem'. Like noticing symptoms of tensions and paradox, you will also begin to notice the surrounding layers and how they have become embedded in the organisation. By understanding the concept of layers, you will be able to identify the otherwise hidden traps that these layers bring.

We will be exploring the following questions:
- How and why are layers built around the original problem?
- What are 'organisational defences' and 'defensive routines'?
- What is the psychology of and motivation for organisational defences?
- Why are organisational defences like double binds?
- What are the layers and/or levels of organisational defences?
- How can you recognise organisational defences?
- How might you address organisational defences?
- What else do you need to bear in mind when addressing these defences?

How Layers Are Built

So far we have explored examples and types of paradox but of course this is not the end of the story. Because polarity, tensions and paradox are apparently difficult to resolve, the people in a paradoxical system will usually seek to find other ways of handling the situation, for example, by avoidance. Over time, a *series of layers* may be created around the original issue. On one hand, this can make resolution more challenging and complex, but on the other, the presence of these layers and 'defensive' behaviours may give us a clue that something is going on *underneath* the layers.

As a learning and development consultant, I am often privy to issues happening within an organisation. Courses and workshops seem to be an opportunity for participants to let off some steam about what bothers them.

On running a 'Dealing with Pressure' course (which often elicits organisational paradoxes), a delegate told me his impossible situation. He was a technician and had to produce a certain number of batches every week. At one time the target used to be *three* batches but after an efficiency study by an external consultancy this was changed to *five* (without any training or explanation to the staff). Then the organisation made redundancies, shedding half the team. Soon after, the organisation gained a new client and so needed *six* batches a week per member of staff. Rather than bring staff back in again, the 'management' wouldn't employ (or re-employ) anyone else as this would have been perceived as a backward step (and may also have created some employment law issues). To solve the problem, the 'survivors' of the redundancy were required to come in at weekends. Weekend work was being considered 'normal' work and hence no longer optional. However, staff were given a 'choice' that they could set up their own rota or be told when they were coming in. Having been forced into this 'choice', the technician asked his manager what would happen if people didn't agree with the 'choice' at all. His manager responded that they would be swiftly moved to another department (which would mean less pay). So not only was the technician in an 'either/or' scenario (neither of which option was good for him), he had a ten year old daughter that he didn't see enough of and having to work weekends was going to make things worse. On top of this, he felt he couldn't 'disobey' the company because he couldn't take a pay cut and he couldn't leave as he was worried he might not get another job elsewhere.

So here we have a man in a forced dilemma (agree a rota or be told which days to work) which he tries to escape ("what if I say no"). He then finds himself in a double bind wrapped around the first dilemma (agree with working some weekends or disagree and be moved elsewhere with a pay cut). He feels he cannot disobey or escape this situation by leaving as he risks not getting another job (or perhaps having to take a pay cut in another company).

Sometimes there are layers upon layers, for example, a double bind around another double bind, wrapped in a no-win dilemma. The value of paradox management is not just recognising that someone has a dilemma; it is recognising the layers that surround it.

Layers can also be in the form of 'cover-ups', where problematic information is hidden, buried or 'forgotten'. These attempts to avoid facing a problem have been labelled 'organisational defensive routines' by Chris Argyris (e.g. 1988).

Organisational Defences

Imagine that a member of staff identifies that there is a problem or a 'dumb rule' (Clemmer 1992) but when they try to talk about it (for example to their manager), they get a response like "don't ask", "just do it anyway", "I don't want to talk about it" or "you're not paid to think".

This "don't ask" response creates a new level of problem(s). There is the original issue (that is perhaps preventing someone from doing their job effectively or perhaps slowing down a system unnecessarily) and then there is the level of "we won't talk about that". This second level may create a sense of further frustration or annoyance.

The reluctance to face the original problem or tension is what is known as an 'organisational defence' and the behaviours it leads to are known as 'defensive routines'. Argyris (1988) defines organisational defensive routines as "any policy or action that prevents someone (or some system) from experiencing embarrassment or threat, and simultaneously prevents anyone from correcting the causes of the embarrassment or threat." Instead of facing the emotions around an issue, people learn to use tactics to rationalise and avoid. But avoiding the emotion around the problem means avoiding the actual problem as well.

Argyris (1990, p138) describes the problem thus: "The dilemma is that the ideas on how to be in control over embarrassment and threat are themselves embarrassing... it creates more embarrassment and threat, which lead to further bypass and cover up. All of these actions and reactions are highly skilful, and thus actors are often unaware of their impact. Or, if the actors are aware of the negative impact, they blame the organisational defensive routines. They report they are in a double bind, helpless but to act as they do."

Organisational defences are rife within business. Take, for example, the humble mixed message. "No offence but..." is usually followed by something offensive. "With all due respect..." will probably continue with something rather less than respectful. "Do as I say, not as I do," is often a cover up for poor management behaviour. Each of these examples of mixed message is designed to protect the speaker from repercussions. In this sense, the mixed message is an organisational defence.

Organisational defences are inextricably linked to 'learned helplessness', where the individual feels helpless to do anything because whatever they do won't make any difference. Even worse, they may perceive that whatever they do will be seen as wrong and will lead to punishment of some kind. When facing a perceived 'lose-lose' situation, perhaps it is natural to want to avoid it.

<u>*Why Organisational Defences?*</u>

If organisational defences (and defensive routines) are self defeating and potentially damaging, why do people continue creating them?

Often the people who engineer and/or maintain the defensive routines are unaware that they are part of the defence because they are unable to step outside of the situation and see the big picture. It is as if they are on a runaway train, with no options but to stay on track, even though it could lead to a wreck at the end of the line.

Even when people *can* see the big picture, they are often reluctant to act due to the emotion of fear. It is likely that fear is at the root of avoidance behaviour and hence at the root of organisational defences. Rather than attempt to tackle an issue, the players walk the steps and talk the script of avoidance. They may be attempting to avoid the problem, the fear of the problem, or both.

The fears that promote avoidance could be mapped onto Maslow's Hierarchy of Needs (1954). At each level, there is a potential fear of losing something or feeling diminished in some way (see table 4a below).

Table 4a: Maslow's Hierarchy of Needs as Motivators for Organisational Defences

Level	Motivation for Organisational Defences
Actualisation	Fear of losing ability to 'realise personal potential'
Esteem	Fear of embarrassment to self and/or others
	Fear of losing face, dignity, credibility
	Fear of losing promotion opportunity
	Fear of appearing inconsistent, unreliable

Belonging	Fear of rejection, alienation
	Fear of losing connection, affection
Safety	Fear of threat to personal safety
	Fear of losing job, income
	Fear of losing freedom
Physiological	Fear of losing house, ability to provide food

At the top of the hierarchy, it is most unlikely for an organisational defence to be engineered in order to avoid losing the ability to 'self actualise'. If it does happen, it is likely to be 'unconsciously' driven since it would seem paradoxical that someone would purposely implement an organisational defence in order to self-actualise. To do so would seem to be like trying to winning a fair play competition by cheating.

Perhaps it could also be argued that organisational defences occur due to people trying to *achieve or gain* something rather than avoid losing something. For example, someone may sweep an issue 'under the carpet' in an attempt to gain a promotion. However, this still appears ultimately to be fear motivated. Even greed is motivated by the fear of not having enough.

Organisational defences often suggest a cover-up, usually a cover-up for mistakes. When people make mistakes in organisations, there is the temptation to give in to fear and bury or avoid the issue. Learning that mistakes are bad comes early on in life (e.g. at school where mistakes equal lower grades and no reward). Most of us learn as small children that owning up to mistakes does not always bring positive results, so covering up mistakes keeps us safer and maintains the belief that covering up is better than owning up.

Organisational Defences as Double Binds

Not only might the original problem be a tension or paradox, but the existence of levels may create new double binds and dilemmas.

For example, a senior manager complains that the well paid managers that report to him are like a bunch of children, seemingly unable to make sensible, professional, thought-through suggestions. Instead, they blurt out ideas in meetings with no substance and expect a pat on the back. The management team complain amongst themselves that the senior manager never takes their ideas seriously, even the ones that could save the company money or increase profits; so there is no point wasting time doing loads of background work before (or after) the meetings. It soon gets to the point where neither party is prepared to discuss it... "what's the point". The tension is maintained and neither side are happy. Both sides are in a double bind now... either we try to discuss this issue, or we carry on not-discussing (avoiding) it. If either side try to address it, it may be seen as 'backing down' or it may invite criticism. If it is not discussed, the problem remains. This double bind is now a result of the original problem plus the new level of "don't talk about it".

Argyris (1990, p45) adds that "Organisational defensive routines create a double bind. If they are not confronted, they will reduce performance, commitment, and concern for the organisation... If defensive routines are confronted in order to reduce them, there is a risk of opening up a can of worms because the players do not know how to do it effectively. Skilled incompetence, the logic of defensive routines, a sense of hopelessness, and cynicism are not sound bases for change." He gives an example (p29-30) of an individual who has a high integrity and wants to accept personal responsibility but "if they do not discuss the defensive routines, then these routines will proliferate. If they do discuss them, they (the individuals) may get in trouble."

Consider a scenario where there is a misunderstanding between a manager and a member of the team. The manager's reaction to this misunderstanding is to pretend it didn't happen and that there is no problem. However, the manager stops asking the individual to get involved in any of the high profile, exciting projects. The individual wants to resolve this but feels in a double bind. If they try and resolve the issue with the manager they will be labelled a trouble maker, or a 'whinger', or accused of 'rocking the boat'. However, if they say nothing, the problem continues. They even consider escalating the problem to senior management but are concerned that this may make things worse. This is not the end of the story because by acting or not acting, new precedents may be set up or reinforced. This type of problem becomes multi-layered and it is useful to establish what those layers are.

Defensive Layers

In the example above, instead of approaching the issue, we don't talk about it. This becomes the first layer or 'shell' around the original misunderstanding which makes it harder to address (as it now has a frame around it). To address it now, we would have to be extra assertive and say: "I know we haven't talked about what happened the other day but I'd like to sort it out..." We may then have to deal with them saying things like: "I don't want to talk about it" or "that's water under the bridge" or "let's not dwell on the past". Now we have to work through this barrier to address the original issue. Of course, the longer we leave it at this stage the harder it gets because we move to another stage of not talking about the fact we don't talk about it! If we do try, it seems like a situation out of context. "Why are you bringing this up now? That was ages ago. Forget about it." Or we might be warned by others: "Don't go there!" As an external consultant or 'trouble-shooter', our job may be to go there anyway. As an employee, we may become labelled a 'troublemaker'. The 'can of worms' paradox mentioned in the introduction is an example of this.

In the realm of defensive layers, we know there is an elephant in the room, and yet we skirt round it. But anyway, let's change the subject...

What are the Layers or Levels of Organisational Defences?

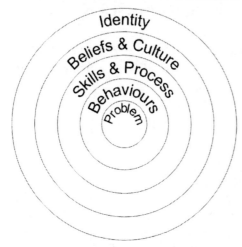

Figure 4b: The Layers/Levels Model

Instead of seeking to resolve or handle the issue, people use behaviours (eg. passive, indirect, aggressive) to avoid actually confronting the original issue. People become so good at avoiding such issues that it becomes an art or a skill; Argyris calls this 'skilled incompetence'. Sometimes, informal, unwritten or unspoken procedures are put in place to maintain the avoidance. So not only does the issue become undiscussable, the undiscussability becomes undiscussable too! This then becomes part of the longer term culture which embeds into the identity of the organisation/department/team/group.

Dilts' Logical Levels model (1990) appears to be a useful descriptor of how the layers of organisational defences are organised. In place of environment is the original issue or tension. This is then shielded by particular behaviours. Behaviours become skills. Processes are in place that become part of the culture and identity of the organisation.

Organisational defences compound the original problem and these defences will often have a number of levels, like layers of an onion. These could be considered 'meta-defences' and when these higher level defences get confused with the original problem, this creates a new type of problem that tends to lock the original problem in place.

The answer lies in understanding that there *are* levels (or layers) involved and what those levels are. Then we can work back though the levels, to address the original issue (if indeed it still exists!).

Let us return to the misunderstanding between the manager and the team member. What are the levels? Firstly, this is perhaps what happens if the individual tries to resolve it:

The manager avoids dealing with the original problem and instigates an 'organisational defence' (i.e. don't delegate). The individual now has two problems, (1) the original misunderstanding that has yet to be cleared, and (2) the lack of delegation. Not only is the individual in a double bind (to confront issue or not), he/she is also facing a dilemma: do I discuss one problem (the original problem or the lack of delegation) or both? If the individual chooses to address the issue(s) and is then labelled a troublemaker, what then? Either learn the lesson and avoid the issue or take the matter higher with the risk of repeating the process at a higher level and making their manager even more unhelpful! If the individual 'learns the lesson' well, they learn that 'we are a team that does not discuss issues'!

What about if the individual does not attempt to confront the issues of the misunderstanding and the lack of delegation:

Quite simply, the issue is avoided, the problem perpetuates and the likelihood of avoiding issues in the future is also perpetuated. The lesson is learnt more quickly that 'we are a team that does not discuss issues'.

Of course, in reality, this scenario might spin off in all sorts of directions and outcomes, but it does show the layers that compound the situation and make the original issue (which may have been quite simple) harder and harder to address.

Situations like this certainly take some intelligent unpicking and courageous action but it *is* possible. The first step is recognising that there is an issue of organisational defensiveness, then understanding (and mapping out) the levels or layers of defences, then asking some key questions, for example:

- What would need to happen for us to become a team that *does* discuss issues?
- What culture and belief shifts do we need to make issues discussable?
- How can we create an opportunity to discuss issues?
- What behaviours can we use to address issues?
- What can we do to prevent issues occurring in the first place or deal with them as they occur?

Recognising Organisational Defences

The nature of organisational and personal defences could be a severe challenge to resolving some impossible problems because it appears that tensions and paradoxes often sit within a series of such defences (Vince & Broussine 1996, Lewis 2000 and Argyris 1986). This makes the identification of the underlying problem significantly more difficult. If one cannot find the hidden issue, one cannot resolve it. However, because tensions and paradoxes may become buried in defences, this may ironically help to identify that there *is* an underlying issue. If we know some of the defences that paradox creates, we can seek out those defences and, with care, dig.

The good news about organisational defences is that although on one hand they muddy the waters, they are also a sign that there is (or was) an underlying tension. Defences do not appear out of nowhere or for no reason. Defences are wrapped around an issue... where we find organisational defences we will also find unresolved tensions. Often the tensions are buried and it is wise to take care as you dig for them. Otherwise, you may find yourself a victim to the very same defences that you are trying to get beyond.

As a starting point for recognising defences, it has been suggested that defences come in a multitude of forms. Siporin & Gummer (1988) give examples of: group denial, goal displacement, group think, collusion, mystification, infantilisation of a member, overt interpersonal conflict, 'vicious circles' of chronic negative interaction, scape-goating and outcasting, empire-building, ritualism, sabotage, exploitation, criminal or corrupt practices. Bobko (1985) gives the example of splitting (i.e. good and bad emotions linked to an object) and Harvey et al (2004) of fabricating information and underestimating the negative consequences of group decisions.

An impossible problem is often impossible because it has been buried in a tangle of organisational defences that prevent access to the original issue. It is worth expanding on the layers/levels model outlined earlier in this chapter (see figure 5b) to help us identify and understand these tangles and layers. Then we may be able to find ways of dealing with the impossible problem by addressing the layers it has created.

<u>*Defensive Behaviours*</u>

From the author's 'Paradox Study', the interviews elicited some very interesting data. This data was in the form of reported behaviours, which appeared to range from passive to aggressive and were all direct or indirect forms of avoiding the actual underlying problem. Each of these avoidance strategies/behaviours were probably stimulated by a fear response (fight/flight/fright) where aggressive is fight, passive-aggressive is flight and passive is fright. Table 4c organises the reported defences along a continuum from passive to aggressive with 'passive-aggressive' as the central column. All of the examples are behaviours that could happen on an individual or group level, hence the term 'organisational defences'.

Table 4c: Organisational defences sorted along a 'passive to aggressive' continuum

Passive	'Passive-Aggressive'	Aggressive
• Avoiding confrontation	• Being cynical	• Being 'overly emotional'
• Avoiding difficult people	• Creating us & them culture	• Blaming
• Compromising	• Getting into negative mindsets	• Claiming top priority
• Not challenging	• Getting stressed out	• Criticising if the new idea fails
• Not delegating	• Ignoring an issue	• Jumping up and down
• Not giving much information	• Looking around to demonstrate how they are hard done by	• Not listening
• Not introducing ideas		• Ranting
• Not making		

decisions • Not saying no • Not speaking up • Not standing one's ground • Working long hours	• Making a joke of it • Moaning, Whinging • Referring back to the past (holding on) • Silo mentality • Taking moral high ground • Taking someone/thing for granted • Thinking 'sod it'	• Taking an entrenched position

Although in the context of the research, the defensive behaviours were about avoidance (i.e. fight/flight/fright), the terms 'aggressive', 'passive-aggressive' and 'passive' are often used when discussing the concept of assertiveness (see 'Addressing Organisational Defences' later in this chapter).

A potentially twisted set of behaviours may emerge around bullying (which itself may be a defensive routine). Bullying might be in the form of aggressive (direct/threatening) through to passive-aggressive (indirect 'psychological' bullying). The *reaction* to the bullying might also become a defensive routine if it is not addressed assertively. Someone might react back with aggression creating a new level of conflict, or indirectly by 'stitching them up later on', or passively by letting it go and not saying anything. When the Chief Executive throws their phone at someone, it takes a brave soul to confront this! However, if nobody does, the behaviour is likely to continue. Silence becomes consent and permission for the bullying to carry on.

Layers Beyond the Defensive Behaviours

As people become acclimatised to the environment and culture of their team/department/ organisation, they generally become more and more skilled at avoiding difficult subjects. Those who want to discuss them are often seen as 'negative' and 'difficult'. This may lead to cynicism and scepticism within such an individual. It is often the case that those who challenge the system are eventually forced out or tolerated as a 'curiosity'.

When staff become sensitised as to what to avoid, they have reached the stage of 'skilled incompetence' Argyris (1988). Not only do people become effective at avoidance, they also learn a range of other skills some of which are direct and some of which are indirect:

Direct ←——————————————→ **Indirect**

Block: "I don't want to talk about it"   Postpone: "Let's talk about it later"
Threat: "Don't mention it or else"   Lie: "I'll think it over"
Deny: "No, that's not what's happening"
Change subject: "Let's talk about something else"
Claim Ignorance: "I don't know – so there's no point discussing it"
Ignore: "I'm not hearing you"
Intellectualise: "There is no evidence for your claim"

Groupthink (Janis 1982) could be considered another form of defensive skill. Each individual within the group learns not to challenge ideas, particularly if no-one else is challenging the ideas. Hence, poorly evaluated decisions are made and the group suffers from the 'problem of agreement'. However, no one specific person in the group can be blamed for the poor idea. Perhaps this is a defensive skill based on the principle of 'safety in numbers'. Argyris (1990, p56) writes about a big picture form of group think when he says: "The irony is that these ODRs [organisational defensive routines] become taken for granted. They are lamented by all players but accepted as part of organisational life. Once the defensive routines take hold, they, in turn, take hold of the players. The players feel helpless about changing them."

Once the defensive routines have become part of the beliefs, values and culture of the organisation, it becomes okay 'not to talk about it'. Indeed, many issues are so well avoided that they are not seen anymore. It is as if staff have to become experts at the art of 'negative hallucination' (sometimes known as the 'elephant in the room'... not seeing something that is obviously there).

It is only when someone new joins the organisation that they see and experience the 'unwritten rules'. Consider the organisations you have worked for in your career. In your first few days have you ever thought: "Why do they do that? Surely there is an easier way!" If you have, you may have been dancing with an organisational defensive routine! To add to the strangeness, sometimes the original tension has gone (moved on perhaps with a previous senior manager), and yet people still abide by the 'unwritten rules'.

Most unwritten rules and organisational defences become self regulating. I heard a story around the year 2000 of which I have never been able to find the original source (or validity). It was probably a thought experiment but it rings true of organisational cultures:

> *A group of five monkeys were allowed into a special enclosure that amongst other things contained a step-ladder with a banana on it. When one monkey went to get on the step-ladder, all five were sprayed with water. Soon, even without the water, if one monkey went to get on the step-ladder, the other four would grab that monkey and 'duff him up'.*

The rule was now self-reinforced. When a new monkey was introduced into the enclosure (and one removed) the new monkey went to get on the step-ladder and was 'duffed up' by the others. The rule was learnt. Another new monkey replaced an original monkey and the process was repeated. Eventually there were five monkeys in a cage, none of whom had ever experienced being sprayed with water, and yet none of them would get on the step-ladder.

As people join the organisation they are soon indoctrinated into 'this is the way we do things round here'. If they have creative ideas from other places they have worked, they may find that we are 'not that sort of company'. If they object or kick up a fuss, they will likely be alienated and ostracised, perhaps being labelled a 'pain' for 'rocking the boat'.

It is a rare and extraordinary senior manager who actively asks new members of staff how things could be improved (and then takes action accordingly).

A big picture view on the nature of organisational defences is highlighted by Joel Bakan in his book 'The Corporation' (2004). Bakan points out that if a corporation is legally bound to the wishes of the shareholders, what if the shareholders' only desire is profit? If profit is the only driving force for an organisation, there is no requirement for it to look after its people or its environment. A corporation is a legal entity unto itself and until recently, no person within the corporation was liable for the misdeeds of the corporation. Bakan reasoned that if the corporation was legally a person, what kind of person was it? Using the DSM-IV diagnostic tool, he reasons that most corporations are psychopathic since they exhibit the following symptoms of psychopathy:

- Disregard for the feelings of other people
- Incapacity to maintain human relationships

- Disregard for the safety of others
- Deceitfulness
- Incapacity to experience guilt
- Failure to conform to social norms
- Lack of respect for the law

If a company is driven at the level of 'spirit'/purpose (Dilts' Logical Levels model 1990) to be psychopathic, it follows that the identity, beliefs, values, culture, capabilities, behaviours and environment of the organisation are also likely to be 'psychotic'. This leads to some words of warning… be careful when addressing organisational defences. Make sure you are well prepared, well planned and carry the appropriate level of authority to make the change.

Addressing Organisational Defences

At the Level of Behaviour - The Assertive Option

Assertiveness is usually promoted as being a positive behaviour, whereas aggressive, passive and passive-aggressive (or indirect/manipulative) are considered more negative. By utilising the dialectic method (see Chapter 11), the author has integrated the 'passive to aggressive' continuum into a quadrant (see figure 4d) which includes assertiveness as the fourth behaviour/concept. The axis, 'empathy' (concern for acknowledging other people's feelings, rights, opinions etc) and 'expression' (concern for putting forth one's own feelings, rights, opinions etc) are arbitrary terms that capture the nature of the behaviours. Low empathy and/or low expression will tend to lead to defensive/avoidance behaviours whereas high empathy and high expression would help to open up 'win-win' discussion rather than hide from it. Figure 5d is designed to be a more accessible framework than previously found in the literature.

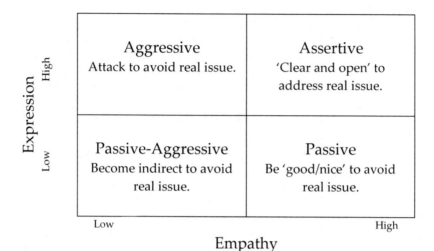

Figure 4d: Organisational Behaviours

Examples of assertive behaviour (i.e. non-defensive) range from active listening to facing up to issues (O'Brien 1997) and from a management/organisational perspective would include most of the solutions covered in table 4e. Assertive management would involve good management practice, for example effective contracting, win-win negotiation, clear direction, supportive coaching and appropriate communication. All of these behaviours are antithetical to organisational defences.

Table 4e: Solutions and interventions (proposed or implemented by those in the Paradox Study)

Category of Solution	Solution or intervention proposed or implemented
Personal	• Push the commercial angle. Back it up with facts. • Express point of view. • Communication, pragmatic approach, compromise or stand up for it. • Say 'no. The decision can be 'no'! • Better to say 'no' so the other person knows • Diplomatic skills to keep directors happy. • Take a holiday. • Talk to manager about what can and can't be done. • Talk to line managers first before setting up.

	<ul><li>Flag it up to manager.</li><li>Escalate to my manager to get info directly.</li><li>Communicate with person then escalate if necessary.</li><li>Prioritise (only works to a point).</li><li>Speaking to people round the back of the meeting.</li><li>Wait for instructions.</li><li>Take moral high-ground but avoid sticking head above parapet.</li><li>Speak up about it – 'get it off your chest'.</li></ul>
Managerial	<ul><li>Gain confidence over time to make own mind up.</li><li>Experience of individual and their needs. Clear targets and objectives.</li><li>Carry on, sort it out and talk to other shift manager.</li><li>Team building.</li><li>Team building, hasn't helped.</li><li>Make a judgement call or get advice and then give clear direction.</li><li>Need to delve to get to the heart of the problem.</li><li>Talk to teams. Meet to discuss issues.</li><li>Consult and train staff more.</li></ul>
Organisational	<ul><li>Drive and integration programme to remind them they are part of the same company.</li><li>Solutions formed for individual situations.</li><li>Compromise. Do customisation without damaging the other side.</li><li>Use same system but communicate differently.</li><li>Get proactive and support other agencies who can handle new or old issues.</li><li>Someone needs to say "we need to share information". Raise that at a lower level at team meetings.</li><li>Integrating services. Training staff.</li><li>Need more org structure to prioritise. Talk to people from other departments, but this is 'topsy turvey'.</li><li>Reframe – sometimes by waiting the outside world makes the decision for us.</li><li>Need direction from the top.</li><li>Stay rational, be aware of competitor but not try and do everything.</li></ul>

Although assertive behaviour might not always resolve paradox, it would certainly help to face these tensions rather than avoid them. It is likely that assertive behaviour would prevent defences (and sometimes prevent tensions/paradoxes) and therefore allow the resolution of the paradoxes themselves through paradox management techniques outlined in Chapters 8-14. It is also possible that these defences might appear during any organisational development intervention and so an awareness of them combined with what they might mean and how to handle them could be crucial to a successful intervention.

Solutions Beyond the Level of Behaviour

In order for the organisation to reduce the level of defensive routines and layers, there needs to be a culture where it is okay to raise issues. I wouldn't necessarily go as far as to say that raising issues should be rewarded as this can create a 'flip' paradox of people creating faults in order to 'find' them and be rewarded for them. However, there needs to be a system in place for people to raise issues without fear of retribution.

Some organisations use a 'suggestion box' approach where people can post ideas anonymously. If this is a new idea, it helps if people are given a structure or template of how to write their feedback. For example, a suggestion sheet with blank boxes with:
1) Issue: Please describe the current issue as you see it
2) Desired Outcome: Ideally, how would you like things to be?
3) Recommendations: What ideas do you have to resolve the current issue to achieve the desired outcome?
4) If you would like to be contacted with regards to this issue, please give your details. Otherwise, your suggestion will be treated anonymously.

It is then important that a senior management team (with authority to make change) collate issues and ideas on a regular basis and published as appropriate (apart from confidential issues that refer to specific managers/members of staff). Action needs to be taken and published or if action is not going to be taken, an explanation as to why. With regards to any issues about specific individuals, HR may need to be involved and action taken (or not) on a case by case basis.

The process of handling issues and defensive routines is part of the creation of a 'learning organisation'. It could be argued that Argyris' (1994) concept of *double loop learning* is perhaps fundamental to the learning organisation. If double loop learning is to work, it needs to become an organisational skill where a process is put in place to regularly challenge the current state (e.g. systems, processes, procedures, products, structure, strategies) of a team/ department/ organisation (depending on the level at which the double loop learning is taking place).

Single loop learning is, in essence, detecting and correcting errors. It is where we establish that something isn't how we want it to be, so we take action to change it. If the outcome is what we want, we then go back to business as usual. If it is not what we want, we try another solution. At worst, single loop learning can be quite reactive, just dealing with the symptoms of problems as they occur. At best, we might ask: "How can we improve X and/or do X better?"

Double loop learning is where we not only acknowledge and fix problems; we look at the situation from a system level and ask if a system needs changing (as opposed to fixing bits of the system). Is the system (process, procedure etc.) serving a function any more or has the need for it changed? Is it still valid, useful and fit for purpose? Does it still serve a purpose (i.e. is the original purpose still there)?

Only by having a big picture view and understanding the fixes we put in place can we truly learn. Otherwise we are doomed to reinvent solutions and remain reactive to our environment. Double loop learning is about going beyond the single loop process and checking out the reason why we started doing the process in the first place (to see if it is still necessary and/or valid). It is also about identifying what prevented us from recognising the issues in the first place and questioning underlying organisational policies, outcomes, objectives and goals. Figure 4f (below) gives an overview of the process of single and double loop learning.

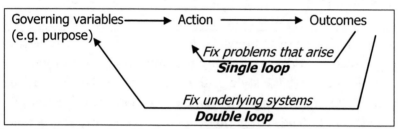

Figure 4f: Single vs Double Loop Learning (Adapted from Argyris 1994)

Although it is challenging, the organisation needs to find ways of moving beyond a blame culture. Rather than focussing on whose fault it was, there needs to be a focus on how do we want things to be different moving forward? In the field of NLP (neuro-linguistic programming) there is a presupposition ('positive belief') that there is no failure, just feedback. If something isn't working, it is not a failure but information on how not to do something! Where this philosophy exists within an organisation, people are more likely to acknowledge 'mistakes' and learn from them, rather than covering them up with defensive routines.

A Final Word of Warning!

As already mentioned in this chapter, caution needs to be taken if challenging the defensive routines in an organisation. The defences have been built and maintained for a reason and are unlikely to be logical and rational. Any intervention or change in the organisation is likely to be resisted, challenged and 'politically manoeuvred'. A member of staff who is embedded in the organisation and who wishes to improve the culture may find themselves ostracised or 'managed out' of the business.

It is usually easier for a consultant or interim manager to challenge 'the way things are done' because that is often their remit. In addition, they will be moving on again afterwards. Even then, there are no guarantees.

A consultant friend of mine was asked to do a five year review of a charity which he did, making sure that any recommendations were couched in the language style of the organisation. This was no easy task since the charity had a history of not encouraging people to give feedback. Indeed, when he handed in the report, the people in the charity would not speak to him again!

Sometimes, cover-ups are purposeful and set up for a reason. If someone has made a mistake (or worse) and does not want to be found out, they will most likely fight back against those who try to uncover the issue. In extreme cases, you may be dealing with people who are 'not in their right mind' (e.g. alcoholism, drug taking, lawbreaking, psychosis) and these people can become very skilled at hiding issues, building alliances and discrediting those who challenge them.

If anyone decides to challenge defensive routines and 'discuss the undiscussable', they need to make sure they have the authority to challenge the system and make the changes. They need to familiarise themselves with the current culture and explore the ripple effect of the 'way things are done' and what would happen if they were no longer in place. They need to consider what might replace the old defensive routine and who would be exposed if the routine disappeared? They need to be aware of alliances... who do these people (who might get exposed) know? Who has power and what kind of power? Anyone seeking to intervene here needs to consider how far they are prepared to go in order to instigate change.

Although on the surface it may appear a 'defeatist' attitude, sometimes the most prudent course of action is to leave the field. If you work for a company in which you feel misaligned, look outside to see what another options may be available. Sometimes the best strategic move is to move on!

Chapter 5

Organisational Models for Scoping & Exploring Impossible Problems

In This Chapter...

In this chapter, you will be exploring six models that will help you to diagnose and understand where problems are coming from within an organisation. This, in turn, will enable you to better communicate the specifics of the issue to other people with a view to finding a resolution.

For each of the six models, we will be exploring the following questions:
- Where is the problem in the organisation?
- What and/or who is the problem between?
- How big and/or widespread is the problem?
- What is the 'ripple effect' of the problem?

Where do Impossible Problems occur within organisations?

When we discover an organisational problem it is important to be able to identify specifically what is going on. By looking at a problem from only a 'big picture', organisation-wide perspective, we run the risk of having something that is too ill-defined and hence potentially impossible to solve. We need to know *what* the specific problem is, what the scope is and *how* is it a problem?

In order to set a context to an 'impossible problem', it is necessary to understand the levels and components of an organisation. Where do problems arise and 'act out'? A useful skill for anyone addressing organisational issues is to be able to move between big picture and details. The models in this chapter will help you to do this by allowing you to explore and ultimately pinpoint where problems actually sit. The idea is not necessarily to use them all in every instance, but to 'pick and mix'. It is probable that you will find certain models appealing to you more than others.

Models for Exploration

Model 1: The McKinsey 7S Model

For understanding more specifically where issues sit within an organisation we will start with the McKinsey 7S model (Peters and Waterman 1990). This was developed by a team at the McKinsey consultancy, after carrying out extensive research of the literature up to that point in time. A question that drove the research was: "What is an organisation?" Is it the people, is it the structure or is it the name? The model suggests seven categories that collectively make up an organisation as demonstrated in figure 5a. Each of these categories is interlinked and so the model is systemic. If a change is made in (or to) any category, the other categories will also be affected either directly or indirectly.

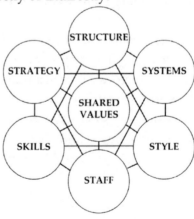

Figure 5a: The McKinsey 7S Model

7S	Definition
Structure	How the business is organised and divided up.
Strategy	The plans the business has in response to the external environment.
Systems	The formal and informal procedures the business has in place.
Shared Values	That which is true of the culture and is most important to people.
Skills	That which the business does best and the skills that people have.
Style	How management comes across.
Staff	Who the people are and how they are currently treated. Concerns, feelings, morale.

The 7S model may be useful in diagnosing where polarities exist within an organisation and hence where tensions are coming from. A tension might exist *within* a category (e.g. conflicting strategies) or *between* categories (e.g. management style is at odds with the shared values and staff morale). The model may also help to determine where the cause(s) and the effect(s) of the tensions are.

An example of the 7S model in action might be that an organisation's IT system has so many issues, that it leads to stress in the staff and a culture (shared values) of cynicism about IT systems. The organisation introduces a new IT system but it is resisted by the staff. The effect of this resistance is a change in management style to becoming more directive which in turn conflicts with the company strategy and values of empowerment and hence staff turnover increases.

Tensions within any system or organisation suggests that something may need to be resolved, improved or changed and using the 7S model to explore tensions and paradox may make it easier to understand and map the conflicting issues. This in turn may make it easier for management and staff to resolve those issues.

Sometimes it is obvious from where issues are originating and then where they are manifesting elsewhere in the organisation. At other times, a problem can be more complex where a series of tensions have been set up. In this instance it is worth setting up an empty grid with the 7S's down the side and also across the top. Then consider each combination to determine where polarities and tensions have arisen.

Once the areas of the problem have been identified within the 7S model, this allows you to drill down further to get to the specific issue(s). For example, if a specific system has caused a clash with the skills, what specific skills are missing and hence required to cope with the system?

The following grid gives a series of examples of organisational polarities and tensions:

7S	Structure	Strategy
Structure	One dept. has a flat structure and the rest of the org. cannot 'translate' it to their own hierarchy.	
Strategy	Current structure does not fit new plans.	Conflicting plans take the org in different directions.

Examples of Organisational Polarities and Tensions using the McKinsey 7S model

	Structure	Strategy	Systems	Shared Values	Skills	Style	Staff
Systems	Restructure conflicts with current HR systems.	Old systems do not support new work-plans.	Incompatible IT systems.				
Shared Values	New structure is at odds with culture of 'who belongs on what floor'.	Cost cutting strategy interferes with 'how we do things' e.g. biscuits in meetings.	A new IT system doesn't allow people access to the internet for personal use even in break times.	Merging teams/ services that have different cultures.			
Skills	Restructure requires multi-skilling which doesn't currently exist.	New company directions require different skill sets.	Staff not trained to use new systems.	Culture of 'you cannot teach an old dog new tricks'	Skills gap in team between what is and what is needed.		
Style	New structure requires a unpopular change in leadership style.	Directive management don't like new 'people centred' future plans.	Management feel restricted by new rules and regulations.	Traditional management style is challenged as ineffective by new MD.	Managers delegate without checking people have appropriate experience.	Different management styles lead to unfair performance reviews.	
Staff	Office move causes upset as people are moved.	Workforce being cut due to new plans.	Staff dislike new system as they have only just learnt the previous one.	Morale drops as workforce is reduced.	Staff are expected to know how to do things they are not trained to do.	Staff do not like the way they are being treated by a manager.	Personality clashes.

Model 2: The Organisational Hierarchy of Concern

As well as looking at the components of an organisation, impossible problems can also occur on or between any number of organisational *levels* as highlighted in the Organisational Hierarchy of Concern (Fig 5b).

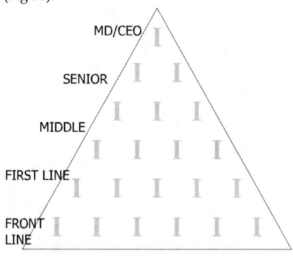

MD/CEO

SENIOR

MIDDLE

FIRST LINE

FRONT LINE

Figure 5b: The Organisational Hierarchy of Concern

During times of change, different levels of the organisation will have different types of issues, concerns, questions and needs. If a change is planned and implemented from the perspective of one or two levels, the resistance from the other levels is likely to be more extreme (and usually more surprising) to those initiating change. In order to prevent 'unforeseen tensions' during organisational change, it is essential to consider the potential concerns at each level of the organisation (no matter where the change is driven from). In addition to the concerns, you may want to consider the potential benefits to each level too which will help to integrate the change.

One feature of the Organisational Hierarchy of Concern is that changes initiated/driven from higher levels are likely to have more organisational impact than those initiated from below. Consider the internal consultant who attempts to initiate a necessary change.

Unless they have the blessing and support of those higher up (e.g. senior stakeholders) they will be limited by their own level within the hierarchy. They will find it very difficult to make people above them do anything if they lack the perceived authority.

As mentioned earlier in chapter 1, the same is also true if you are an external consultant. If you are called in to change something, what level is the person calling you in? Who are you reporting to? You may find yourself prevented from going beyond that level. It is also probable that as a consultant you might get pulled into the system and politics of the organisation. So, if you are coming in from the outside, how can you remain external and maintain your credibility? A consultant I met a few years back had this kind of 'impossible problem' as he was brought in by a director to help make change happen. However, they soon found that the MD was against the change. Although the change would have dramatically improved the situation, the organisation wasn't going anywhere.

For each level of the organisation, we can consider the issues, questions, concerns, needs and expectations in relationship to the problem at hand. For example: What has not yet been taken into account? How might some of the concerns etc. of one level clash with another? What specifically is at odds and what still needs to be addressed?

Model 3: The Buffer Zone

Pressure can come at someone from a number of directions. Any manager in an organisation will most likely know the pressures coming from above, below and sideways in the form of needs and expectations. Figure 3c below gives a visual representation of the manager's plight. The manager has to meet the needs and expectations of the organisation (including their own manager) but also has to meet the needs and expectations of their team. Do the needs of the team always match up with the needs of the organisation? Of course not! Often these needs and expectations are diametrically opposed and hence there is a tension. To add to this, if a manager deals with internal and external customers, there is another set of tensions. The manager becomes the 'Buffer Zone'.

Fig 5c The Buffer Zone: Needs and expectations on the manager

In the diagram above (Fig 5c), tensions can occur between and within any of the areas. For example, individuals in the team may have conflicting expectations of the manager and the manager's manager may have different needs to the organisational objectives. The pressures on a manager will never go away, but experience can provide more efficient solutions.

Of course it is not just managers that are in a Buffer Zone of pressures. Senior management report to the chief exec and the chief exec has to report to the shareholders (or members). At the front line, there is pressure from management and from the customer.

For any management level (or for a particular manager), consider the needs and expectations that act upon them, coming from the organisation (including their own manager), their team and the internal/external customers.

- Do those needs and expectations always match up?
- What issues does that create when they don't match up?
- How might those issues be resolved?
- Are the needs and expectations of the customers, organisation and team on management realistic?
- If they are not realistic, what can you do to resolve that?

Consider also the management's expectations of the customers, the organisation and the team.

- Are the expectations aligned?
- What issues does that create for management when they are not aligned?
- How might those issues be resolved?
- Are the management's expectations of the customers, organisation and team realistic?
- How might management be challenged to check their expectations are realistic?
- If they are not realistic, what can be done to resolve that?

Model 4: Organisational Scope

Linked to the levels of the Organisational Hierarchy of Concern is the Organisational Scope of the problem. How local or global is the issue? Is it happening within or between individual staff members (who could be anywhere in the organisation, from front line to senior management) or is the issue happening on a larger scale between groups or departments?

Organisational Scope Of Problem	Example
Personal	An internal conflict might cause an individual to feel split between a number of options.

Interpersonal	Two or more people might fall out with each other, or take different positions on an issue.
Team	A team becomes dysfunctional, perhaps because of conflicting priorities and unrealistic workloads.
Inter-team	Two or more teams are in competition with each other to achieve results. For this reason they end up sabotaging each other.
Departmental	The structure of a department is changed (e.g. from hierarchical to flat) and some of the staff don't like it.
Inter-departmental	One area of the business wants to produce quality items and so needs time to do this, whilst another department want to get sales in and products out the door as quickly as possible.
Organisational	An organisation is losing market share and so becomes confused about its identity and core market.
Inter-organisational	Two or more organisations within the same group are direct competitors and so try to undercut each others prices.
Market place: Competition	An organisation gets caught in a 'dirty tricks' campaign with a competitor because the competitor 'started it first'.
Market place: Customer	In a bid to attract new customers, the organisation has a special introductory offer. However, loyal customers are not offered such a good deal and so they go elsewhere.

In a given context, how widespread is the problem? How many people are involved and/or affected. What are the consequences if the problem is not resolved? At what level of the organisation will this need to be addressed?

Model 5: Dilts' Logical Levels

The Logical Levels of Change framework (also known as the 'Neurological Levels') was developed by Robert Dilts and originally published in "Changing Belief Systems with NLP" (1990). The framework was 'inspired' by Gregory Bateson's (2000) work on 'Logical Types' which in turn was based on Whitehead and Russell's (1970) 'Set Theory' and 'Theory of Types'. The nature of logical levels in general and their applications to paradox management are explored further in chapter 7.

Dilts presents the model as a pyramid style hierarchy (see Figure 5d) where each level is a category or set that contains the level directly below (e.g. a capability or skill is a collection of behaviours). It could also be said that a higher level cannot develop without the immediate level below (e.g. a skill cannot develop without behaviours). A change at any level will impact on those above and below (i.e. the model is systemic), although a higher level change tends to have more effect on the lower levels than vice versa. The key principle of the framework is that each level organises, governs, contains and categorises information from the level below it. For this reason, it is advisable to seek solutions at a higher level above which the problem sits (as this should give you more leverage on the problem). As an aside, although Dilts' model has been criticised for not representing 'true logical types/levels', it can be extremely useful nevertheless when used as a tool for exploration and problem resolution.

The model consists of six hierarchical levels comprising of Spirit (bigger picture purpose beyond the individual organisation) which is supported by Identity supported by Beliefs and Values supported by Capability supported by Behaviour supported by Environment (see Fig 5d).

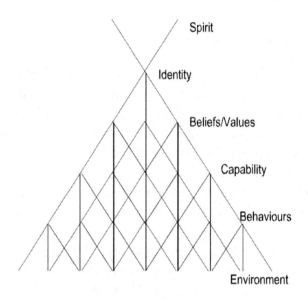

Figure 5d: The Logical Levels

7S	Definition Question
Spirit	Who are we here for?
	Who are we here to serve?
Identity	Who are we?
Beliefs & Values	Why do we do what we do?
	What do we believe in?
	What is important to us?
Capability/ Skills	How do we do what we do?
	What are we good at?
Behaviours	What do we do?
Environment	Where and when do we do what we do?

The key benefits of Dilts' Logical levels model are that it will help you to:

- explore different levels of an issue,
- see if certain levels are out of alignment with others,
- detect where conflicts may be occurring,

- establish possible solutions by going to another (preferably higher) level.

An example of Dilts' Logical Levels model in action was a County Council that was being unified with the District and Borough Councils in the same county. The staff in many service areas (departments) felt that they were losing their identity, particularly since they were being split into two possible districts (or having no job at all). The result of the 'loss of identity' was a decrease in motivation and belief in what they did. Things were not getting done and people were getting irritable with each other. Given the notion of getting to the level above the problem, we explored the level of 'spirit' ('for whom') and helped them to realise and accept that what would not be changing was the service they provided to their customers (i.e. the people they were there to support and help). By focussing the staff on this higher level, they regained a sense of (albeit changing) identity.

For exploring polarities and tensions within and between the logical levels, I have developed the model further to include an **internal/external** distinction (Cheal 2007). This helps to resolve such confusions as to whether the environment of an organisation is the décor, the appearance of reception and restaurant etc. or whether it is the market place and/or the geographical site. Obviously, the **internal** describes the inner environment and the **external** describes the outside world.

Internal & External Aspects of the Logical Levels

Level	"In Side" (Internal eyes)	"Out Side" (External Eyes)
Spirit *For Whom?*	Common vision between staff Internal partnerships	Published Company Vision Corporate Social Responsibility Partnerships Customer satisfaction and loyalty
Identity *Who?*	Collective of people Culture: paradigm – what is true of this	Company name, brand, logos, image, mission statement. Generalised public experience of

	organisation? E.g. "We are competitive." Purpose	individual staff members/representatives of the organisation. The face of the organisation (eg. Branson = Virgin)
Beliefs/Values *Why?*	Culture, rules, policies Motivation Staff satisfaction (e.g. surveys)	Published value statements, policies Advertising/promotional material, brochures. Strap-lines, slogans Customer satisfaction surveys
Capability *How?*	States, memory, imagination, innovation, skills, abilities, knowledge, thinking. Systems, procedures, training, induction Performance, competency framework, objectives, plans, goals Resources, workforce, time, money, power, authority, tools, technology, IT	Customer service Effectiveness in marketplace Published/written procedures What is offered: product, service.
Behaviour *What?*	How people treat each other What people talk about What people do to try to get what they want Implementing action points/plans	Publicly visible actions, reactions, responses, interactions. Takeovers, buyouts. Reducing/increasing prices. Releasing new product Carrying out the service.
Environment *Where/When?*	Décor, reception, canteen, physical surroundings, buildings	Marketplace, geographical location, competitors, suppliers, customers, potential customers, partners and potential partners.

This hierarchical model allows you to explore at what level(s) the two ends of a polarity sit (and hence where/how the tension is being created). Do the tensions sit at the same level or different? Does the organisation do internally what is says it does publicly (externally)?

The Logical Levels model can help you to identify (in a given context and/or issue) where the issue sits predominantly. It may also help you to highlight conflict (or a number of conflicts) between the levels. When you have identified the level of an issue, you can go to the level above and notice what ideas come from this higher level in helping to resolve the issue.

Model 6: The Rational - Emotional Divide

Another important consideration when addressing impossible problems (or any form of problem) is that an organisation has both a rational *and* emotional side. Although addressing both sides may seem common sense, it is certainly not always common practice. The emotional side is often neglected as the focus is placed upon rational solutions. However, by their very nature, impossible problems are usually 'irrational'.

To explore the difference between rational and emotional, let us look at it from an individual perspective. When someone is in an emotional state, what happens to rationality? For most people, it 'goes out the window'. In this sense, when the balance tips over and we 'lose it' to emotion, we become more irrational. It could be said that emotions act like lenses, distorting what we experience and the way we think. And what happens if you try to deal with an emotional person in a rational way? Usually it acts like pouring petrol onto flames in an attempt to put out the fire. Indeed, Fine (2007, p44) suggests that "our decisions, opinions, perception and memory can all be set adrift by our emotional undercurrents – often without our even noticing that our anchor has slipped." It is apparent that when talking about emotions (particularly in a professional setting), we rely heavily on metaphor. It is as if we are sometimes reluctant to express and talk about emotion directly.

What if we apply the Rational–Emotional model to an organisation? Impossible problems, particularly when 'irrational' will tend to sit in what Wagner (1978) calls the *affective* side of the organisation as opposed to the rational. It is worth exploring further the idea of an organisation having a rational and emotional (affective) side because this may help to provide a context to impossible problems and their resolution. It should be noted that the categorisation demonstrated in the table below is more useful when considered as conceptual as opposed to representing reality. Although it is not designed to represent 'how the world really is', it may be a useful way of explaining why rational interventions are not always successful.

Examples of the Rational and Emotional sides of an organisation.

Rational	Emotional
Systems and procedures	Paradox and tensions
Objectives	Values, symbols and metaphor
Structure, roles & responsibilities	Ambiguity and uncertainty
Management of task and process	Leadership of hearts and minds
Procedural/planned project side of change	Natural change and resistance

Although the rational-emotional distinction is expressed here as a polarity (either/or), it is important for an organisation to understand, utilise and synthesise both aspects. It is also true that other components of an organisation will not necessarily fit neatly into these categories, for example from the McKinsey Seven 'S' model (Peters & Waterman 1990): staff, strategy and skills might each range across a rational-emotional continuum.

What happens if an organisation is too rational?
Would it help us if we were purely rational? Perhaps not, as this would return us to a state of depersonalisation, a loss of sense of self. Following this train of thought leads to the inevitable analogy of people being like logical robots, with no genuine motivation, no creative spark, no evolution, no 'joie de vivre'. Perhaps this is a debate for the philosophers, but it suggests that we require both the

rational and emotional, working in balance and harmony with one another, both informing the other.

A particularly useful element of the Rational-Emotional model as a metaphor is in explaining what happens if the emotional aspects of an organisation are ignored. For example, during times of organisational change, the level of resistance is likely to be higher if people do not feel involved, or perceive that their feelings have not been taken into account. Perhaps people do not always resist *what* is changing, but instead *how* the change is being carried out. Vince & Broussine (1996, p18) suggest that "It is difficult for managers to work with, and even sometimes to admit to, the existence of either emotional or unconscious aspects to their role... if these remain denied and unacknowledged, then attempts to make change happen will be restricted and ultimately unsuccessful."

What happens if an organisation is too emotional?
What happens to an organisation when emotion overrides reason? It is likely that an 'over emotional' organisation is unproductive, acting like an individual who goes into an emotional state and becomes irrational, losing touch with the rational side. Values without objectives have no direction. Constant change without stability creates exhaustion.

It is likely that an 'overdose' of negative (and indeed positive) emotions will have an adverse impact on the organisation. On the other hand, emotions in balance can be very helpful. The following gives an example of some organisational emotional states and what happens when there is too much and also when there is a balance:

Organisational Emotion/State	Emotional 'Overdose'	Balanced
Fear (concern)	• Uncertainty & worry • Panic and risk taking • Increased absenteeism & staff turnover • Decision avoidance • Procrastination & inaction	• Awareness of environment • Desire for reality checking • Identify and manage risks • Contingency planning
Anger (frustration)	• Hostility • Aggression • Increased levels of bullying	• Identify things that are not right or working properly and drive for change/improvement • Focus on fairness and justice
Joy & Excitement	• Euphoria • Childlike 'loss of control' & loss of perspective • Distraction • Unwarranted/blind optimism & hence higher risk taking	• Love and enjoyment of the work (and/or the people, outcomes etc.) • Motivation (want to do more)
Contentment	• Complacency • Lack of attention to detail & miss the 'what could go wrong' when planning.	• Satisfaction and fulfilment

The Rational-Emotional model in Paradox Management

There is an irony here; although paradox management deals neatly with the emotional side of the organisation, in order for it to be taken seriously, it needs to be practical and logical (i.e. rational). And as a discipline, for it to be put into practice, 'paradox management' needs to appeal to managers within organisations (rather than be perceived as a theoretical 'academic exercise'). It would also be of benefit if 'paradox management' can be accessible to (and within the control of) all individuals in the organisation. Price Waterhouse (1996) propose fifteen rules of managing paradox but they can only be achieved at an organisational/director level. Although perhaps useful at the top level, surely this leaves the rest of the organisation drowning in paradox, hoping that someone at the top will notice. If a paradox is only really affecting people at 'lower levels' of the organisation, the director level will usually be the furthest away from the implications of such paradoxical problems, and therefore the least aware (and probably the least motivated to find resolutions).

It is essential to understand the nature of paradox without losing sight of the practical business application. At the same time, it is important not to simplify paradox management to the point of being ineffective and unusable.

In a given context (e.g. organisational change) it is worth taking note of the following:
- What are the emotions and feelings being expressed and acted out? How are people talking and behaving?
- What is the organisation currently doing to handle these emotions (on an individual and group level)?
    - Are these approaches rational (e.g. put a system in place) or emotional (e.g. facilitated workshops to engage staff)?
- What else could the organisation be doing?

Chapter 6

Deeper Understanding: The Thinking and Language of Paradox

In This Chapter...

In this chapter, you will discover some of the reasons we seem to perceive the world in either/or terms. Although this section is not essential to the resolution of impossible problems, it is designed to give some ideas as to why and how we think the way that we do.

We will be exploring the following questions:
- Why do we polarise the world into opposites?
- How does our thinking and language create duality?
- Is paradox cultural?

Duality Thinking, Beliefs and the Self Fulfilling Prophecy

On a moment to moment basis, our thinking affects how we feel (and vice versa). If our thinking leads us to feel trapped and/or less than positive in some way, then it is worth identifying that in order to change it. On a larger scale, our thinking affects our belief system (and vice versa). Our belief system becomes our psychological playground, complete with fences and boundaries. Our beliefs can help us, but our beliefs can also hinder and limit us too. If we are aware of the kind of thinking that traps us in paradox, we may begin to understand how we can step out of it again and think differently.

As already discussed, the basis of paradox is polarity. It would seem that we have a built in tendency to see the world from a perspective of opposites, e.g. night and day, this or that, big or small. This duality thinking appears to be our way of making sense of the world. We sort things into categories and place value judgements on them... good or bad, right or wrong. We then generalise, for example: "Fred is a good manager," so we have placed Fred in the position (pole) of 'good manager'. We may disagree with someone else who takes the opposite view: "Fred is a bad manager". In order to maintain the stability of our belief (generalisation) that "Fred is a good manager" we may unconsciously ignore some of Fred's less desirable behaviours and focus on the positives thus justifying our belief. Our colleague on the other hand finds themselves focussing on Fred's less than desirable traits and is blind to Fred's strengths. Each of us creates a self fulfilling prophecy by maintaining our generalised belief about Fred and so we both get to be 'right'.

Why do we see and process the world in this dualistic way?

Subject and Object

From the earliest, simplest sentences we learn, there is a subject and an object. Someone (or something) is usually doing something in relation to someone (or something) else. This immediately sets up a *difference* as we now have a duality between the doer and the done to. For example, the statement 'my manager praised me', gives us a duality – there is a difference between my manager and me. Inherent in this subject/object split is the potential for tensions. We have the subject (the manager) and the object (me). We know that there is a manager and something that is not the manager (i.e. me).

When a sentence has no apparent object, it is usually implied or deleted in some way. We tend not to feel satisfied with the statement, as if it is missing something. Take the statement 'Fred walked'. The mind wants to ask questions here to complete the picture. Where did he walk? When? How? How long for? 'Fred walked around town' now gives us our subject (Fred) and our object (the town). Now we have Fred and something that is not Fred (i.e. the town).

Of course, something could be the subject *and* object, but even then, we seek differentiation. For example, 'Fred hit himself' means that Fred is both subject and object. However, imagine Fred hitting himself now. It is likely that you will get an image of Fred's hand hitting some other part of his anatomy. In this sense, we still have subject (Fred's hand) and object (other body part).

The point here is not to give the reader a lesson in grammar; it is to point out that the fundamental building block of our language, which in turn affects our thinking, is based on separation, division and difference. This is neither right nor wrong, neither good nor bad... it simply is. It is important however in considering that we are programmed to differentiate.

The Embodiment of Thinking and the Dualistic Brain

Physiologically, we are two parts that work together. The brain is in two halves, left brain (which controls the right side of the body) and right brain (which controls the left side of the body). In most people, the left brain is 'dominant' in the sense that it is responsible for language and thinking. It is therefore responsible for most of our experience of consciousness and self awareness and hence it plays a more immediate role in our processing of the world.

Under 'normal' circumstances we have two eyes, ears, arms, hands, legs, feet etc. It is not surprising that we experience and process the world in duality. Have you ever been in two minds about something? On one hand you might do this, but on the other hand you might do that. Have you ever noticed in organisations where the right hand doesn't seem to know what the left hand is doing?

In the same way that our binocular vision is converted into one picture in our minds eye, the beauty of the body is that it works in unity (particularly when fully healthy) as the system transcends the parts. Although the components of the body are in duality, the whole of the body works as one unit. This is an excellent analogy for how we will be seeking the resolution of paradox later in the book.

In the fields of Embodied Cognition and Cognitive Linguistics (e.g. Shapiro 2011, Evans & Green 2007, Lakoff & Johnson 1999), it is suggested that language is embodied (i.e. the body influences and is influenced by language and thoughts). Notice the difference internally between "in the room" and "out of the room". How about your internal experience of "on the table" versus "under the table"? The prepositions we use in language shift our physiological experience of them. When someone is 'under' pressure, they need a way to get back 'on top' of it all, so that they can get 'over' it. For most people, there is a significant physical difference between feeling 'below' standard as opposed to 'above' standard.

Once again, with our language and our use of prepositions, we are in the realm of opposites... for example: up/down, in/out, above/below, to the left/right, one side or the other, back/front, forward/backward.

Our body (including mind) is the only tool we have for creating meaning about our relationship with the world. Our language has a direct impact on our physiology. Even at the most basic level, we hear a word and it stimulates a set of neurons to fire off. We can even *think* a word and those neurons will fire. Consider the word 'elephant'. When you hear, read or think the word 'elephant', certain neurons in the brain will 'light up' and you might even get an image of an elephant. However, the words have made a direct link to the body. If our body is dualistic, our language and thinking is likely to be as well. The two things are systemically linked, affecting one another in a cybernetic loop.

Either/Or Thinking

The problem of polarised thinking appears to trace back to Aristotelian logic which, in turn, has influenced Western thinking to the present day. The Aristotelian 'exclusive or' has become known more commonly as 'either/or' thinking and it creates polarities (e.g. either right or wrong, either win or lose). Why does polarity lead to paradox? A common description and/or definition for paradox (e.g. Berg & Smith, 1995, p107) is that it "describes a particular relationship between opposites. It is, in its simplest form, a statement or state of affairs seemingly contradictory but expressing a truth." Polarity equates to two contradictory opposites, either X or not X.

The notion of either/or thinking might sometimes be perceived as a quest for truth... dividing, sorting and categorising to establish what is real and what is not. So, in order to categorise and make sense of the world, we often sort things into either/or terms. We could also call this black or white thinking. Something is either one thing or another, it cannot be both. A fridge is a fridge. A cooker is a cooker. A fridge is not a cooker. The appliance you might be thinking of is either a fridge or a cooker.

Some people seem to find it hard to move beyond seeing things in black or white terms whilst others are very happy with shades of grey. Here again we have a potential polarity... those who want to see things in absolute terms of one thing or another, and those that say things are rarely that simple. Our notion of science has the same polarity: at one end we have the 'positivist' school of objectivity with absolute right or wrong answers. At the other end is the 'phenomenologist' school of subjectivity where each person has their own answers.

Positioning – Right and Wrong

When people are in conflict with one another, they tend to get stuck in their position, placing a value judgement on something as right or wrong. One of the key tell-tale signs to know if you are stuck in a position about something is when you 'know' you are right. You know someone else is stuck in their position because they obviously 'know' they are right and they are likely to keep repeating their position again and again.

When we get ourselves into this need to feel right, we tend to find it very difficult to see or even acknowledge the other person's perspective. We go into absolute thinking and at that point become very limited in what we will accept or hear.

This is true of negotiations where one party has an absolute fixed outcome they want and will not budge from that. This kind of negotiation soon turns into a conflict, where the other party decides not to budge either. Positions are taken and everyone stares at each other across the table. A paradox is born!

Negation

Paradox is based on the existence of two opposing concepts, both of which seem valid. This can be an impossible problem… which side do we sit on when both sides are equally valid? Can we accept two opposing concepts as true at the same time and live with that tension?

The concept of 'not', or negation may be at the heart of paradox. Andreas (2006, p58) suggests that "negation is an easy way to create an oversimplified world of 'either/or' categorical opposites, limiting choice to one of the two." In formal logic, as soon as a position is

116

taken on something, there will be a negation, an opposite, a contradiction and hence a potential paradox. As soon as we define or frame something, there will be a 'not that thing', i.e. everything that sits outside of that frame. As soon as we focus on something, it becomes foreground; everything else becomes background.

The negation of X (i.e. not X) could mean one of three things:
1) an apparently mutually exclusive, specific, logical opposite (e.g. on/off),
2) a notional opposite (e.g. autocratic/ democratic, manager/leader, option a/option b),
3) a general opposite which could be anything other than 'X'.

This is useful to identify as it gives us three levels of negation from very specific and 'tight' to more general and 'loose'. A looser paradox is usually easier to resolve than a tight one.

Nominalisations

As well as the polarity of negation (thing or not-thing), there is another subtle duality that appears in our language and our experience of the world we live in.

To simplify our experience of the world, we could break reality down into two key components: things and relationships. Perhaps our reality is simply a collection of things in relationship to other things. Usually, in our language, things are represented by nouns and relationships are represented by verbs.

There are plenty of things out there that we can experience directly and interact with (e.g. rocks, chairs, worms, molecules, bottles and sausages). Indeed, we measure these things and make a science of it. But what of the immeasurable things: what of love and change and empowerment and possibilities? These are nouns and yet they are harder to quantify. These tricky nouns are known as 'nominalisations'. To 'nominalise' is to turn a verb into a noun and to 'denominalise' is to turn the noun back into a verb.

How do we know something is a nominalisation? What is the difference between a nominalisation and a 'normal' noun? In the *Structure of Magic*, Bandler and Grinder (1975) give us two methods of testing for nominalisations. The quickest way to identify a nominalisation is the 'wheelbarrow test': "can I put this thing in a wheelbarrow?" At times, this may have to be a very big wheelbarrow because, for example, a planet is not a nominalisation; it is a 'concrete' thing and it *could* sit in a wheelbarrow if the wheelbarrow was big enough. 'Empowerment' on the other hand cannot really be put in a wheelbarrow. The other test is the 'ongoing' test: "does it make sense if I place the word 'ongoing' in front of the thing?" If I can, then it is likely a nominalisation. Hence, 'ongoing empowerment' works but 'ongoing apple' does not. The 'ongoing test' is a useful reminder that a nominalisation is a process that has been converted into a thing.

Part of the human mindset appears to be the need to convert processes into things. We like to label things, even things that aren't really things at all! For example, take the word empowerment. We treat empowerment as if it is a thing, but can we actually point to it? Can we put it in a box? Empowerment is based on the verb 'to empower' and empowering is a process more than it is a thing. This is the nature of nominalisations, they are a kind of 'fuzzy' language, where words are used but the listener or reader has to fill in their own meaning.

To nominalise is to convert a verb into a noun - indeed, even the word nominalisation is a nominalisation, converting the process of nominalising into a conceptual thing! Although they are convenient, allowing us to 'freeze frame' and label, nominalisations also cause confusion. Ask a room full of people to talk about empowerment and you will get a roomful of differing answers.

Why do we nominalise? It is likely that we need to nominalise in order to grasp and measure the world around us. It is perhaps convenient to see the changing world as a series of snapshots and talk of 'things'. However, the downside is that we are creating things that are not really things at all; we are trying to reify or solidify something that is an action or process. This is like watching a moment of a game of football and abstracting that we now know what football is. It would be like seeing a photograph of a game of chess and then thinking that this is what chess is, a frozen set of pieces. As we will see, it is likely that the process of nominalising actually creates paradox.

Understanding 'nominalisations' in the context of solving impossible problems is useful for two key reasons:

1) Words like tension, paradox, dilemma, double-bind, ambiguity, polarity are all nominalisations. Therefore, it depends on the listener/reader's map of the world as to whether these problems are resolvable at all. It certainly makes these things more difficult to define.

2) When examining a list of polarities in organisations, all of the examples appear to be nominalisations (as in Stroh & Miller 1994, p31, Marsh & Macalpine 1999, p645, Pascale 1990, p53, Peters 1992, p473 and Quinn & Kimberly 1984, p301). A sample list appears below in table 6a.

Table 6a: Example list of organisational polarities

Empowerment	----------	Control
Autonomy	----------	Partnership
Internal focus	----------	External focus
Decentralisation	----------	Centralisation
Short term	----------	Long term
Order	----------	Creativity
Plan	----------	Opportunity
Stability	----------	Change

Competition	----------	Collaboration
Simplicity	----------	Complexity
Analysis	----------	Synthesis

Perhaps one thing that distinguishes a nominalisation from a 'non-nominalisation' is that it has a meaningful polar opposite. For example, 'desk' (a 'non-nominalisation') has no meaningful polar opposite, whereas 'empowerment' (a nominalisation) does. A list of values is also likely to be a list of nominalisations and "nearly all values have a polar opposite value that is also positive" (Quinn & Cameron, 1988b, p292), for example: spontaneity and predictability. So to add to Bandler and Grinder's (1975) two tests, we also have the 'opposite test': if it has a meaningful opposite, it is probably a nominalisation.

Although not essential, an awareness of nominalisations may be useful. Considering the amount of potential nominalisations in the English language, it would be a case of picking up on those that are troublesome in a particular context, for example the word 'empowerment' or 'leadership' where tensions might arise due to lack of an agreed/shared definition.

Cultural Thinking

Is this either/or thinking a cultural phenomena? Pascale (1990, p142) proposes that "the stumbling block is our Western mindset. We have been trained since childhood to think in absolute categories: good/bad, either/or, black/white. We are taught to argue positions: 'for or against'; the middle ground is suspect… Either/or lies at the heart of the old paradigm, and it cripples our ability to manage effectively". Handy (1994) reports that the Western approach to business (and negotiations) stems from an Anglo Saxon win/lose mentality.

Culturally, there seems to be a difference between Western and Eastern thinking. According to Eisenhardt & Westcott (1988, p172) "Eastern thinking emphasises the timeless eternal qualities of life... One does not think in terms of opposites, but in terms of harmony of the whole." Buenger & Daft (1988, p195) agree that "Westerners think in terms of opposites and tradeoffs, while Easterners think in terms of the harmony of the whole." Hampden-Turner (1990, pxv) adds that Asians "neither see separate atoms as we do nor stubborn antagonisms among these, but are sensitised to complementarities... they create from that struggle a more elegant and efficient combination than they had before." And so polarities only appear as opposites when we don't understand their interrelationship.

The yin/yang symbol is a nice example of where the Eastern mindset seeks to transcend polarity in favour of a view of the whole. It is not that they don't have polarity and either/or scenarios, but they have another option of looking beyond the duality and seeing the bigger picture relatedness of the whole.

Perhaps we could stereotype the Western mindset as sorting for difference, drilling down to establish an intricate system of knowledge of what fits with what and what doesn't fit where. The Eastern mindset is about sorting for similarity and connection, seeking the bigger picture relationship between things.

Neither the Western nor the Eastern thinking styles are particularly better than the other. Each has a time when it is useful. Perhaps the skill is in moving between the two as the circumstances require it.

Chapter 7

Thinking Patterns That Transcend Problems

In This Chapter...

In this chapter, you will gain more of an understanding of the levels of thinking we can go to and use. This will help you to shift your thinking outside of a problem to see it from another perspective.

We will be exploring the following questions:
- What is 'meta' and why is it important?
- How does it help to think in terms of levels of thinking?
- What is the opposite of 'meta'?
- What is the impact of a hierarchical organisation?
- What happens if we remove the hierarchy?

Thinking Beyond the Problem – 'Going Meta'

Put a robot in a round room and tell it to sit in the corner.

If a robot knows what a corner is and is searching for it in a round room, it will carry on searching until its power supply fades. In this instance, the robot has not been programmed to think outside of the problem. It has a routine to run and it will continue until it has found a corner. As a human being, most of us have the ability to see the irony in the instructions because we can also see the instructions in the context. We can reason that the task is impossible because we have the ability to see beyond the content of the instructions.

As a child at school, I remember someone handing me a piece of paper with the statement "How to confuse an idiot" written on it. In the bottom corner was the instruction "P.T.O" (i.e. "please turn over"). On following the instructions, the other side read exactly the same with the same instructions. At this point, I got the joke and handed the paper back (or perhaps passed it on to someone else to see if they 'fell for it'). As with most people, I had made a jump outside and beyond the piece of paper. I had found another level of meaning that I was able to jump to. This 'jump' is known (particularly in the field of NLP) as 'going meta'. This is an amazing skill that perhaps we rather take for granted. We are able to mentally step outside of ourselves and our context to escape a problem and look at it from a new level of perspective.

'Meta' can be an elusive and confusing concept. Its main meaning outside the field of NLP is 'about', for example, meta-communication is communication *about* communication. In this sense it is an adjective, telling us what kind of communication we are talking about. Of course, by communicating about meta-communication, we are meta-meta-communicating. This could go on ad infinitum, adding levels and levels of meta.

In NLP we also talk about meta as meaning 'beyond' or 'outside' and we use the term 'going meta' as if it is some kind of destination or direction. Here, 'meta' means stepping outside or further away from the situation, seeing something as if we are a 'fly on the wall' or disassociated from the process/event/thing.

If we were unable to step 'outside' of a problem or system, we would become stuck in a loop. Like the robot, we would go round and round, searching for the corner. Like the 'confused idiot', we would keep turning over the piece of paper. Fortunately, we have the ability to decide when an instruction is valid and when we need to go beyond it. If there is a sign on the back of the office toilet door that says: "Now wash your hands", we know that if we have not yet washed our hands, we should go back and do it. Then, as we leave, we see the sign again but we ignore the instruction. The comedian, Lee Evans, once said that there was a 'do not disturb' sign hanging on the inside of his hotel room door... he read that and realised that he couldn't leave his room. Presumably the outside world did not want to be disturbed. We see the silliness in this because he is pretending that he is caught in a kind of paradox.

Amusing though this may be when it is pointed out, the very same thing happens within organisations but no-one seems to realise or see the funny side of it. Staff within a department keep doing something that doesn't work or add value because they have not been told to do otherwise. Forms are filled in online and go nowhere as the person who wanted the data originally has moved on and no-one else wants it. Some companies have regular meetings (e.g. the Monday Morning Meeting) because they have 'always' had these meetings. No-one questions it because it is 'how things are done'.

In a *New Scientist* article about theoretically 'rebooting' our civilisation, Bob Holmes (2011) writes of the current state of affairs: "It all just about works, but it's hardly a model of rational design – instead, people in each generation have done the best with what they have inherited from their predecessors. As a result we have ended up trapped in what, in retrospect, look like mistakes." This would also describe most organisations where systems, policies and procedures are built on the knowledge, skills, technology and resources of previous 'generations'. What if some of those systems (etc.) were to be changed, overhauled or removed? The only way we might do this is to go meta to that system.

Here we are into the realms of Chris Argyris' 'Double Loop Learning' model (see Chapter 4), where the department is trapped in 'single loop learning', perhaps fixing issues as they crop up within the system, but never challenging whether the processes themselves are still fit for purpose (or indeed if the 'purpose' of the process is still valid). If the staff took the time and courage to question the process (and/or purpose) of 'how we do things', they may find that there is a better way altogether. This would be 'double loop learning' and would also be an example of 'going meta'.

Many organisations suffer from 'repetitive mistake syndrome' because they fail to learn. A typical example here might be projects, where the recommendations/learning points from review meetings (if the review meeting happens at all) are not shared with the rest of the business. Often the learning points are put in a filing cabinet somewhere and forgotten about. A similar project runs six months later and experiences the same problems and/or makes the same mistakes. The process of review and reflection requires us to 'go meta' in order to talk 'about' and reflect 'upon' the project. By communicating the recommendations across the rest of the organisation we can create transfer of learning on a system-wide scale. With the existence of company intranets and search engines (with other technology and software being developed all the time), there is really no excuse for 'recommendations for future projects' not to be shared.

Layers of Meta

If we 'go meta' to a process or system, where are we then? We are outside the original system and in a new one. This new system is a layer out or a level up from the original system. So what happens if we 'go meta' again? We will now enter another system that is outside or above the original two systems. In this sense, there is a whole system of systems, one above or outside the other. Alfred Korsybski (1956) called this process of moving from one level up to another 'abstraction' and he called this system of systems the 'ladder of abstraction'.

Another way of looking at this 'system of systems' is to consider a model called the 'Hierarchy of Ideas' (e.g. James & Woodsmall 1988). If we take a concept or thing we can ask "what category does that concept/thing fall into?" For example, a duck falls into the category of 'bird'. In order to shift from duck to bird, we need to 'go meta', where we begin to talk about a different order of concept. Bird sits above duck in the sense that duck is an example of bird but bird is not an example of duck. There are many other examples that fall into the category of bird, for example: robin, thrush, swan, eagle. Of course, bird sits in the larger category of 'animal'. Animal sits at a higher level to bird.

The process of moving up a category is known in NLP as 'chunking up' (taken from early computer terminology). The process of 'drilling down' or seeking examples within the category is known unsurprisingly as 'chunking down'. So, when using the term 'chunking' we are talking about changing the level we are referring to. 'Chunking up' means taking one step up the ladder of abstraction (into the bigger picture, general, broad terms). We are asking: "what category do the things we are looking at now fall into?" or "what is this an example of?" If we 'chunk down' we are going down one step of the ladder into more detail (specifics). We are then asking: "what belongs in this category?" or "what is an example of this?"

If we take the example of 'dog' - to chunk up might take us to 'mammal' because 'dog' falls into the category of 'mammal'. To chunk down might take us to 'beagle' because 'beagle' belongs in the category of 'dog'.

Obviously, we could keep chunking up to the broadest abstraction or down into the minutest detail. This would create a whole system from top to bottom. If meta is the same as chunking up then 'dog' would be meta to 'beagle'. Alternatively, meta might also be looking at the whole system of levels from the outside, completely stepping back from the system of mammals and dogs and beagles etc. There appears to be a potential confusion with meta, in that it doesn't refer us to one particular place or direction. It could be a small step up one level of a system or a massive leap outside a whole system. To add to this, it could be argued that going outside a whole system is simply going up one level of abstraction to that system. So we might have levels of abstraction within levels of abstraction... or abstraction about abstraction... or 'meta-abstraction' perhaps!

Logical Levels

The nature of going meta or chunking up and down categories provides us with a series of distinctions that Gregory Bateson (2000) called 'logical types' or 'logical levels'. Bateson's concept of 'logical types'/'logical levels' (terms that he seemed to use interchangeably) was based on the work of Russell and Whitehead's 'set theory' and 'theory of types'. Whitehead and Russell (1970) brought this notion into mathematics to avoid the problems of paradox. They surmised that *a set cannot belong to itself (or be a member of itself)...* a category cannot be a category of itself otherwise this creates the circular logic of self reference.

The category of dog may contain 'beagle' and 'basset hound' but it cannot contain 'dog'. The category of 'dog' does not belong on the same level as beagles and basset hounds. It sits at a different logical level. Once again, we are saying that 'dog' is meta to 'beagle' and is of a different logical type.

If we try and place 'dog' into the category of 'dog' we are creating a confusion of levels and hence a paradox. If a company offers services x, y, and z, the fact that they offer services cannot be considered a service in and of itself. If a company suggests that: "Our USP [*unique selling point*] is that we have no USP", it is generating a paradox that not only confuses logical levels but appears to contradict itself. This would be a paradox on a par with the liar's paradox (e.g. "I am lying right now!"). Perhaps it is a clever marketing catchphrase, but it does appear rather meaningless.

According to Kostere and Malatesta (1990, p4): "The theory of logical types states that there is a discontinuity between a class of information and the members of that class. This theory is used to delineate levels of abstraction and states that one logical level is about (meta-to) the logical level below it." This would also include the label we give something (i.e. its name) as Bateson (1979, p229) states: "The name is not the thing named but is of different logical type, higher than that of the thing named."

When referring to logical levels, going meta takes us a level up to a 'second order' (Watzlawick et al 1974). It takes us to the category that contains the place we have come from. As discussed, if we start with 'dog' and go meta, we may arrive at the category of 'mammal' or any other set that has 'dog' as a member of that set. Herein lies the power of going meta. If you change something in a category, for example by redefining it, it usually has an affect on that one thing only. In the late 1800s, a new breed of dog was developed by crossing the Flat Coated Retriever with the Tweed Water Spaniel, the Bloodhound and the Irish Setter. It was originally called a Golden Flatcoat and in the 1920s, this breed of dog was officially recognised as the Golden Retriever. Before that time it didn't officially exist as a breed by this name. Whilst the new category of Golden Retriever affected those dogs that would now fit into the new breed, the category of dog remained unchanged. If however, we changed or redefined the category of dog, for example to add a new condition that dogs have to have golden coloured fur (in order to fall into the category of 'dog'), this would have a massive impact on the current canine set.

If you make a change at a meta, higher order or higher logical level, it will have a significant impact on the levels below. This then becomes a major tool for change work with individuals and organisations.

For a thorough exploration on this topic, I would recommend a book titled "NLP: Going Meta" by Michael Hall (2001). Drawing from the work of Robert Dilts, Hall (p82) separates out five criteria for logical levels, which will provide a useful summary here:

1) There is a *hierarchy* of experience.
2) Higher levels organise and control information on lower levels
3) Higher levels will necessarily affect lower levels
4) Lower levels will not necessarily affect higher levels (although it is possible)
5) Higher levels encompass and impact more than lower levels.

When exploring and resolving paradox we will find that going meta to the issue will allow us different perspectives to separate out the polarities of the paradox and may even blow out the illusion of paradox entirely. According to Van de Ven et al (1988, p23) the concept of logical levels (and hence meta) "resolves paradoxes by clarifying levels of reference and the connections among them."

A concise summary to this section is to be found in Watzlawick et al (1974, pp9-10): "1) logical levels must be kept strictly apart to prevent paradox and confusion; and 2) going from one level to the next higher (i.e. from member to class) entails a shift, a jump, a discontinuity or transformation – in a word, a change – of the greatest theoretical and... practical importance, for it provides a way *out of* the system."

The Organisation as a Hierarchy

A traditional organisation tends to work as a hierarchy, with the MD/CEO at the top of the organisational chart and front-line staff at the bottom. Even if one chooses to turn the whole thing upside down so that the MD appears to sit at the bottom 'supporting' the organisation, there is still an implied hierarchy. Indeed, we can go so far as to say that an organisation is a hierarchy of 'logical levels'. If we use Hall's criteria (mentioned earlier this chapter), we can see that an organisation meets each criteria. However, what does this mean in practice?

If we imagine that Amy is the manager of a team consisting of three people, from an organisational/system perspective Amy will sit at a logical level higher than the team. She has a higher authority level and decisions she makes will govern the team and what the team does.

As we move up the 'corporate ladder', the degree of control and impact on the lower level becomes greater. The decisions of the MD/CEO will govern the whole organisation. Of course, the MD/CEO may be governed by an 'external' level of e.g. shareholders, governors or councillors. When the external level has its own agenda or no emotional stake/connection with the organisation or what it actually does, this can cause paradoxical problems. As Bakan (2004) points out in The Corporation, if shareholders are only interested in financial return, the company is legally obliged to put profit first. Sadly, this can lead to a rather 'psychopathic' organisation that (for example) may harm itself and its environment. Corporate social responsibility (which usually incurs a cost of some sort) in this sense could be seen as contradictory to the company's legal obligation to make profit.

Although not strictly linked to the 'logical levels' nature of organisations, there is a model I use called the 'Organisational Hierarchy of Concern' (introduced in Chapter 5). The idea of the model, although rather simple, is to remind management that when they are planning change they would be advised to consider the issues, concerns, needs and questions of each level of the organisation since each level may have different requirements. If a change is planned and implemented from the perspective of only one or two levels, the resistance from other levels is likely to be more extreme and more surprising to those initiating the change.

No matter where the change is driven from, it is essential for change managers to consider the concerns of (and the benefits to) each level of the organisation.

Consider for example the introduction of a flexitime system into an organisation. The MD may want it to raise the profile of the organisation as an 'employer of choice'. Senior management (along with the MD) may be interested in the 'bottom line' improvements (i.e. how it impacts financially). Middle

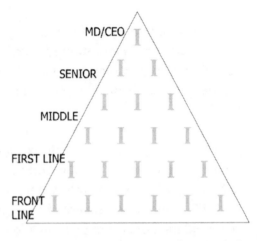

management may want to see an improvement in attendance and delivery. First line management may see it as an extra duty to monitor staff and perhaps as a risk that the system will be misused and abused. Front line staff may welcome it or be concerned that they will have to 'clock in' and be monitored by 'big brother'.

Any organisational change has the potential to create new unforeseen problems (i.e. falling foul to the Law of Unintended Consequences). By exploring the 'ecology' of planned change on each level (i.e. the ripple effect), some of these issues could be prevented and/or catered for. This concept is explored further under 'Contingency Planning' in Chapter 13.

The second aspect of the Organisational Hierarchy of Concern is connected to the nature of logical levels in that changes initiated/driven from higher levels are likely to have more organisational impact than those below. It is hence advisable for change managers to elicit the support of some senior figures in the organisation. John Kotter (1996) suggests that in order for a change to be truly effective, it needs 75% of the management on board.

When there is a 'confusion' of logical levels in the organisation, there is likely to be a paradoxical problem. According to Ford and Backoff (1988, pp91-92) "when different levels collapse, intercross or otherwise become entangled... individuals experience a sense of paradox."

For example:

1) A middle manager instructs the front line staff (or front line staff go to the middle manager) without including the first line manager in between. This can be frustrating for the manager in between and may cause extra work for the front line staff since the manager is unaware of the additional tasks delegated by the middle manager. Of course, the front line staff may feel unable to push back when the middle manager is offloading tasks.

2) A manager ends up managing one of his friends. This seems fine until the friend begins to come in late and stops 'pulling his weight' at work. The manager finds himself torn between being a friend (hence turning a blind eye) and being a manager (hence addressing the issue). If the manager decides to be the friend, he is not doing his organisational duty and is acting at the wrong level.

3) A recently promoted manager continues to do her old job instead of the role of being a manager. When she does 'step up', she monitors the staff closely for the job she used to do very well. The staff find her to be too 'hands-on', to the point of being a 'meddling micro-manager'.

In addition, if information is not handled by (or 'raised' to) the correct level within the system, those below may continue to implement unhelpful or redundant strategies. For example, I heard about a team that painted the lines on roads and each year they would paint over a diamond shape in one of the back roads of the town. No-one knew what the diamond shape was for or what it meant, but they painted it regardless. One year, a young man asked 'why?' and the question went back to the manager who eventually tracked down the originator of the diamond shape. The original painter had retired, so they called him up. He was amazed that they still painted the shape since in his last year he spilt some paint on the road and tidied it up by making it symmetrical. Until a 'higher' authority level was made aware of the 'glitch', the diamond shape continued to be painted. A loop was set up that could only be broken by someone above in the system.

In many ways, a project manager is liable to suffer the paradox of confused logical levels. She is told she is responsible for the project and is made accountable. The failure of the project will be held against her and the success will be met with praise. However, she is not given full authority to carry out the project. All budgets must be agreed by senior management and a group of stakeholders keep moving the goalposts around. Any changes to the project must be authorised by a board who are also requesting reduced timescales. All these people are above the project manager in the system of the organisation and so she feels powerless to fight back (as she perceives that this may be a career limiting move).

As well as the organisational hierarchy type of logical levels, there are other types of logical levels that create problems when confused. For example, a facilitator is brought in from another area of the business to allow a team to get some action planning done. It is agreed that the role of the facilitator is to focus on the *process* of the meeting, to help keep the team on track. However, the facilitator begins to offer solutions and suggestions for how the plan could be implemented. At this point, the facilitator is focussed on the *content* of what the team are doing and so becomes a potential hindrance. No-one is keeping an eye on the process and so the facilitator becomes redundant.

Removing the Hierarchy?

Can we remove the organisational hierarchy altogether as a way of preventing logical level paradox? It is an interesting decision to flatten out the structure of an organisation or department. Even when this happens, there is usually still a director or MD. The challenge is how other (more hierarchical) organisations address them. Who are they meant to contact and talk to that is on their level? When a department goes flat, other departments don't always understand who they should be communicating with. Who do senior management talk to: the director of the department or someone who appears to be a front line member of staff?

The problem of hierarchy is sometimes seen as the problem of authority. Many people when told what to do will give up autonomy (even if they can see how it is not necessarily in the best interest of the organisation or broader environment). Here we have shadows of the Milgram studies (1997) where people conform to authority figures even when someone else's welfare is at stake. When challenged later, people will simply respond that 'they were following orders'.

So does removing hierarchy remove this problem? Certainly, a flat structure appears good for equality. It appears to encourage and promote ownership and responsibility of actions and tasks. However, it brings with it a problem of discipline. If someone is not doing what they should do (or doing what they shouldn't), who takes them to one side and reprimands them? As soon as somebody does, we reintroduce a logical level hierarchy when one person governs another. Can the group as a whole reprimand the individual? Possibly, but you might want to read *Lord of the Flies* to see how that turns out.

Ironically, by removing the paradox of authority, organisations may create a new paradox by replacing one authority with another. It seems that the 'problem of authority' simply gets transferred to a consensus of the group. In a group setting, people tend to behave less rationally and empathetically than they would alone. Studies on group conformity (e.g. Cialdini 1993) seem to show that the pull of the group norm is equally persuasive to the following of authority figures. In these studies, people have consistently behaved in ways they wouldn't do if they were on their own because the group 'norm' makes it okay. For example, people will sit in a burning building if no-one else seems bothered about leaving.

Of course, there are other types of organisational structure and we are not going to analyse of all of them here. Each type of structure will bring its own challenges. A matrix structure, for example, may seem efficient for resource management. But since there may be no line management authority a culture of self interest, conflicting priorities and unrealistic expectations often prevail.

Sorting Out Levels and Hierarchies

A hard-line definition of paradox tends to contain simultaneously opposing positions (e.g. Buenger & Daft 1988). However, with the slightly looser concept of 'social paradox' we allow that the contradiction might happen at slightly different times or come from different levels. Can paradox (as Poole & Van de Ven 1989 state) take into account "the spatial and temporal nature of the social world"? Ford & Backoff (1988) respond to this question by postulating that combining the spatial and temporal aspects creates four forms of paradox:

Directional

		Horizontal (Same Level)	Vertical (Different Level)

Temporal	Synchronic
	(Same Time)
		• same level,
		   same time
		(eg. two managers ask a staff member to do two equally important tasks now)
			• different level,
			   same time
			(eg. a manager asks a member of staff to do something that contradicts company policy)

	Diachronic (Different Time)	• same level, different time *(eg. a manager changes their mind and says 'no' when they said 'yes' earlier)*	• different level, different time *(eg. a director asks a member of staff to do something that conflicts with what their own manager told them to do earlier)*

It would be expected that a problem that has a different level and/or different time duality should be easier to resolve than a problem that sits at the same level and at the same time. When there is a difference in time or level in the paradox, it would seem to be 'looser' and hence easier to resolve.

The directional/temporal (same/different) model is a useful distinction in that it may help to understand the dynamics of a paradox and hence how to approach it. For example, if the problem is 'caused' by disagreement between (or mixed messages from) a manager and senior manager, we might defer to seniority as having higher priority. If we receive an apparently contradictory instruction from the same person but at a different time, rather than accusing the person of doing a 'u-turn', we might instead consider that new information has come to light causing a change in plan. Remember that a 'change of mind' is really usually just a progression of thought. In this instance, it would probably be prudent to check that the 'old' instruction has been superseded before carrying out the new order!

Chapter 8

Four Thinking Logics

In This Chapter...

In this chapter, you will gain an overview of the nature of logic and why this is essential in understanding how paradox is set up and how it can be resolved. This will help you to shift between logics when problem solving.

We will be exploring the following questions:
- What is a logic?
- What types of logic are there?
- How do the logics differ?
- What are the advantages and disadvantages of each type of logic?

Methods of Thinking: Logic

Some people want things to be simplified to either/or terms; they want it black or white, win or lose, succeed or fail, with us or against us. Others talk in terms of a 'scale', shades of grey, finding a balance between things (e.g. a work/life balance). Some want the best of both worlds, seeking a 'third way' to integrate both/and; they want *both* black *and* white, on *and* off, cake *and* eat it. Then there are those who like to see things from another perspective, knowing that there is always another way of looking at things. Maybe it's not about black or white or grey, but another colour altogether.

Each of these methods of thinking could be described as a logic. The word 'logic' is derived from the Greek *logikos* (meaning 'of speech or reason') and it could be defined as the method, system and principles of reasoning applied to a particular context. It could also be seen as the relationship and interconnectedness of a series of events or facts.

With regards to the management of paradox, Ford and Ford (1994) discuss three key methods of thinking: formal logic, dialectics and trialectics. Each of these approaches is a logic which ultimately affects the mindset/thinking model of the individual. For this reason, the difference between these logics is an important distinction to make. Ford and Ford (1994, p758) suggest that: "When a person is 'operating in' a particular logic, he or she takes its rules and boundaries for granted. Logics pose the problems, provide the language for explaining and understanding them, and determine their solutions. Logics give people their 'reality', the truth, the way things are... when people are unaware that they are using a logic, or are 'trapped' in only one, this point of view becomes an unwitting limitation to what might be seen or understood, restricting their observations and offering no really new alternatives."

We can also add a fourth logic called 'fuzzy logic' which could be seen as somewhere between formal and dialectic logic. Here, we are proposing that 'fuzzy logic' is a type of logic distinct from the other three. The four logics are summarised in the table below.

Table 8a: Types of Logic (adapted from Ford & Ford 1994 and Kosko 1993)

Type of Logic	What is this?
Formal Logic	Working in the framework of either/or, maintaining a polarity between two seemingly opposing positions.
Fuzzy Logic	Allowing for a scale or continuum between the polarities.
Dialectic	Creating a 'third way' or synthesis from the polarities (which are known as thesis and

	antithesis).
Trialectic	Shifting outside or beyond the polarity (e.g. by reframing).

As approaches, each type of logic appears to have its advantages and its drawbacks and these are discussed below. The next four chapters then explore formal, fuzzy, dialectic and trialectic logics as methods of resolving paradox.

Formal Logic

Formal logic is the predominant thinking pattern of the Western world. It is the driving force behind the positivist, quantitative scientific approach where things can or have to be quantifiable, repeatable and provable. It has its roots in the teachings of Aristotle who put forward three laws of formal logic:

First Law $A=A$	**Second Law** $A \diamond B$	**Third Law** $A \diamond (A+B)$
Law of identity A thing is what it is.	*Law of contradiction* A thing cannot be something else.	*Law of the excluded middle* A thing cannot be itself and something else nor something in between.

The three laws of formal logic are designed to reduce ambiguity by making things more concrete and absolute. This is done by defining something specifically and determining that *it is what it is* and that *it is not something else nor anywhere in between.*

Formal logic (or Aristotelian logic) attempts to deal with the paradox by maintaining the either/or frame which means that although it may help to *understand* a paradox, it does not *resolve* it. Formal logic has also been criticised for its inability to account for change (e.g. Korzybski 1958), and as such is not necessarily a useful method for organisational development and change management. Not only does formal logic struggle with the nature of process and time, it also appears to struggle with the idea of 'levels' of change. Watzlawick et al (1974, p11) concur that second order change (i.e. logical levels, 'going meta') are "the very phenomenon whose existence Aristotle denied so categorically."

Horn (1983, p7) argues that : "The basic limitation of the formal logic point of view is that there is no convenient and consistent way to consider time and change within that point of view." The problem for formal logic when it comes to change is that something is either one thing or another. According to formal logic, when something changes, it suddenly shifts from A to B, but there is no explanation for its transition. There is no allowance for steps in between. Given the organisational example of a restructure, it is as if at one moment the organisation has one structure and the next moment it has a different structure. There is no sense of 'during' the change.

Formal logic would require that a light is *on* or *off* – there appears to be no room here for a dimmer switch. Even if we argue that a change from A to B is a series of measurable steps A1, A2, A3, A4...B, there is a problem of how did A1 'suddenly' get to A2? What exists between A1 and A2? Is it A1a, A1b, A1c, A1d...A2? This could go on and on without ever explaining the transition from one step (or sub-step) to another.

Formal logic is designed to *avoid* paradoxes but, paradoxically, it seems to create them. Kosko (1993, p102) argues that: "Paradoxes are the rule and not the exception. Pure black and white outcomes are the exceptions... There are two Aristotelian extremes of black and white, 0 and 1, and many shades of grey between them." It could indeed be argued that paradox shows up the problem of binary/formal logic thinking.

Formal logic is also the driver for 'Occam's Razor' (also known as 'lex parsimoniae' – the law of parsimony) which disregards multiple explanations for an event. To put it crudely, the philosophy of 'Occam's Razor' is: Given multiple explanations, select the simplest one (that makes the least assumptions) until we find something that has greater explanation power. On one hand, this is generally useful advice to prevent hundreds of nonsense explanations when we already have a logical and/or measurable explanation. On the other hand, it limits us to a single explanation where we have to choose the 'right' one amongst many possibilities. In the medical profession, the law of parsimony is expressed as 'on hearing hoof-beats, think horses not zebras'. Although this works well for most cases, it does not help when there is a more exotic illness with 'common symptoms' or for when there are multiple causes (i.e. layers of illness). This is also true of organisations where problems are often systemic, complex and have multiple layers. Although parsimony is convenient, it may be too simplistic to really understand the issue.

The benefit of formal logic is that it encourages us to focus on what something is and to define its identity. It helps us to problem solve most of the time, defining the specific issue and its root cause (although it may struggle with multiple causes). It helps us set precise goals and outcomes, to imagine a steady state of how we want things to be. It encourages us to be scientific about our explanations rather than creating fantasies and fairy tales as to why things work as they do. The problem is that it simply does not allow us to work through polarities and tensions other than to choose one end or the other.

Fuzzy Logic

If formal logic is 'either A or B' then fuzzy logic would be 'from A to B'. Rather than 'black or white', fuzzy logic is about 'shades of grey' which allows people to think and be between the polarities of either/or. When dealing with people and their mixed feelings about particular topics, this seems to be a more realistic approach. For example, have you ever been somewhere between 'for' and 'against' an argument because you can see both sides? The 'shades of grey' approach is the driving force behind the more qualitative, phenomenological side of science. Fuzzy logic allows for the more subjective and interesting possibilities between the absolutes of the positivist formal logic. It gives us a chance to be creative and inventive.

The disadvantage of fuzzy logic however is that it may lead us to seek a compromise when further win/win (dialectic) exploration may be useful. The continuum of fuzzy logic only allows for a one dimensional plane, a result of somewhere between one polarity and another. In negotiation terms this is known as 'splitting the difference' or meeting someone 'half-way'. Compromise can lead to people feeling exactly that, 'compromised' where they only get some of what they were wanting. Although there is a greater fairness to this than the 'win/lose' approach of formal logic, a compromise is not as good as the more two-dimensional 'best of both worlds' that is 'win-win'.

Another drawback of fuzzy logic is that it may encourage us to seek a rigid balance point half way between one end and another. For some people, the effort to find a perfect 'work/life balance' may be a stressful endeavour. To try and then maintain it could be even more stressful! To want to hold on to some idealised midway point is perhaps to miss the point altogether, since a half-way point may lead to the problem of not doing either thing very well (e.g. feeling guilty about not spending enough quality time with family nor meeting the ever demanding targets of the job). When both ends of the polarity are pulling at a person (e.g. job vs. family), maintaining a status quo may take an inordinate amount of energy. Somehow, a new paradox is created in that trying to find a place to rest becomes very tiring in and of itself.

144

Perhaps a healthier version is to see the continuum between the polarities and then seek to work within a range, depending on the situation; for example, to allow oneself to be pulled towards work for a while and then towards family. Keeping an eye on how much time we are spending towards each polarity may give us clues to whether we are in balance or out.

Dialectic logic

Dialectic logic is to think in terms of 'both A and B' rather than either/or. It seeks to find integration of opposites in order to create the 'best of both worlds'. It was the philosopher Hegel that saw the potential of taking a concept and its opposite and from that creating a third uniting concept. Although often attributed to Hegel, it was another philosopher (arguably either Kant or Fichte) who developed Hegel's dialectic method in the form of 'thesis - antithesis - synthesis'.

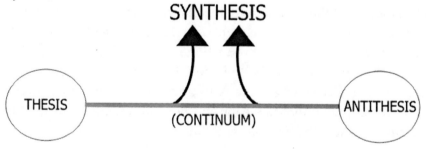

Koestler (1978) linked the dialectic method to creativity where innovation is the spark between polarities. He coined the word 'holon' to mean a whole and a part (i.e. something is complete in itself whilst being part of something bigger). He suggests (p57) that: "every holon is possessed of two opposite tendencies or potentials: an *integrative tendency* to function as part of the larger whole, and a *self-assertive tendency* to preserve its individual autonomy." This suggests that within a dialectic system there is a force for synthesis and a force for independence.

Dialectic logic has its critics (e.g. Ichazo 1982, Horn 1983) as it is perceived to create an endless struggle driven by the sense that 'more is better'. For this reason, it has been said to underpin capitalism (Ichazo 1982) and to lead to "the paradox of Malthusian growth in a finite world" (Voorhees 1983). This argument seems to stem from Hegel's desire to demonstrate the relationship between quantity and quality which he called 'Measure'. Consider a project where the project is designed to achieve x, y and z. It could be argued that if the project delivers x, y, and 90% of z, the project is still a success and quality is maintained. However, if we are missing most of y and the whole of z, the quality has indeed suffered. At what specific point does the quantity affect the quality? The project might overrun by a day and this may not affect the quality. However, if it overruns by 20 days, this might seriously impact on the quality (e.g. because service delivery is delayed). This dynamic between quantity and quality could be perceived that 'more is better' (i.e. more quantity equals better quality), however, Hegel talks about a 'definite quality' which appears to be the quality that is defined (e.g. the specific outcome) for a particular thing. He suggests that when there is a reduction in quantity, there will still be quality but not necessarily the 'definite quality' defined at the outset. The real challenge here is to understand (e.g. when setting up a project) what quality means and how we might define quality in terms of time, specifications and 'finish'.

Dialectics does not suit the formal logic quest for absolute truth because it allows (and seeks) that every truth should have an equally true opposite. Horn (1983, p13) argues that dialectics promotes conflict and "lends itself to justification of struggle, violence and constant fights." This however is a far cry from Hegel's idealism of synthesis and unity where "it is in the nature of spirit to sustain contradiction and to maintain itself precisely therein as the speculative unity of things opposed to each other" (Gadamer 1976, p16). Whilst it may be true that the dialectic method seeks the opposition, it seems that the reason to do this is not to justify conflict but to raise awareness of the potential for conflict and then to help aid in its prevention and resolution. Hegel seemed to want to use the dialectic method as a way of expanding understanding.

Horn (1983) also criticises dialectics in that the 'negation of negation' (i.e. the integration of the opposition) can lead to unhelpful unintended consequences. Of course this is also true of choosing one side over another. This is an important point and so must be taken care of when using synthesis as a form of tension resolution. The point here is to make sure we take the best of the oppositions' positions into account when creating a synthesis and then check the potential consequences of the synthesis.

Another problem for dialectics is that as a synthesis is formed from the thesis and the antithesis, that synthesis will also have an opposite. This means a new polarity is created at the level of the synthesis and hence a new potential paradox. For example, if we synthesise directive leadership with non-directive (i.e. supportive) we get (according to Blanchard et al. 1994) 'situational leadership' where one adapts to the given situation. However, the antithesis of situational leadership is a kind of 'trait leadership' where one remains constant throughout all situations. We might take the 'best of both worlds' and create a higher level concept of leadership but this too will have its opposite.

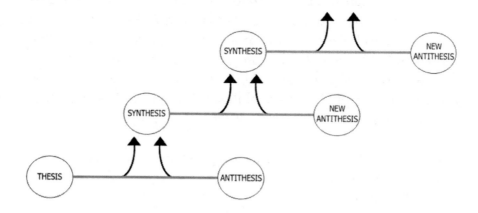

It seems that this synthesis series might go on ad infinitum and this appears to create another problem. However, rather than seeing this as an infinite series of synthesis levels, Hegel saw the *whole* as a complex system, calling it the 'Absolute' where the synthesis of thesis and antithesis ultimately comes to an end at the 'Absolute Idea' (Russell 1954).

It is also possible that the 'more is better' and 'infinite synthesis' criticisms of dialectic thinking are valid when applied to Dialectic materialism, developed by Engels and Marx, but it is less clear that they apply to Hegel's original works on dialectics which was proposed as a model of idealism and was designed (according to Gademer 1976) to be a positive reframe on what the Ancient Greeks had seen as a negative concept (ironically, that for every concept there is a conflicting opposite).

Trialectic logic

If dialectic logic is thinking in terms of 'both A and B', trialectic logic might be thought of as 'beyond A and B'. Trialectic logic does not see polarity in terms of opposition, but more that both sides are parts of something else. By using trialectic logic we are 'going meta' and seeking an alternative system where both sides are true. Indeed, opposites are called 'apparent opposites' since in this logic things only *appear* to be in opposition. Ford & Ford (1994, p770) suggest that the polarities we experience are "part of a larger whole that relates them. The predator and prey, or competitor and competition, are two roles in a larger, whole system of relationships." So opposition is simply in the eye of the observer, i.e. subjective rather than objective.

The creator of this logic, Oscar Ichazo (1982) proposes that there are three 'laws' of trialectics:
1. The law of circulation
2. The law of attraction

3.   The law of mutation

1. The Law of Circulation

The law of circulation considers that a concept will contain the seed of its apparent opposite. Horn (1983, p21) suggests that opposition and contradiction are only apparent and tells us that the "trialectic position sees opposites as containing each other, or interdependent with each other." The notion that the polarities in a tension contain each other is used by Caswell (1983) to suggest that 'cycles of causation' (i.e. paradoxical loops, vicious circles etc.) are caused by each side holding the seed of the other. Caswell draws connections between trialectics ("a logic of cycles," p164) and cybernetics and states that (p167): "It is only possible to single out variables as 'cause' and another as 'effect' by recognising the seed of the opposite within each. This is a form of self-reference and self-reference leads to fascinating problems."

2. The Law of Attraction

According to D'Andrade and Johnson (1983, p80), trialectic logic "rejects conflict as the mechanism of change, and describes change as a process of attraction." This is an interesting idea that leads to the notion that there is no such thing as resistance, just attraction to an alternative. Consider this in terms of change management where people who appear 'resistant' may simply be attracted to the old/current way of doing things or to an alternative solution going forward. If you are able to tap into what attracts them, you may be able to incorporate this into your proposal. It is also a more psychologically 'positive' experience for both parties to consider what so called 'protagonists' are *attracted to* rather than what they don't like.

Ford & Ford (1994, p768) expand the law of attraction by suggesting that change is a result of the attraction between 'attractives' (which are like magnets) and 'actives' (which are like receptors): "Attractives are only attractive to things that are 'active' (i.e. things that are looking for, listening for, or open to what is being offered, made available, or given off by the attractive)." When there is a balanced flow of active-attractives there is equilibrium. When there is unbalance, there is a jump to a new state. In change management, people may be attracted to the proposed change or to an alternative. As previously stated, there is no resistance, only attraction to alternatives... and not enough active-attractive. It is like the 'active' creates the sense of dissatisfaction and need. The 'attractive' is like the positive vision and benefit of the change (though the benefit/vision still has to appeal to and fit the 'active'). This is reminiscent of the 'formula' for change management (Beckhard & Harris 1987) that (a) *dissatisfaction with the current state* multiplied by (b) *shared vision* multiplied by (c) *clear first steps* needs to be stronger than *resistance* in order for change to be accepted and successful.

3. The Law of Mutation
The law of mutation suggests that there will be a change or jump from one frame ('material manifestation point') to another when there is an unbalance between an active and an attractive. It is a like a piece of metal sitting next to a magnet that has lost its power suddenly being attracted to an alternative magnet. In real terms, this means that if a position/proposal is no longer attractive, people will look elsewhere if there is an appealing alternative.

To sum up the process of change according to trialectics, Ford & Ford (1994, p776) propose establishing: "(a) the desired result, (b) the active and attractive forces, and (c) the function or process that can engage both the active and attractive forces to produce the desired results."

One potential criticism of Trialectics is that it is not always easy to distinguish it from the idealistic dialectics of Hegel (as opposed to dialectic materialism of Marx), which is ironically close to the philosophical idealism of trialectics. Others have also noted that the distinction between dialectics and trialectics can appear blurred (e.g. Carini et al 1995). The nature of 'going meta' (i.e. second order/double loop thinking) appears to be a feature of both dialectic and trialectic thinking. However, the results of 'going meta' may differ. Dialectic logic would 'chunk-up' to a specific outcome of a synthesis of the polarity below. With trialectic logic, 'going meta' might take us to any number of outcomes. For example, if two colleagues are hooked into an escalating 'revenge war', the dialectic method might seek the route of mediation to generate a win/win solution. The trialectic method may take us to mediation or to many other possible places like creating a Bullying and Harassment policy to resolve such cyclical problems of inappropriate behaviour.

In conclusion, trialectic logic is a rather new and obscure concept that is sometimes hard to quantify, model and reproduce. If dialectic materialism could be compared to a Cartesian/Newtonian dualistic, mechanistic paradigm, then trialectics would be comparable to a holistic, quantum physics paradigm (Dell'Olio 1983). In organisational terms, trialectics would link with complexity theory, cybernetics and systemic thinking. A tool that reflects trialectic logic might be 'reframing' and this is an area where NLP (neuro-linguistic programming) might add value (e.g. Dilts 1999, Hall & Bodenhamer 2002) in helping to understand and resolve paradox.

Chapter 9

Maintaining Polarity:
The Formal Logic Approach

In This Chapter...

In this chapter you will explore the first set of techniques for working with polarity, tensions and paradox. The approaches here are based on remaining within and utilising our traditional logic, known as Formal Logic.

We will be exploring the following questions:
- How, when and why would you hold a paradox open?
- What would be an example of an open paradox?
- When would you want to close the paradox?
- How might you utilise polarity as a method of movement and change?

Dilemma or decision?

When we face a one off dilemma where we want to choose one side over another, there are many classic decision making techniques which could be considered part of 'paradox management'. Examples include: force field analysis, cost benefit analysis, grid analysis and decision trees. These have been covered extensively elsewhere and so are outside the scope of this book. When the dilemma has an immediate conclusion and is really a decision, these techniques are excellent (even if there are a range of options to select from). For example, if we need to decide whether to select Fred or

Daphne for a job, once a decision is made, the dilemma has gone. Some paradoxes, however, are rather less easy to resolve! In addition, it may be that by deciding one over the other we are missing out on a myriad of other possible options.

Holding the Paradox Open and Keeping the Tension Going

Why resolve paradox? Why not simply keep it open and maintain the tension?

An interesting (usually Eastern) approach *is* to hold the paradox open. There is a distinct difference however between holding it open purposefully and simply not addressing it. Holding a paradox open purposefully means focusing on the tension to generate a spark of creativity. Innovation tends to come from synthesising two opposing or different things that are not already working together. The innovation can then be shared as best practice until another innovation comes along.

Some organisations purposely hold paradoxes open rather than try and resolve them. This is particularly true in some Asian companies, for example those that use Just In Time methodologies. It is recognised that if management provide solutions and processes for everything, there is no possibility of learning, growth and development. So, tensions are held open to generate new ideas. For example, if the workforce is asked to cut cost without taking more time or losing quality, it is likely that someone will eventually come up with an idea of how to do that. Some bright light will have a spark of inspiration and generate some new thinking beyond the current processes.

Arthur Koestler (in 'the Act of Creation' 1964) proposes that creativity often results from the tension between two things. When a paradox is held open, it encourages unconscious creative sparks to ignite (sometimes at unexpected moments). Have you ever had an idea that came to you in a flash when you were somewhere other than where the problem is? A great strategy for doing cryptic crosswords (and lateral thinking puzzles) is to put them down when you are stuck (rather than sit staring at them) and then come back to them later; it is amazing how more answers may come to you then. Sometimes ideas might come to us just as we wake up; we get that 'eureka moment' as a new set of neural connections are made. Guy Claxton (1988) writes about this process in: 'Hare Brain, Tortoise Mind' where the hare brain is our moment to moment conscious thinking and the tortoise mind is our slower unconscious processing. Because the tortoise mind is working away in the background, it tends to be responsible for 'eureka moments'. Although perhaps the tortoise mind should not be rushed, there is no harm in giving it 'synthesis-ready' data to speed up the spark of innovation which leads to a creative synthesis/solution. We will be exploring this in chapter 11 (on 'dialectic logic').

Because the Western culture teaches us to think in either/or terms we tend to want to look for the best option out of the two sides of polarity. When we try and select one side over the other, the dynamics of the paradox will take us for a rollercoaster ride. In addition, when staff are not aware that there *is* a polarity/tension, or don't understand it, they feel the chaotic forces of a mismanaged paradox. This tends to mean people getting frustrated and stressed because they are being hindered in getting their job done. People may then feel split and/or that they are going round in circles, leading to the unhealthy symptoms discussed in chapter 3.

Remember:
> *Mismanaged tensions and paradoxes lead to stress.*
> *Well managed tensions and paradoxes lead to innovation.*

More often than not, in an environment where paradox is mismanaged, sparks fly around but do not settle on a solution. This is because people put into the tension do not know they are there and so they get stressed out. Sadly, those above are usually unaware that they have created a tension for the staff! For example, staff in many public sector roles are asked to 'do more for less'. What does this mean? As far as vague instructions go, 'more for less' is a winner!

The key to holding a paradox open is to:
a) Inform staff that there is a tension, be explicit as to what it is and tell them why it is being held open
b) Tell them the desired outcome(s) and what is expected of them
c) Set up a system that allows and encourages ideas to be shared easily throughout the organisation with credit attached to the creator
d) Acknowledge and praise staff for innovative ideas
e) Reward any innovative ideas that are put into practice or held as a best practice model
f) As a general approach, teach staff techniques on how to manage paradox and tensions.

In summary, if there is a rule for purposely holding open a paradox, it would be:

Inform the staff that the tension exists
AND reward innovative ideas.

If staff are not acknowledged or rewarded, they may feel that their ideas are being stolen from them.

For example, a lady was working for a small company where the environment was rather chaotic. To make things simpler for herself, she created a checklist form so that there was an order to what she had to do and nothing got missed. Someone at head office saw it and said: "We'll use that for everyone." She was not acknowledged or thanked for her idea. She also created some activities to help customers understand their service. Again, head office said: "Great, we'll use that!" Having received nothing for this, she stopped telling head office about her ideas and became more secretive about what

> she was doing. Then she realised that she had stopped having any
> new ideas at all... so she left!

Some people may have random flashes of inspiration when they
work in the environment of tensions, others may not. It would help
staff dramatically if they were taught techniques for managing the
paradoxes they face, both those that are being held open
intentionally and those that crop up more randomly. Tom Peters
(1989, p396) suggests that we should: "Promote those who deal best
with paradox... If the ability to deal with these paradoxes is the key
to success, then we should promote, at all levels, those who show
the greatest facility in doing so." However, he doesn't say *how*
people might deal with paradox. Paradox management is a skill, not
a trait; some people may be naturally good at it, but that does not
mean it cannot be learnt by others.

Another hurdle for the traditional Western business culture is how
managers manage and leaders lead when it comes to tensions and
paradox. 'Management' seem reluctant to push decision making
down to the lowest appropriate point. This means managers make
decisions about things they have little knowledge of since they are
not customer facing. It is rare that a senior manager comes down to
the shop floor and wanders about, observing, talking to staff and
getting their sleeves rolled up. On the other side, staff are expecting
management to come up with the ideas, make decisions and solve
their problems for them. So staff make management responsible for
solving their problems. The expectation on leaders to lead by
solving all the problems (and their continuance of doing so) keeps
things stuck. This is perhaps where 'empowerment' comes in.

Empowerment can create its own paradoxes, however, and if
people are told: "you are now empowered" but are not given the
training that goes with it, chaos will often ensue. In order to devolve
responsibility the organisation needs to equip staff to solve the
problems themselves. This means providing briefings as to what is
going on, why it is going on and training on how to go about things.

They then need to be equipped with the appropriate resources and given a growing level of authority as their confidence and capability increases. The nature of empowerment and delegation are discussed further in chapter 13.

In an ideal company, each manager might be left to manage certain tensions (e.g. the team reward versus individual reward paradox). They are told that these tensions exist and that they are expected to keep staff motivated. Some may succeed and others initially might not. Those that succeed need to be rewarded *and* the best practice needs to be shared through the company. All managers then have a range of ways of handling these tensions. If this seems unreasonable, then train the managers how to understand and resolve paradox! Give them the skills.

What would be an example of a working open paradox?
A classic three way paradox (introduced in chapter 2), particularly for project managers, is the Time-Cost-Quality triangle. If we need to reduce time, this will generally mean lowering quality (e.g. a reduced finish or fewer features than originally specified) and/or increasing cost (e.g. bringing in additional resources to speed up the process). If we want to reduce cost, this may mean lower quality (e.g. cheaper components) and/or time increase (e.g. having to do more oneself). If we want to increase quality then it will usually take longer and/or cost more. If we try and focus on one corner of the triangle it tends to throw the others into flux. Although it seems that stakeholders often want 'perfection for nothing now', something has to give.

If we were to stereotype for a moment, it appears that different cultures focus on different aspects of the triangle. Americans seem to focus primarily on time (the urgency of short termism... a 'fast buck'). This has created paradox for some British companies (used to long term planning) that have been taken over by American companies who want to know how each decision will affect the next quarter's bottom line. The British have a tendency to focus on cost (the cheapest deal... 'look after the pennies and the pounds will look after themselves'). This creates paradox when (e.g.) government bodies and local authorities select contractors by the criteria of cost. Those people tendering have to put in a low cost bid to stand any chance of winning the tender but sadly have no way of achieving the outcome on that budget. Project costs overrun dramatically since the local authority is then stuck in the 'investor's paradox' (where they have invested so much money/time/resources into a project that they will continue to fund it in order to complete it).

An example of a culture that focuses on quality is Japan. Most of the organisational quality movements appeared to start with Total Quality Management (which ironically was inspired by an American called William Edwards Demming, a man who had to take his ideas to Japan for them to become widely recognised). This quality movement has led to such practices as Toyota's Lean manufacturing and the methodology of Just in Time. The focus on 'quality as primary' will, of course, throw cost and time into a potentially paradoxical flux. However, the notion of holding and working with paradox would seem to fit with the Eastern culture, where it is used for innovation rather than allowed to become chaotic. As an aside, to demonstrate that no stereotype is absolute, the quality strategy of Six Sigma (i.e. for every million opportunities for failure in a process, only 3.4 defects is allowable) was developed by the American company Motorola.

To conclude here, the time-cost-quality triangle is an ongoing open paradox. If it is managed effectively it will generate new ideas, but if it is not it will usually lead to chaos, stress and overruns.

When someone finds a workable solution, why not close the paradox at that point?
Sometimes, this may be a wise option in order to give people time to move on to other innovations elsewhere with new paradoxes to solve! However, if an organisation closes a paradox (e.g. by saying: "We now have the answer") it may be limiting the possibility of a

future innovation that would be even better. An example would be the motor car. The internal combustion engine was invented in the mid 1800s and when the first car was patented in 1886 it used the already invented engine. The engine design of a car has never really radically changed since then. This may have been in part, due to the abundance of oil and hence petrol and diesel. However, we are now heading towards a new tension where oil reserves are depleting and there is pressure globally to reduce emissions. Only now, over one hundred years after the internal combustion engine was invented are other types of car engines being taken seriously. As well as the hybrid cars, which still use oil (albeit less) we have the innovation of the hydrogen car. If the paradox had been held open before, perhaps the hydrogen car (which is apparently significantly better for the environment) might have been invented sooner.

Some paradoxes we might resolve through an innovation and for others it will not make sense to close them. The answer to this may not necessarily be an 'either/or' however, as we shall explore in the next chapter. Even if a paradox is closed or resolved, it may be important for management to monitor the success of the innovation. This will link with Argyris' Double Loop Learning, where the innovation needs to be monitored on a number of levels:

Level 1:   Does the innovation work and can it be 'continually improved'?

Level 2:   Does the innovation actually serve the purpose for which it was originally intended? For example, you can make a typewriter better and better, but a PC serves the purpose much more effectively.

Level 3:   Is the original purpose still fit for purpose? Does the purpose meet the needs of the current context/environment?

When the original purpose is no longer valid (e.g. customers don't want rental televisions anymore regardless of the excellent service and payment plan), then this shifts the whole issue to finding the new paradox/tension and hence a new innovation.

Polarity Management

The term 'Polarity Management' was coined by Barry Johnson (1996). As already discussed, a polarity is a pair of interdependent opposites that cause ongoing problems. Too much of one side or the other can be damaging and picking one side over the other doesn't really work.

Polarity management is a useful tool when handling strategic differences where one side likes one approach and the other side likes the opposite. However, when you look at it both polarities are valid and have value. In this instance, if the paradox is like saying: "Which is better, breathing in or breathing out?" then this tool is well worth utilising. Sometimes, both sides of the polarity are necessary but not at the same time.

To summarise the process, we look at the pros and cons of each side and then (rather than make a decision of one over the other) we use this data to inform a movement from one side to the other when appropriate. We are seeking to get the *best of each option over a period of time*.

As a working example, imagine an organisation struggling for position in the market place. One group of executives want to find ways of expanding the company perhaps by diversifying and investing in marketing/advertising. The other group want to find ways of contracting by cost cutting, reining in and focussing on the core of the business. In this situation, if were to use polarity management, the process (as outlined by Barry Johnson) might be:

(1) Establish the polarity *(e.g. expansion vs. contraction)*

(2) Write the pros & cons of each polarity in a grid as below:

Pros **L+**	Greater market presence Increase profits Broaden services Be more appealing to customers	Cut costs: use fewer resources Core focus: brand strength Re-evaluate what market wants Release less effective staff	**Pros** **R+**
L- **Cons**	Rising/spiralling costs Unclear brand in market Loss of control of business	Worry shareholders – shares drop Poor image + reduced credibility Customer confidence down Sales go down	**R-** **Cons**

(left axis: **Expansion**; right axis: **Contraction**)

Then in the 'real world'...

(3) when facing L- symptoms, shift attention to making R+ happen

e.g. if experiencing rising costs, unclear brand and/or loss of control, then shift attention and efforts to Contraction

(4) when facing R- symptoms, shift attention to making L+ happen

e.g. if experiencing drop in share prices, poor image, low customer confidence, reduced sales, then shift attention and efforts to Expansion

(5) Go to (3)

Hence there is a flow in alternating between the polarities when the threat of the negative side of the current polarity begins to show.

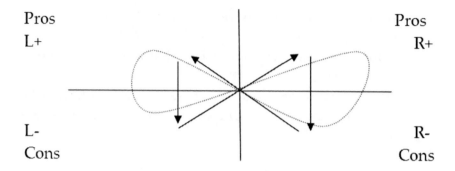

Pros
L+

Pros
R+

L-
Cons

R-
Cons

According to Johnson, if there is too much focus on one 'pole'/position, the cons of that position will begin to occur. If there is continued focus on that pole/position, the *negative of the opposite pole is also likely to occur*. In this way: "you get what you are afraid of by clinging to its apparent opposite." (p157).

The advantage of this process is that it allows people to see the full picture of the paradox. It tells people that change is necessary and the movement of change can be predicted and controlled. By focusing more time in the top quadrants, we can optimise the advantages of each side over a period of time.

It is important however, that this oscillation is reviewed over time to make sure that it still fits the environment. Sometimes a paradigm shift is required (i.e. Argyris' double loop learning). For example, although it seems that in the UK we swing back and forth between Labour and Conservative, if we never shifted beyond the polarity of the two main political parties we would still be stuck with Whigs and Tories!

When implementing polarity management back in the real world, here are some useful questions to ask:

Ongoing questions (Johnson, p132):
   a) What do we need to do to keep us in the upper two
      quadrants?

b) At this moment, how do we measure pros of both poles and give recognition?

c) How do we know when it time to shift focus from one pole to the other?

d) How do we communicate most effectively with those who want to focus on the current pole when we want to shift focus?

System questions (Johnson, p137):

a) What communication systems need to be in place to alert the system when it slides into one of the downsides?

b) What additional system practices would be in place if this polarity was being well managed (moving back and forth with relative ease and staying primarily in the upper two quadrants)? What steps could you take to move in that direction?

To give another example of Polarity Management, we might use the polarity of Change vs Stability.

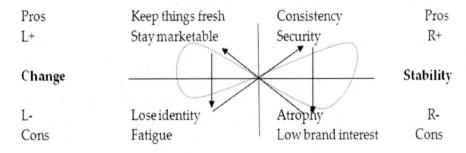

Pros	Keep things fresh	Consistency	Pros
L+	Stay marketable	Security	R+
Change			**Stability**
L-	Lose identity	Atrophy	R-
Cons	Fatigue	Low brand interest	Cons

As an organisation, if we are seeking to understand our relationship with the polarity of Change – Stability, we would look at the flow: where are we now? Are we in the 'fresh and marketable' or 'losing identity and fatigue'? If the latter (disadvantages) we would seek to actively 'Stabilise' in order to get the benefits of 'consistency and security'. If we then saw the early signs of 'atrophy and low brand interest' we would seek the benefits of change and so on *ad infinitum*. In a real world setting we would put this to a group and have lots more factors on each side that were pertinent to the business.

If a group is in conflict, it is good to start by separating each side of the group to write the positives of their polarity. Then ask them to be honest and write the potential negatives of their side. After this, bring both sides together to debrief and apply the movement from one side to the other.

For more information about this technique I recommend Barry Johnson's "Polarity Management".

Chapter 10

Somewhere in the Middle:
The Fuzzy Logic Approach

In This Chapter...

In this chapter you will move from the 'either/or' of Formal Logic to the 'from/to' continuum approach of Fuzzy Logic. This will open up more possibilities in your approach to resolving paradox and ethical dilemmas.

We will be exploring the following questions:
- What is fuzzy logic?
- What happens when we see polarity as a continuum?
- How might we use fuzzy logic to approach ethical dilemmas?

Fuzzy Logic – Seeing the Continuum

To take us a step beyond the polarity of 'either/or' thinking (e.g. something is either black or white, right or wrong) we might utilise 'from/to' thinking. This is called 'fuzzy logic' where we are creating a line between the two polarities. This gives us a continuum with a spectrum of positions and possibilities, each with pros and cons. So we move from 'black or white' thinking to 'shades of grey'.

Some polarities although interconnected appear to be mutually exclusive. How about the humble polarity of 'on' or 'off'... surely this is an absolute polarity? By using fuzzy logic, where there is a continuum between on and off, we have dimmer switches for lights and for televisions, we have a 'standby mode' where the TV is, in effect, on and off at the same time.

As opposed to the absolute, either/or type language of formal logic, the language of fuzzy logic is much more in the realms of *possibilities* (that indicate a place *between* the opposing poles). Examples of 'fuzzy language' might include: quite, very, possibly, nearly, often, might, may, maybe, frequently, sometimes, almost, perhaps. When we use formal logic and take a position, it becomes very easy for someone else to take an opposing conflicting position. With fuzzy language, there is less to argue with since there are degrees of possibility involved. When speaking in fuzzy language we tend to be more honest that this is opinion (i.e. 'my truth') rather than fact (i.e. '**the** truth'). We are acknowledging that there are shades of grey.

When someone gets themselves caught in 'either/or' they tend to see themselves limited to two options, for example:

If we assume that X and Y are polar opposites, by using the idea of the continuum we allow for a range of possibilities in between the 'either/or' (i.e. creating a 'from/to'). By writing down the paradox as above (placing each side in a circle some distance apart) it is interesting to note what happens when we draw a solid line from one to the other.

In the context of a particular example where the line has been drawn between the two sides, it is then worth exploring the following questions: What does this immediately give you? What connections does this make? What other options are available to you now? How might it be for you that the two sides are interconnected and part of a greater whole?

For most people, particularly when they have been locked into an either/or, this changes their internal processing. Instead of seeing 'this' or 'that', by drawing a joining line in between they open up a massive amount of possibility. This is like going from a zero dimension solution (one of two dots) to another dimension of understanding and resourcefulness. The continuum gets rid of the exclusion of one or the other and makes a link where 'there may be other things we can do in between'. Smith & Berg (1987, p218) suggest that when a group is "struggling with a paradoxical tension, the discovery of the link between two apparently contradictory opposites provides a 'reframing' of the relationship between the two. This reframing brings with it new ways of looking at the conflicts that have formed in the relationship between the two extremes."

The drawing of the continuum has an additional psychological effect of shifting from two separate things to the unity of the bigger picture. It links up the polarity and begins to collapse the paradox by demonstrating that it is one thing and not two. It becomes one picture, like the yin-yang symbol. For some people, it is this that unlocks the impossible problem as they begin to see other possibilities and the spark of innovation is fired off.

By seeing the whole as a continuum, it allows us to comment from a higher order of thinking (or higher logical level). For example, when running appraisal skills courses, some delegates seem to want to attack the system and/or the paperwork. After hearing the various perspectives, I often respond: "There is no such thing as a perfect appraisal system. If at one end it is a prescribed set of questions with spaces for answers, then some people would feel this is too rigid and restrictive and doesn't apply completely to themselves. If we go to the other end and give people blank paper and say: 'do it your own way', lots of people would be lost and not know what to ask or write. Each variant between those two points will have its pros and cons. What this course is about is taking the system you have and making it useful for you and your staff." I usually find that this puts the 'positioning' to bed.

Another area where fuzzy logic can be useful is in questionnaires and personality profiling. Have you ever filled in a 'yes/no' or 'agree/disagree' questionnaire/survey and found yourself thinking "it depends" to nearly every question? An advancement on the formal logic binary style questionnaire is to have a scale and/or scoring system. For example:

- Do you visit the library: Never – rarely – sometimes – often - nearly always – always?
- On a scale of 1 to 6 (where 1 is low and 6 is high), how much do you like peas?

These approaches (although somewhat subjective) are likely to give a truer response from the person being asked the questions. Of course there are many other ways of asking questions and seeking response data, however, this is simply an example of where fuzzy logic might be useful.

Fuzzy Logic in Ethical Dilemmas

Ethical dilemmas are those that create a moral uncertainty where it is not always clear what is right or wrong. People at either end of the dilemma can put forward persuasive arguments and we might take 'one side' or another. Alternatively, we may end up confused as to the right position or course of action. Consider the following examples:

- Should a member of staff have the right to not use soap or deodorant when the consequence of that right has an impact on other members of staff?
- Should organisations ban their staff from using airplanes when they could travel long distance by train?
- Should there be a company ban on all swearing?
- Is banter acceptable in an office environment?
- Do managers have the right to implement a 'silence' policy on their staff (to stop them from chatting)?

Fuzzy logic can be useful when considering ethical dilemmas where the focus is usually on right or wrong. As soon as we take a position, there will be a counter position and hence potential conflict. By shifting to 'from/to' thinking, a continuum is created, where there is no absolute right or wrong.

In any instance, if we call the extremes of an ethical dilemma 'a' and 'b', then how do we make ethical judgements along the continuum from 'a' to 'b'? Without view of the whole continuum, we tend to draw a line in the sand and then seek to justify and defend that position. In addition, when attacking other people's positions a common trick is to use the 'argument by extreme' (i.e. to compare the opposing side with the *extreme* end of the continuum). For example, a vegetarian might accuse a meat eater of being a murderer or a cannibal.

By using fuzzy logic, we can see the whole range of arguments as a continuum. This allows us to step beyond the argument and see the whole picture, hence thinking at a higher logical level. It is then our choice to comment upon the continuum as a whole or to go back and argue our position.

There is an interesting paradox in an ethical dilemma when we consider it a continuum: at what point does something move from being right/okay to wrong/not okay? This is known as the Sorities paradox: at what point does a heap become a heap? How many grains of sand does it take to make a heap of sand? If we have a heap and we take one grain away at a time, when does it cease to become a heap? At what point is a man considered bald? The Sorites paradox is the 'problem of a gradual continuum'. In terms of organisational behaviour or performance, if there is a scale from 'okay' to 'not okay' at what specific point does it suddenly tip from one to the other? If a member of staff's performance *gradually* gets worse, at what point should the manager have them under review? A sudden drop is easier to distinguish but a gradual drop is sometimes harder to spot and comment on. To make matters tougher, what if you have a member of staff who hovers around the okay/not okay tipping point? Of course these situations are resolvable and most managers may have to face that situation at some point. However, it does make it more challenging!

A final note on ethical dilemmas and on continuums as a whole: wherever you decide to draw your line in the sand, *consider the potential consequences of that decision*. For example, as a manager, if you decide that it is okay for people to come in a little late if they make the hours up by staying behind at the end of the day, consider the impact on the service you run, consider the precedent it sets for others, consider how late is late?

Here are some steps for approaching an ethical dilemma:
1. Consider: What is the dilemma? What is it between? What are the extreme ends?
2. Draw a continuum to see the complete picture of all possible positions.

3. Along the continuum, consider the consequences of holding some of the possible positions.
4. To escape the dilemma, go meta and comment on the continuum/ big picture. (e.g. "This is a continuum between X and Y and we seem to have different positions along that continuum.")
5. If desired, decide on a stance and consider the implications of that stance.

Last Thoughts

The advantage of fuzzy logic is that it allows for a midway point solution, a balance or a compromise. However, although a 'from/to' continuum is an improvement on 'either/or' (in the sense that it provides more options), it might still be considered rather one dimensional. For example, if the result of a negotiation could only be somewhere between win/lose and lose/win, then the best result for all parties could only be a compromise – win/win can only occur if a second dimension is added as we will see in the next chapter.

Chapter 11

Synthesis: The Dialectic Approach

In This Chapter...

In this chapter you will learn some of the dialectic approaches to resolving paradoxical problems. You will also discover how to create useful models from polarities. This will help you in generating creative solutions when faced with polarity, tension and paradox.

We will be exploring the following questions:
- What is dialectic logic?
- What are some dialectic tools and techniques?
- How might we use the dialectic method in making models?

What is Dialectic logic?

When people are stuck in a dilemma, they may feel split or feel that their thinking is going round in circles between the two options or positions: *This side is good but that side has good points too... The trouble with that side is that it has some negatives... But having said that, so does this option.*

Being stuck in a dilemma (caught between two options) is usually the result of 'either/or' thinking, *either this option or that option.* As we have seen in chapter 9, there can be merit in holding a polarity open or understanding it so that we can predict the circularity. However, with dialectic thinking, we are seeking 'both/and' rather than 'either/or'. We are seeking to synthesise the options to create a 'third way'. It could be said that in seeking or holding the possibility of 'both/and', we are setting up an environment for the creative spark to happen. This is the point of inspiration - or as Arthur Keostler (1964) called it, the 'act of creation'. We accept that both sides of the polarity have a value (even if it doesn't immediately appear that way) and then we seek to blend the 'best of both worlds'. Every position will have a counter position that has some value.

If we simply accept a paradox, hold it open and wait, it could take some time for inspiration to come. During that time there may be a significant amount of stress while the poles of the paradox are disconnected. With the dialectic method, we are focussing the synthesis and generating a 'third way' when we want it.

The nature of the dialectic method is in taking a 'thesis' and its 'antithesis' (opposite) and transcending both to create a 'synthesis', a third way. Rather than being a fuzzy logic 'continuum' solution somewhere between thesis and antithesis, the true synthesis creates a second dimension by taking us up a logical level, to transcend the paradox. (The word 'transcend' is an interesting word here in its phonological ambiguity as it sounds like 'trance end', i.e. ending the trance, the illusion of the paradox.) Einstein is reported to have said that a problem will not be solved on the level it was created. Dialectic synthesis takes us to another level in order to 'solve' the problem.

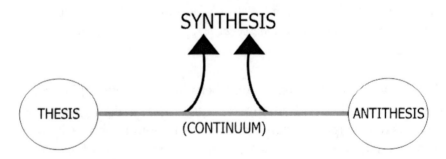

A question that could be asked of dialectic synthesis is that in only looking at the positives, is there not a danger of 'pollyanna'ing and not living in the real world? Isn't it rather risky to not consider the downsides of each option?

When people use phrases like 'between the devil and the deep blue sea' or 'between a rock and a hard place' they are looking only at the negative sides of each end of the paradox. It is the process of focusing on the negative aspect of each horn of the dilemma that keeps us stuck at the level we are on. When we explore the positives, this has the potential to lift us to a synthesis at the next logical level up. There we can allow ideas of having 'both/and' with new potential solutions. We can *then* explore the downside of our new solution in order to understand the ecology (potential ripple effect) and the risks and hence put contingency plans in place.

The dialectic synthesis moves us past the circular trap of focusing on *positive* then *negative* then *positive* etc., or *positive* but *negative* but *positive* etc. With the synthesis, we look at the positives of both sides to stimulate fresh thinking and new ideas; then we can look at the negatives of the new idea and work from there.

The mishandling of difference is usually a result of each side focussing on the negatives of the opposite position. When this happens, the two sides will usually spiral downwards into conflict (a negative spiral of: yes but, yes but, yes but... etc.).

Side A's
Perspective   O

Side B's
O Perspective

Seeking the negative
aspects of each
other's perspective

CONFLICT

However, when each side focuses on the positives of the opposite position, there is an opportunity for an innovation spiral.

Dialectic Techniques

Technique 1: 'Dilemma Integration Technique'
The Dilemma Integration Technique (DIT) is, in my opinion, one of the simplest and most effective approaches for generating new ideas when a polarity/tension/dilemma is identified.

As well as working effectively for individuals, the DIT works very effectively for teams and groups. All you need is a large piece of paper (e.g. flip chart) or whiteboard and then answer the following question for each side of the dilemma, writing the answers randomly around on the paper/whiteboard: "What would I gain from this option?" or "What does this option give us?"

It is important to intersperse the words and use the same colour for both sides. By doing this, you are breaking down the either/or thinking and creating new connections in the minds of those involved. By answering the question for both sides, you are capturing the full set of 'positive intentions' (benefits, gains, advantages). When working with a group, it is important to get everyone's input. As Bandler & Grinder (1982, p144) propose: "In order to successfully reframe a system, you have to take into account the needs and wishes of all members of the system."

By intermingling and amalgamating the answers, you are leading to a synthesis. When you have all the 'positives' of both sides ask: What alternatives does this give you? What other options are available to you now? What third solution might meet this (*pointing at the words on the paper/whiteboard*)? What could you do now?

If the client/group is still stuck here are some methods for moving on:

1) If there are only a *limited amount of answers* (or limited from one side) ask "And what else does that give you?"

2) Look at anything *still conflicting* in the mix and for each of the conflicting items ask: "What does that give you?" writing the responses in place of the conflicting words.

3) Look for any *material/tangible* items on the list (e.g. a Ferrari) or anything to do with *other people* and ask: "What does that give you?" writing the responses in place of the old words.

4) Look for any *negations* ('not' words – e.g. 'not stressed'). Ask: "If you weren't being/doing/having that, what would you be/do/have?" Replace the words on the page.

5) Look for any *judgements* (e.g. good job) or *comparisons* (e.g. better house) and ask: "What does that give you?" writing the responses in place of the conflicting words.

6) If necessary, scoring each of the positive intentions on a scale of 1 to 5 where 1 is less important and 5 is most important. Then look at your 4s and 5s to generate a third way.

Here are two examples where this simple technique has been effective with a group

Case study 1: A team or not a team?
A team of senior managers were having problems since they were also heads of units that were in competition with each other. There was a lot of confusion between competition and co-operation. They were being told to do both by their manager (a Vice President of the company) but without any indication what was expected. Their manager expected them to work this out; they were after all on very

179

good salaries! One of the problems that was manifesting (aside from a kind of 'sibling rivalry') was that the manager would run with an idea from one of the managers and remove budget from other projects in order to fund it. A day or two later, he would do the same again with a different proposal. This meant that the 'team' of managers ended up competing with each other for a limited (albeit large) pot of money. On working with the team, the issue of 'team vs unit heads' came up again and again and this was a serious source of the tension.

We did the Dilemma Integration Technique with the team, looking at the benefits of working as a team and working in competition. There was soon a discussion happening between colleagues who previously had been isolated and aggressive. Seeing the best of both sides, they realised that the problem was not really team vs units but how they collectively 'handled' their manager. They agreed that if he was looking to move a budget of more than £50,000 they would contact each other to discuss what they thought was best. They also agreed that other problems they would resolve as they went along by setting up a communication system between them. At this point they could happily work in their units, knowing that if there was an issue, they could 'jump up a logical level' and joint problem solve. This allowed for a dynamic way of working that they had all agreed on. Conflict practically disappeared and now they were working in a kind of 'co-opetition' (a mindset that combines competition and co-operation - Nalebuff & Brandenburger 2002)

Case study 2 - Sales or integrity!
A team of sales consultants in a small company were having problems in the market place because their central value (integrity) meant that they were losing out on tenders to less scrupulous companies. It seemed to them that they could 'have integrity but no business' or 'business but no integrity'.

We looked at the 'win/win' for them; what did they get by winning business and what did they get by maintaining integrity. Through capturing the best of both, they began to see a strategy of using their integrity to win business. This meant turning things they did anyway into selling points, for example, money back guarantee for up to six months if the client was not totally satisfied. As a strategy, this was almost unheard of in their industry.

Technique 2: 'The AMBO Model'
The AMBO model is an analysis tool designed to elicit the positive aspects of an option. It is a more thorough version of the Dilemma Integration Technique, bringing in benefits to the individuals and the organisation as well as values and potential applications. The model might be useful in decision making and in weighing both sides of a dilemma.

AMBO stands for:
- A - Advantages (to you personally)
- M - Meanings (motivations and values)
- B - Benefits (to organisation/bigger picture)
- O - Opportunities (and applications)

The following table gives an explanation for each component of AMBO and a key question for each:

AMBO COMPONENTS	EXPLANATION	KEY QUESTION	EXAMPLE: Rewarding Team Performance
Advantages to You	This is about the positive consequences we would experience by taking an option. It may also link to the positive intention – what positive purpose might the option serve?	*What would you gain from this option?*	Motivation of team, team works together, productivity up.

Meanings	This is about our motivations, values and criteria in relationship to an option, i.e. what is important to us.	*What is important to you about this option?*	Fairness, everyone is given a chance and acknowledged.
Benefits to Organisation	This is about the resources, strengths, tools, skills, capabilities and qualities that the option brings to the organisation.	*What benefits and resources does this option bring to the organisation?*	Provides a measurable system, consistency, structure.
Opportunities	This is about the contexts and situations in which an option adds value, some of the potential applications.	*Where would this option be useful?*	Team oriented tasks/activities.

The words 'ambo' is Latin for 'both' and in this context, the AMBO model can be used to create a both/and synthesis from an either/or dilemma. The model is used initially in the same way that a SWOT analysis is used.

Use the AMBO quadrant (below) to elicit information for both sides of the dilemma. **Combine the data from both sides into each quadrant** (mixing the data up and using the same colour). Use this synthesis of data to generate some new options.

	Gain	Value
Personal Perspective	Advantages to You	Meanings
Organisational Perspective	Benefits to Organisation	Opportunities

Using the Dialectic approach for Model Making

Most management books and training courses will introduce a 'quadrant' or 'four box matrices' at some point and a few of these are discussed later in this chapter. The four box model is often a convenient way of expressing ideas, particularly when there are one or two continuums being explored. Part of the 'Paradox and Tensions Management' toolkit is in making models to explore paradox.

The technical term for the quadrant model is a 'dialectic construct' as it allows us go beyond the 'either/or' and the 'from/to' continuum and explore other 'boxes'. In this sense it adds another dimension that gives us two new areas: 'both/and' and 'neither/nor'.

The dialectic construct is particularly useful when seeking to create models and/or explore conceptual paradoxes, for example, which is better:

- o Autocratic or democratic leadership?
- o Using in-house consultants or external consultants?
- o Forging change or seeking stability?

One approach to resolving tensions and conflict is to find the middle ground, the balance point. With many tensions however, although this half way point along the continuum is very convenient, it doesn't encourage us to access any 'third way' solutions. For example, the half way point between using in-house vs. external consultants might be to use each 50% of the time. This might be rather costly to employ a group of people and pay for externals.

The dialectic construct allows us to explore the other areas of 'both/and' and 'neither/nor'. What would happen (or what would it mean) to have use both internal and external consultants? Perhaps it leads us back to the 50/50 balance point but it also allows for much more. Both/and might mean having externals train the internals, or using externals as a reference point during a project, having them add advice into a planning meeting rather than have them do the planning. What would happen (or what would it mean) to use neither internal nor external consultants? Perhaps allow staff to solve their own problems and get involved in their own projects, to form their own workgroups and propose and implement changes as they see necessary.

From my experience of working with others, the 'neither/nor' box can often be the hardest to answer or 'get ones head around'. It is apparently the place of vacuum, emptiness and void. It is the null space. Do not underestimate it, however. The 'neither/nor' box can be extremely powerful and liberating, allowing a person or group previously stuck in a dilemma to transcend 'stuckness' and enter a place of potentiality.

<u>Creating a Dialectic Construct</u>

1)   Start with a polarity. This could be in the form of X vs Y (e.g. individual reward vs team reward or X vs not X (e.g. employed or not employed)

2)   Draw a quadrant with each side of the polarity as axes from low to high:

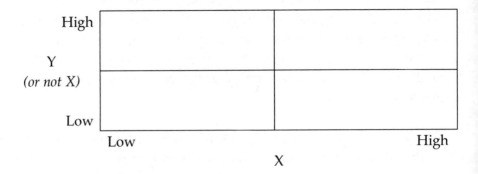

3)   Label the boxes:

High	High Y, Low X	High Y, High X
Y	*(Either/Or)*	*(Both/And)*
(or not X)	Low Y, Low X	Low Y, High X
Low	*(Neither/Nor)*	*(Either/Or)*
	Low	High

X

In a real example, it is useful if each quadrant can be labelled in positive or neutral language. For example, if we were creating a quadrant for individual reward versus team reward, we might label the 'neither/nor' box as 'Alternative to reward' rather than 'No reward' or 'Don't reward'. This allows for potential value in this area.

Sometimes your examples might initially look, sound or feel clumsy and hard to comprehend. For example the 'neither/nor' box for the dilemma *employed vs not employed* will become: 'neither employed nor not employed'. This can be like hearing the question: "So what wouldn't happen if you weren't employed?" However, stick with it.

Examples of Dialectic Constructs

Type 1) Top right quadrant = best

  a)   The Negotiation Quadrant

Both the approaches and results of a negotiation can be turned into a quadrant. For this example, I am starting with the formal logic version, the fuzzy logic version and then the dialectic construct. This is to demonstrate the movement from one logic to another and also to show where the one dimensional fuzzy logic continuum fits in a two dimensional dialectic construct.

185

According to Handy (1994) the Anglo Saxon approach to negotiation was/is 'win-lose' (i.e. I win, you lose). It is competitive rather than collaborative, designed to get the best deal you can regardless of the other party's needs. This approach is very 'results' oriented. The opposite to 'results' oriented appears to be 'relationship' oriented where we give more away and do more simply to maintain the relationship. It could be argues that the polarity behind a negotiation is 'results' vs 'relationship'.

Formal Logic: Polarity   (Either/Or)

RESULTS Vs RELATIONSHIPS

Fuzzy Logic: Continuum   (From/To)

RESULTS   RELATIONSHIPS

(Compromise)

Dialectic Logic: Quadrant   —   (Both/And)

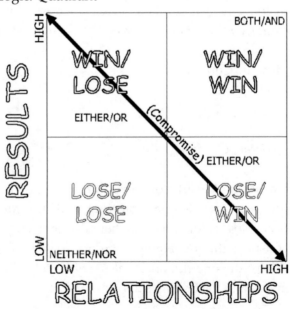

As you will see from the above, the fuzzy logic continuum will run from corner to corner in the dialectic construct (from high X to high Y). It is sometimes interesting to consider a continuum running from low/low to high/high. In any particular context you might ask yourself: "What might this suggest?"

b) *The Managerial Grid*

Robert Blake and Jane Mouton (1966, 1981, 1985) developed a model using the dialectic construct. They used two continuums, 'concern for people' and 'concern for production' to create a grid with scores that led to five 'management styles'. The model is excellent and I recommend their books, however, I am showing their model here to demonstrate what you can do with a dialectic construct.

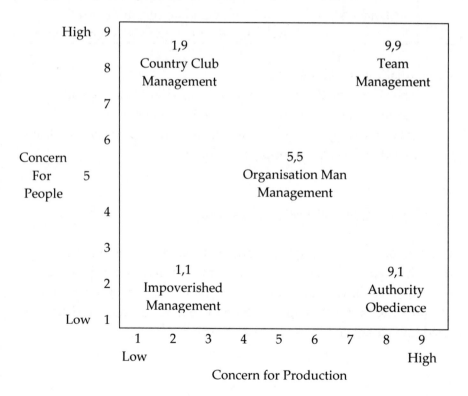

The resulting five styles of management can be used as a guide to the types of managers in an organisation. The five styles are described as:

1,1	Impoverished Management	Seeks to do the minimum required to stay in their job.
1,9	Country Club Management	Seeks to make sure that staff are happy and enjoying themselves potentially at the expense of results.
5,5	Organisation Man Management	Seeks to maintain status quo. Do what needs to be done to get along. Works at a satisfactory level.
9,1	Authority Obedience	Seeks to achieve results through power and control. Seeks compliance in staff.
9,9	Team Management	Seeks to produce quality results through their team. Good at informing and involving the team for high commitment.

Other quadrants include:
- The Organisational Behaviours quadrant (see Chapter 6) based on the axes of empathy and expression.
- Steven Covey's (1994) time management priority quadrant based on the axes of important and urgent.

Type 2) Contextual: All quadrants have value

If the polarity is ongoing (i.e. there are times when 'either is better'), then this type of quadrant allows you a situational approach. By drawing a list of pros and cons for each quadrant, the pros become a 'best fit criteria' for that approach and the cons become the risks that need to be managed if taking that option.

a) Situational Leadership

Ken Blanchard and Paul Hersey created a well known model by looking at two types of leadership: autocratic and democratic, and then updating them to directive (giving specific instructions and close supervision and controlling) and supportive (listening, encouraging, guiding and coaching). This is another classic management model and I recommend reading Ken Blanchard et al's "Leadership & the One Minute Manager" (1994).

By running these two types of leadership through the dialectic construct, they developed four *styles* of leadership (directing, coaching, supporting and delegating). Each style has its own relevance and use depending on the situation (hence the label 'situational leadership'). The idea is that the leader would *adapt* his or her style, leading different people in different situations in different ways, depending on the member of staff's experience, ability, confidence and motivation. No one quadrant is better than the others.

b) Modes of Communication

The Modes of Communication model is an aid to planning a communication strategy during times of change. When managing change, there are two key aspects of communication: informing (telling, updating, briefing, giving information) and involving (consulting, seeking input/feedback).

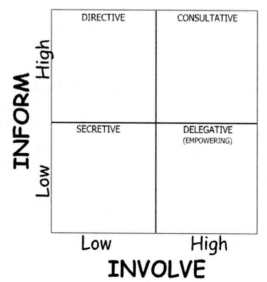

As the change progresses,

communication modes may change, depending on whom you are communicating with. The level of information you communicate (and at what point during the change) will depend on the impact of the change on the market place, organisation, department, team, individuals. The style will affect the 'what' you communicate and 'how' you communicate, so it is worth considering "what would happen if we used this style with this group at this point?"

If we look at the pros and cons of each mode, the pros will help to determine which is the most appropriate to use with a group of people. The cons will tell us the risks that will need to be managed. For example:

DIRECTIVE		CONSULTATIVE	
+	-	+	-
Fast. Clear. Reach many people simultaneously.	Less buy-in. Have to do more persuasion/ selling to get people on board/ committed.	Buy-in. Range of ideas. Input from people who will have to implement change.	Time consuming. Possible unrealistic ideas. Unrealistic expectations. Demoralising if ideas not implemented.
SECRETIVE		EMPOWERMENT	
+	-	+	-
Maintain control. Prevent market sensitive info from leaking.	No buy-in. Surprise and break in trust when announced. Possible grapevine/ fantasising.	Total buy-in. Ownership. Motivation & commitment. High likelihood of action.	Less control. May go in unwanted direction & staff on-board with 'wrong option'.

So if at some point during change you need buy-in from a particular group with a range of ideas and input from the people who will have to implement the change then the 'consultative' mode may be the best approach. However, you will need to manage the time frames and the expectations of the staff coming up with ideas.

Type 3) Information gathering: All quadrants provide a useful point of reference

o   *Change Response Model*

This dialectic construct was developed to determine people's attitudes and/or positions about a particular topic. I was working with a group who were responsible for a brand change within their organisation. They were getting angry with people they felt were not on board with the change. They were of the opinion that people were either with them or against them and they were looking for ways to overcome the resistance. Sadly the direction they were headed was in the form of punishing and disciplining those that were not on board and who were not using the new branding.

Seeing an either/or polarity, we drew up a quadrant with 'On Board' as one axis and 'Resistant' (i.e. not currently on board) as the other. Each axis was given a range from low to high. Each quadrant was then labelled with positive language (to help shift the group away from their antagonism).

High	Bought in	Challenger/Innovator
On Board	Apathetic/Undecided	Independent
Low	Low High	

Resistant

The group's ideal box was the top left, i.e. 'Bought In' (on board with low resistance). The other three boxes gave them some insights into where other people might be. They realised that some people might be on board but didn't necessarily appear to be. They saw how someone could be supportive but uncomfortable with part of the branding, perhaps because they were unsure about it or didn't understand it.

The group now saw the four quadrants as different places people could be during a change. They began to use it as an information gathering exercise, considering how to win the hearts and minds of the 'undecided's, the independents and the challengers. In a bid to bring them on board and help them to buy in, they also spoke about listening to the other groups to find out what they needed in order to work with the new brand.

A Synthesis

The dialectic construct can be a useful way of creating models from paradoxical problems. It allows people to see more options and perspectives than just the logic of 'either/or'. Remember that each quadrant in the dialectic construct is an *area of possibilities* and not just a single solution. For example, we might get a win/win result from a negotiation, but there may have been all sorts of other possible wins that we could and would still have been delighted with.

Whenever you face an 'either/or', change your language and your thinking to 'both/and'. Consider what other possibilities and solutions are available to you when you consider having the 'best of both worlds'. For example, I was working with a fellow trainer a few years ago and we were trying to decide how we should split up an activity where there were three groups and three areas for discussion. Should we have each group do all three discussion areas, ready for a 'key points' debrief afterwards, or should we focus each group by giving them one subject area each, so they could present back to the others? The benefit of the first option was a familiarity with all the discussion areas. The benefit of the second option was to get the groups to focus and make sure they came back with something ready to present. So we 'synthesised' and got them to discuss all areas knowing that they would present back on one of them (which we would randomise when they returned). This way, they familiarised with all the discussion areas *and* focussed on quality feedback ready to present. Whilst this may not be a groundbreaking example, it makes the point of using dialectic thinking in resolving a simple 'daily' dilemma.

Chapter 12

Changing Perspective:
The Trialectic Approach

In This Chapter...

In this chapter you will learn about the trialectic approach and develop you use of reframing and denominalising in order to resolve paradox. This will help you to go beyond the paradox to solve it from another perspective.

We will be exploring the following questions:
- What is trialectic logic?
- What is reframing and how do you utilise it?
- What is denominalising?
- How do you loosen a paradox through denominalising

What is Trialectic Logic?

Aside from formal logic that seeks to hold an 'either/or' position and dialectic which seeks to synthesis 'both', we have a third, relatively unknown and abstract notion of trialectic logic where we go 'beyond' the problem. The trialectic approach is to consider that there are no positions of either/or and hence no synthesis to be had. The poles of the polarity are illusions created by our desire to make the intangible tangible, to turn what is in flux into a 'thing'.

According to Ichazo (1982, p74), trialectic logic is about "the change from one material manifestation point to another" and the movement from one point to another point appears to be that of one frame to another frame. A change of perspective will tend to change what we are perceiving. In this sense, 'reframing' captures the essence of trialectic logic.

It seems that the aim of trialectic logic in the resolution of paradox is to return a 'problem' back into its 'flow' state and then see what is now a process from another perspective. There are two key thinking processes which are both well developed within the field of neuro-linguistic programming (NLP), known as 'reframing' and 'denominalising', which may be of use here.

As to how trialectics can 'reframe' a paradox, here is a general example:
1. We know that a paradox has a position and a counter position.
2. We could say that the tension in a paradox is a result from one side being resistant to the other.
3. A belief within trialectic logic is that resistance is simply attraction to something else.
4. So rather than two positions in opposition (which leads to a stuckness like 'stalemate'), we have attraction in other directions.
5. By following the attractions we enter back into the flow and out of the stuckness.

Another helpful reframe about paradox comes from one of the presuppositions ('useful beliefs') of NLP: "Confusion precedes understanding." Whenever we learn something significant or have a breakthrough 'aha!' moment, there is usually a point before that where we 'don't get it'. Then neurons connect and we have a new learning. We know that paradox brings confusion and so when managed effectively, it will tend to lead to significant learning. Indeed, Charles Handy (1994, p17) suggests that: "Framing the confusion is the first step to doing something about it."

Reframing

A frame is how we look at something, like looking through the eye-piece of a camera. We might focus in on something, or pull back to a wide angle. Obviously, where we look is what we'll see. Bolman & Deal (2003, p12) refer to 'frames' as "windows, maps, tools, lenses, orientations, and perspectives... mental models, maps, mind-sets, schema and cognitive lenses". Frames are important because they help us make sense of the world. Dilts (1999, p23) suggests that: "Frames direct attention and influence how events are interpreted." Bolman & Deal (2003, p13) also add that: "A good frame makes it easier to know what you are up against and what you can do about it."

Reframing is changing the way we perceive an event/thing. We might not be able to change the event, but we can change the way we perceive it. When we change how we perceive it, we change the meaning. This then tends to change our response state and behaviour relating to that event (giving us more choices). Watzlawick et al (1974, p97) argue that reframing operates on the level of *meta*reality, where "change can take place even if the objective circumstances of a situation are quite beyond human control." In this sense, when we reframe, we 'go meta' to the real world issue and hence 'beyond' it. Bartunek (1988, p138-9) adds that reframing "is a qualitative, discontinuous, second order or double loop shift in the understanding of some domain, not an incremental shift in the previous level of understanding."

Apparently, Epictetus, a first century philosopher said that: "It is not the things themselves which trouble us, but the opinions that we have about these things." An event or thing has no meaning of its own. We attribute meaning to it depending on our own perceptions, beliefs, attitudes, behaviours, map of the world etc. As well as personal perceptions, meaning is also context dependant – the meaning of something may change depending on the situation or environment.

When someone is focussed on their problem, they are 'problem framing' (or seeing only the problem frame). The real problem comes when they get stuck with that frame, only able to see the world that way (in the context of their situation). One of the key principles of reframing is to help someone feel differently about their problems; hence we help them to see outside their problem frame. Dilts & Smith (1999) tell us that in order to get a solution, we need to get the client(s) out of their problem space first and then lead them to an 'outcome frame' (i.e. what they want instead of the problem, how they want to be different).

Another way of looking at a problem is to presuppose that *a problem is only a problem if it is perceived as a problem*. By reframing we can change the perception and hence potentially remove, resolve or at least loosen the problem. Ford & Backoff (1988, p89) suggest that a paradox is "some 'thing' that is constructed by individuals when opposite tendencies are brought into recognisable proximity through reflection or interaction... this definition implies that paradox can be dissolved through reframing or the revision of conceptual schemes wherein the apparent paradox is transcended." Smith & Berg (1987, p16) also suggest that reframing can help to resolve paradox: "Frame contradiction differently and the self-referential, self-renunciating circularity may well be broken." Quinn (1990, p20) suggests that the reason why reframing helps to resolve paradox is because: "Reframing means moving to a different kind of comprehension. It is the emergence of a new view or theory that suddenly makes sense of a contradictory situation."

Reframing taps into a rich source of material and hence provides a useful resource for paradox management. Bandler and Grinder (1982) differentiate between two types of reframing called 'content' and 'context' and these are outlined below:

Content	The event/thing that you are looking at. • What else could this mean? What could you learn from this? • What is good/bad about this? • How could you perceive this as positive/useful? or • How could you perceive this as negative/problematic?
Context	The situation in which you are placing/viewing the event/ thing. • What might this mean in another situation? • When else might you...? or When else might you not...? • In what situation might this be positive/useful? or • In what situation might this be negative/problematic?

A seemingly common polarity for many people in a job is 'do I stay or do I go'. They tend to see the positives and negatives of each side, reframing back and forth within the paradox. It might be argued that it is reframing that is keeping someone stuck in their dilemma – back and forth, back and forth. However, if we use reframing in a more purposeful and structured way, we can help the person transcend the problem. In this situation, we might seek to reframe the dilemma itself to shift it away from being perceived as a problem (which will in turn stop it from being experienced as a problem). For example:

Content reframes:
- (*What is good about this?*): Having this choice is a strong position to be in... it is often easier to get another job if you are already employed.

- (*How is this useful?*): Having this choice gives you the opportunity to check out the marketplace and update your CV.
- (*What else could this mean?*): This means you can make the decision or look for other options whilst you are still secure in a job and being paid.

Context reframes
- (*What might this mean in another situation?*): Many people don't have a job at all, so it is a positive position to be in.
- (*In what other situations might this be useful?*): You may find yourself looking back someday, glad that you had this opportunity to take stock of where you are now.
- (*When else might you choose to have this dilemma?*): It is a good to be in a situation from time to time where you are looking at your options. Some people stay in jobs they hate for years because they don't realise they have a choice like you have now.

Of course, we can also use reframing to explore the pros and cons of both sides of the dilemma. This is a dialectic approach as discussed in the previous chapter. If we want to take this further, we might look at each of the cons and seek to reframe them. For example, if the person wants to leave because they don't get on with their manager, we can reframe on that level: What could they learn from this? What are some other ways of working with their manager? How might they seek to resolve differences? What is *good* about not agreeing with their manager all of the time?

As an aside, you would reframe positively if you want you or others to feel better about the event/thing (and hence this might also be used to persuade yourself or others). You would reframe negatively if you want you or others to feel worse about the event/thing (and so this might be used to dissuade yourself or others).

Most times, when someone is 'in' a paradox they are seeing it negatively. They tend not to see the positive side of the paradox (content) or see where the paradox might be useful (context). When the owners of a company see a dilemma like 'lay people off' or 'struggle in the market place', they rarely consider the fact that they have the dilemma means they are still in business. Marketplaces often shrink and grow again. Companies that innovate, diversify and survive a slow market will usually be in a strong position when things pick up again. Tough decisions are one of the responsibilities that come from enjoying the profit of running a company. Is this really a problem? Now of course, the owners of the company will still need to take action rather than sit back and say: "everything is okay". However, is it not better that they do so from a point of strength, courage and positivity rather than timidity, fear and negativity?

A Final Cautionary Note on Reframing

It is important that 'reframing' is not just a tool to make things 'look better' when there is a real underlying issue that needs to be resolved. This is where government 'spin doctors' get a reputation of manipulation and deception. As well as managing perception, we also need to make sure we manage the reality! If people wander around with blinkers saying: "Everything is okay! Everything is okay!" when it is clearly not, we are back to the problem of 'organisational defences' as discussed in Chapter 4. Reframing could prove detrimental if overused and so needs to be used selectively and carefully. Quinn & Cameron (1988b, p304) warn that reframing (like organisational change) "if exclusively pursued, will lead to exhaustion of resources and collapse of the system."

According to Bolman & Deal (2003, p309) it is important not to get too attached to one single frame since: "For a given time and situation, one perspective may be more helpful than others." They go on to say (p331) that "frames are powerful because of their ability to spur imagination and generate new insights and options. But each frame has limits as well as strengths, and each can be applied well or poorly... The essence of reframing is examining the same situation from multiple vantage points. The effective leader changes lenses when things don't make sense or aren't working. Reframing offers the promise of powerful new options, but it cannot guarantee that every new strategy will be successful. Each frame offers distinctive advantages, but each has its blind spots and shortcomings."

Remember that paradox is often a *result of conflicting frames*. Bolman & Deal (2003, p305) remark that: "Organisational life is full of events that can be interpreted in a number of ways... Multiple realities produce confusion and conflict as the individuals view the same event through their own lenses." Smith (1984, p290) suggests that the real problem with reframing comes when contradictory frames are forced together: "So long as the frames are kept separate, there is no logical dilemma. However, when the multiple frames are collapsed into a single, unidimensional structure, problems of self referential logic emerge." So be aware that reframing without sensitivity to the rest of the system may create the very phenomenon you are trying to resolve.

From an 'Organisational Development' perspective, reframing may be a challenge at an organisational level. Dilts & Delozier (2000, p1071) states that to reframe something means "to transform its meaning by putting it into a different framework or context than it has previously been perceived". Bartunek (1988, p151) suggests that reframing in organisations means a change in perception at an organisational level, i.e. "shared meaning or culture". This means organisational reframing is more complex due to interaction between different groups with different perspectives and sub-cultures. There is also a confusion in the concept of reframing which is perhaps more crucial when applied to an organisation – does reframing mean a change of perception, a change of the perceiver, a change of the thing being perceived or a combination? Bartunek

(1988) appears to use reframing as a way of changing the organisation from one form to another but this then becomes indistinguishable from classic organisational change management. Perhaps it might be useful to distinguish between reframing an organisation (i.e. change management) and reframing an organisational issue (i.e. seeing that issue from another perspective perhaps in seeking how the issue could actually be a strength). Although it might ultimately lead to some change management intervention, the reframing approaches highlighted above apply to reframing organisational issues as opposed to reframing the organisation itself. The question of who or what is actually changing in reframing is an interesting one, but beyond the scope of this book.

Denominalising: 'Unsticking' the Paradox

> *"As human beings we seem to be looking for something static,*
> *the answer to everything.*
> *And the undoing of a paradox...*
> *is actually to recognise that it is movement."*
>
> *Sallie Crawley.*

As discussed in Chapter 6, to nominalise means to turn a verb into a noun, for example 'empowerment', where the process of 'empowering' has been turned into a thing. Most nominalisations are abstract nouns because they represent an action (or set of actions) that has been converted into a concept. Nominalisations are sometimes tricky as they can be hard to quantify and seem to mean different things to different people. 'Change' is a classic organisational example where many people treat it as if it is a 'thing' that they will have to face. People often refer to change as if it is 'something' that is coming, looming up ahead somewhere like we are going to bump into it or be hit by it. Perhaps one of the reasons that people fear change is that they have mentally nominalised it.

To denominalise is to turn the noun back into its verb form, to convert the 'thing' back into being a process. When 'change' is denominalised and treated as a process, it becomes less threatening since it is something we go 'through' (and hence out the other side). As a process we can enter the stream and 'go with the flow'.

Of course, paradox itself is a nominalization. For this reason it will mean different things to different people. This may account for the variety of interpretations and descriptions of paradox. It would appear that one's interpretation of paradox may determine whether it is something that can be managed or not.

Paradox, like all nominalisations, is a 'thing' and a 'process'. How might paradox be denominalised? Rather than invent a new word (e.g. 'paradoxing') we might consider contradicting, polarising, opposing. If one thing is contradicting something else, this allows for a time when this may pass and not be the case anymore. It certainly gives us more room to play with than the simple but permanent sounding "it's a contradiction". This means that by denominalising a paradox, we may be able to loosen or shift it.

It is important to remember that we are not saying that denominalising is better than nominalising, otherwise we would be creating a new either/or polarity. Each is useful in a certain context... there is an appropriate time for one or the other and sometimes there is an appropriate time for both!

The process of denominalising is often linked to NLP (e.g. Dilts & DeLozier 2000) but it is also referred to by Hampden-Turner (1990) who argues that "by adding ing to...words we convert the noun form to the present participle; not decisiveness but deciding... Once expressed in this way, they are process words... the oppositions are softened and the adversary structure disappears." (p131). Ford & Ford (1994) inform us that: "According to trialectics, there are no 'things' in the world other than change, movement or process. Things, such as people, organisations and ideas, are all names given to abstractions of what are identifiable and relatively constant patterns of movement" (p765). Trialectics would therefore imply that paradox is a process and not a thing.

> One senior manager I encountered was having trouble making a tough decision. He procrastinated to the point where his team was becoming frustrated and angry as all they could see was a lack of decision. He then began to doubt his leadership. Not only had he nominalised the 'decision' (as had the team) he was also nominalising 'leadership'. He had mentally created a box in which there was a decision and he was not addressing that mental box. He had also put leadership in a mental box and placed himself outside that box. In his mind, it had become an either/or. *Either* he makes the decision and has leadership *or* he does not make the decision and does not have leadership. He was asked to consider that in *leading* his team through this situation, what was he *deciding*? This he was able to answer and he realised that deciding was an ongoing process of gathering data and giving direction. The team could go in a particular direction and if there was a better way they could change course.
>
> Another team I worked with had a new buzzword of 'benchmarking' but in their minds and language it had become a thing. They had then got stuck on what a benchmark is and what it meant. They had forgotten to ask 'how' are we benchmarking? When they remembered that benchmarking is a process, they were back in flow.

Can we denominalise an organisation? Kurt Lewin (in Senior 2002) proposed that in order for organisational change to be effective, the change process needs to go through three key stages: 1) unfreeze the organisation, 2) make the changes and 3) refreeze the organisation. In a sense, Lewin is suggesting the organisation be denominalised (into flow) in order to make changes and then 'renominalised' when the change has been made. According to

Senior's (2002) OD (organisational development) Model, this translates into:

1) Unfreeze the organisation (*denominalise*):
    - Diagnose current situational (present state)
    - Develop vision for change (future state)
    - Gain commitment to vision
    - Develop an action plan
2) Make the change (*intervention*)
    - Implement change
3) Refreeze the organisation (*renominalise*)
    - Assess and reinforce change

The Reframing/Denominalising Relationship

When we nominalise and denominalise, we change the perspective and meaning of that thing (to a process and vice versa). For many people, when they nominalise a process to a thing it becomes like a photograph, still and constant. When they denominalise a thing to a process it becomes like a video, moving and ongoing. In this sense, nominalising and denominalising are both forms of reframing.

At the same time, from a trialectic perspective, we might consider that reframing is a process of letting go of one frame ('deframing') and seeking another. This could be perceived as denominalising from one frame and then 'renominalising' into a different frame. Bartunek (1988, p145-6) echoes this idea by suggesting that "reframing commences with events that signal that the present framework for understanding no longer works. This challenge to the present frame, if sufficiently strong, 'unfreezes' the present understanding and initiates the process of developing a new adequate one."

Chapter 13

Managing Uncertainty
and Ambiguity

In This Chapter...

In this chapter you will deepen your understanding about the nature of uncertainty and ambiguity in organisations and how to handle and prevent them where possible. This will give you a set of tools to use for yourself and others when there is a lack of information and clarity.

We will be exploring the following questions:
- What is uncertainty and what is ambiguity?
- How is uncertainty useful?
- What are some of the types of uncertainty and how might you handle them?
- How might you prevent uncertainty?

Handling Uncertainty and Ambiguity

Uncertainty could be defined simply as *'not knowing'*. This might be about the 'what', the 'where', the 'when', the 'who' the 'why' and/or the 'how'. We tend to experience uncertainty when we cannot predict what will happen. We might also experience uncertainty when there is information missing or if there is *too much* information. Ambivalence (from the Latin 'ambi' meaning 'both' and 'valent' meaning 'strong') can also cause uncertainty as we are not sure which way to go since both sides seem compelling in some way.

Ambiguity is a special form of uncertainty that could be equated to *'not understanding'*. When something is ambiguous, we will tend to be unsure of its full meaning, again perhaps because detailed information is missing. Instructions like "we must communicate better" or "change the system" do not give us enough detail to allow us to satisfy that instruction. What do these really mean? As they stand they are too broad, too big picture and open to interpretation.

The problem with uncertainty and ambiguity is that we end up with what people have described as a gap, a void, empty space, grey areas, nothing to hold on to and no familiar reference points. Being uncertain can create a sense of doubt which at best may knock our certainty and confidence, but at worst may for some people cause severe anxiety and worry.

In the first part of this chapter, we will be looking at different types of uncertainty with some strategies for moving through the uncertainty or at least feeling in control again. However, before we do, are there any positive consequences of uncertainty?

The Positive Side of Uncertainty?

It seems that there is a place for uncertainty and when handled effectively, it can lead to new innovative solutions. Ellen Langer in her book Mindfulness (1989, p121) suggests that uncertainty results in more creative solutions than certainty. This is because certainty causes the mind to take the same old roads and the brain to fire the same old neural networks. Uncertainty provokes us to learn, to make new connections and to innovate. Uncertainty takes us outside our safety/comfort zone and off our 'map' of what we know already. For some people, being off their map means 'here be monsters'; for others, it is an opportunity to create a bridge back, hence expanding their map. Consider walking in a forest each and every day. Some people will walk the same path, ignoring the side routes. However, they would be easily lost if they ever found themselves off that main path. Of course they are also missing some of the wonderful features of the forest. Other people find out where the side routes go and begin to expand their map of the forest. Over time, it becomes harder for them to get lost as they have so many reference points. Time for them to check out another forest perhaps! There is of course a third way and that is to model where others have been, to buy a map, to use a compass.

In the face of uncertainty there are at least three overarching positions or attitudes, the third being a synthesis of the first two:

1) The Stabiliser: Stay with what we know. If we are faced with the unknown, we will wait and see what happens. We can then make informed decisions.
2) The Pioneer: Innovate and set trends. Explore where others have not been, particularly when times are easy. Take the lead and develop new approaches so we are unlikely to be affected by the unknown. If we are faced with the unknown, we are already ahead of the game.
3) The Modeller: Watch where others go and follow the path that best suits the situation. If we are faced with the unknown, we have plenty of role models to draw experience from.

Since it is the Stabiliser who struggles the most with uncertainty, the following strategies are based mainly on the approaches of the Pioneer and the Modeller.

Types of Uncertainty

Uncertainty of Problem

Often, an impossible problem is a problem of uncertainty because it is seemingly outside of the control of the people involved. Perhaps the Government makes a decision, the market takes a downturn or senior management instigates organisational change. The people affected cannot control or influence these situations. They may feel trapped or become a 'victim' to their environment. They believe they cannot do anything about the issue and so they might give up and label it an 'impossible problem'.

In reality, everyone has a sphere of control and influence (i.e. things they can make happen by themselves and things they can make happen with the support of others). The reason a problem may seem 'impossible' is because it appears to be beyond the person's 'boundary of influence'. However, in order for it to be a problem for the person, it *must* directly affect them (and impact on them) in some way. The answer here is to move the focus of *where* the problem can be solved.

When working with a person who has a problem outside their control, ask: "How does that affect you directly?" This usually elicits the 'real' problem for the person (i.e. how the 'outside world' problem is an issue for them personally). I call this the 'impact point' between them and the

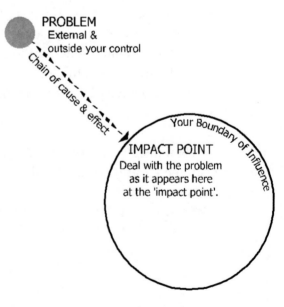

PROBLEM
External &
outside your control

Chain of cause & effect

Your Boundary of Influence

IMPACT POINT
Deal with the problem
as it appears here
at the 'impact point'.

outside world.

The reason the 'outside world' problem is an issue for us is because there is a mini chain of cause and effect that then impacts on us in some way. If it didn't impact on us, it wouldn't be a problem for us. Indeed, there are lots of problems 'out there' that are not problems for us (although they may be for someone else).

If we cannot control the situation 'out there', then we will need to deal with it at the 'impact point'. Sometimes this is straightforward. We might need to introduce a solution or system to handle the issue or we may need to change how we feel about it.

Uncertainty of Clarity/Direction

Within organisations, staff often suffer from lack of clear direction. This can come in the form of vague goals, objectives, targets and priorities. Under these circumstances, there is a sense of puzzlement and frustration. What do they want? Where am I meant to be going?

a) No Clear Outcome
A significant problem of problem solving is trying to solve problems where the outcome has not been clearly established. Whilst there are definitely problems out there that are seemingly impossible to resolve, sometimes the impossibility comes about from the way we are trying to solve the problem. In this instance, it is not the problem that is the real problem; it is *the way we are trying to solve* the problem.

Have you ever experienced the following (or something along these lines)? In a group scenario, someone raises an issue or problem. Others react by throwing in ideas and solutions. Then you begin to hear phrases like: "The problem with that is..." or "the difficulty there is..." or "yes, but..." or "the trouble with that is..." Any new

211

solution is immediately rejected with a 'yes but' of some sort. The group goes round in circles often reaching a frustrating impasse.

The reason for the above scenario is *reactive* problem solving. When we encounter a problem, our first response seems to be 'fix it'. Perhaps it is a cultural mindset. When faced with a problem, what do we tend to look for? Solutions. Those that have been trained or conditioned in problem solving protocol may first analyse the problem (i.e. look for root causes). Others may look for someone to blame! However, our reactive mindset is often:

Problem – Solution.

The trick here is to move to *responsive* problem solving. When a problem is raised, by all means seek to understand the problem (and root causes) first; then shift to *outcome.* The mindset needs to be:

Problem – Outcome – Solution.

Imagine that there is a hole in the floor and your manager says: "we've got a problem here... so sort it out". If you don't know the desired outcome, you might spend ages coming up with solutions (e.g. fill it in, cover it, put a barrier round it or put water in it). Even with all your possible solutions you may or may not get the desired answer. This may seem to be an odd example, but it is the kind of thing going on in organisations every day. The system is down, fix it. The photocopier doesn't work, mend it. This member of staff is under-performing, sort it out. We are losing business, come up with ideas to solve this. Without a clear desired outcome, we are still in the realms of uncertainty and ambiguity.

When faced with a problem, seek to understand the problem and then determine an outcome. What outcome are we looking for here? What specifically do we want (or want to achieve)? How will we know we have achieved it? What will that outcome look/sound/feel like?

Working towards an outcome is significantly easier and more productive that working away from a problem. We need a destination point before we begin the journey. The problem is the current 'origin' state (i.e. where we are now). The outcome is the desired 'destination' state (i.e. what we want/where we want to be). The solution is then the process/steps/plan/route (i.e. how we get from here to there). When faced with an impossible problem, ask yourself: What outcome am I looking for here? What do I want instead of the problem?

Thinking about this another way, how can we possibly find a route ('how') until we know the destination ('what'/'where')? In this situation, the Stabiliser wants to know what the desired outcome is before they take any action. They will tend to work with the risk-averse philosophy of "I can't until I'm told I can".

The Pioneer, on the other hand, has a strategy to handle a lack of clarity and direction. If they are not being given a clear outcome or destination, they will work with the philosophy of "I can until I'm told I can't". Obviously, if they simply go off in their own direction without a thought for the consequences, this 'maverick' approach could lead the Pioneer into trouble.

The Modeller seeks a third way, a risk-averse method of taking action:
- Consider the situation and the bigger picture, then do any research that seems appropriate,
- Decide upon a reasoned direction and approach,
- Inform relevant parties (e.g. the manager) of the proposed direction and approach, outlining the purpose of the action (i.e. in order to achieve what?),
- Take action.

- If the party who is not giving direction doesn't like the approach, they will soon respond. If not, the modeller has given fair warning.

b) Negative Commands

One other important thing about setting an outcome is to make it positively stated. What do you want (as opposed to what do you *not* want). Whilst it is perhaps helpful to know what you don't want, this could become an infinite list! In addition, it gives us no-where to go, nothing to head towards. Indeed, it usually brings us straight back to the problem. A business owner who says: "I don't want this business to go down the pan" is still focussed on the problem rather than the outcome.

Sometimes, a lack of direction can be in the form of a negative command. A manager who tells a member of staff not to use the blue forms is not giving clear direction. Perhaps it is obvious if there is only one other type of form, e.g. a red one, but does the manager mean, "use the red form instead" or "don't use a form"? Here we have an example of ambiguity where the meaning is unclear. This carries a (usually) straightforward solution... ask the manager: "Do you mean use the red form or don't use any form?" This could be considered a simple form of 'contracting' which is explored later in the chapter.

With some management styles, a lack of direction is cunningly disguised. When a senior manager says to their staff: "If you don't hear from me, you are doing okay," what does this mean? Perhaps it sounds reasonable on one level... at least staff know where they stand. Or do they? Unpacking that communication suggests: "If you are doing well, I will ignore you. But if you do something wrong I will be having words with you." And what are the consequences? Whenever the senior manager is around, everyone hopes that they are ignored! In addition, why would anyone be proactive, take a risk or go the extra mile? If it goes well there is no acknowledgement or reward. If it doesn't go well, there is trouble. How motivational is that? The end result of this style of management is no-one taking leadership, responsibility or ownership of issues and opportunities unless they are told to do so!

c) Lack of Priorities

Lack of clarity can also be due to a reluctance to prioritise. Any manager who tells their staff that everything is a priority is creating uncertainty. I worked for a manager years ago who wrote "Urgent" on every document he passed on to me. Being young and cheeky, I pointed out that since *everything* was urgent, it meant that *nothing* was urgent (compared to everything else!) He then began to write "Very Urgent" on some documents and then escalated to "Top Priority" and "Critical" and then "Emergency". At least he had a sense of humour!

The problem of no priorities means that it is impossible to determine what is more important relative to everything else. There is nothing to start with, nothing to focus on, nothing to hold on to. Someone once described this experience to me as like swimming in water with no edges, floats or platforms. Decisions become arbitrary and action becomes rather meaningless. So what can you do? One solution is to seek 'purpose'. This might be at the immediate level of 'purpose of my job'. If you know the purpose of your job ("I do what I do in order to what?"), then you can ask: "How well does this task, activity or project help me to achieve the purpose of my job?" Take whichever task most fulfils the purpose of your job and put that to the top of the priority list. Alternatively, you can take a 'bigger picture' perspective and ask: "What is the purpose of this organisation? What is its overall desired outcome?" Then follow the same process. Take the actions which best fulfil the purpose of the organisation and treat them as the highest priority. Another solution is 'damage limitation'. For each item on the list, ask: "What would happen if this didn't get done?" Treat the one that has the worst consequences as the highest priority.

There are times when people know what they want but they don't know how to get it or how to go about it. This is the realm of classic problem solving which has been written about in hundreds of publications. The steps are usually as follows:

- Determine your 'origin' (where are you now) and then your 'destination' (where do you want to be).
- Explore some possible routes. If no options are immediately forthcoming, you might try out some *creative problem solving* approaches (e.g. modelling creative people or modelling nature - see below).
- Decide on a favoured route or combination of routes.

Another angle on finding solutions is to ask yourself: "Who else has achieved it?" and/or "Who else is good at this kind of thing?" A friend of mine had an excellent manager and when he himself became a manager he faced all kinds of problems. If he faced something he couldn't fathom, he would ask himself: "How would my old manager have dealt with this?" Often the answer was there. When I first started training in 1993 I was running workshops for people who were long-term unemployed and were told that if they didn't attend the workshop they would lose their benefit. We had a range of 'problems' and 'problematic behaviours'. Faced with a hostile audience I would ask myself: "How would my mentor deal with this?" My mentor at that time was an Australian chap who I thought was an excellent trainer. I found that by stepping into his shoes I was able to 'borrow' some of his skills and deal with the hostile audience. I even had an Australian accent for a couple of weeks! Then I was able to be me in front of the audience.

The idea of 'borrowing' skills from someone or something else is known as 'modelling' and is the centre-point of the field of NLP (neuro-linguistic programming). If you can think of someone who is good at solving these kinds of problems, think about how they would handle it. If they are around, you could of course ask them for an answer. Remember also to ask them *how* they solve these problems as well as being appreciative of an answer.

Have you noticed that there are times when you yourself are creative and able to solve problems...when ideas just 'spring'? What makes the difference? How are you when you are effective at solving problems? How might you model yourself when you are resourceful and successful? What emotional state and physiology do you hold? For some people, being relaxed is an important part. For some, they like to be under pressure to fire out the ideas. For others, they need to leave it alone for a while and come back to it later. For an excellent explanation of the relaxed vs. urgent approaches to problem solving, have a look at Guy Claxton's "Hare Brain, Tortoise Mind" (1998).

In addition, you will find that you can model more than just people. You could, for example, model nature. Think about it... nature has solved just about every problem that ever existed. Nature thrives on problems and uses them to create new branches and dynamics. The following case study was based on a facilitated workshop I ran some years ago...

A Case Study

A store was losing custom (and therefore money) to a number of smaller competitors in the area. Each of the competitors had diversified a little, which created an overlap in products. The different competitors each sold only one or two similar products, but customers bought from the competitor because when they were in the competitor's shop buying other things, it was convenient to buy there and then.

Comparing this situation to nature generated the following (with food being used as a metaphor for money and custom):

When food is being taken, what do organisms do to survive and thrive?

217

- o   Mark territory, put up fences, set up boundaries
- o   Seek new food supply
- o   Seek new territory or place
- o   Grow higher/bigger/quicker/stronger and out-compete the competition.
- o   Fight/destroy competition
- o   Form alliances, symbiosis, swap, barter
- o   Move/live nearer food supply
- o   Use competitions' food supply
- o   Be more attractive to food supply e.g. more colourful
- o   Infiltrate, get competition to feed us/supply food
- o   Block the sunlight, leave competition in the shade
- o   Grow/rear our own food
- o   Go further afield for food
- o   Form deeper roots
- o   "Poison"/taint the area so that only we survive
- o   Hibernate
- o   Mimic competition
- o   Mimic predator
- o   Mimic food supply to attract it/make it feel safe
- o   Camouflage – disguise as something else

Using this metaphor from nature, the group then used the above list to generate and suggest real world solutions they could utilise to gain and maintain customer loyalty.

Examples included:
- o   Mark territory, put up fences, set up boundaries.
    - ▪   Seek to be clearer in advertising as to what we actually sell.
    - ▪   Make ourselves the company that people think of when they think of the products we sell.
    - ▪   Put up signs locally (where legal!).
- o   Seek new food supply
    - ▪   Seek new customers – advertise where we have not advertised before.
    - ▪   Consider alternative advertising streams.
    - ▪   Advertise to different local populations (e.g. class, gender etc).

o Seek new territory or place
- Look at alternative locations for selling (e.g. out of town super stores, motorway service stations).
- Look abroad for potential gaps in the market.
- Expand presence and product line on the internet.

The solutions were assessed as to how they might be built in to the future business strategy.

Uncertainty of Future

In 'Uncertainty of Problem', we looked at 'impossible' problems that seem outside our control. This led to the question: "How does/will/might this affect me directly?" However, when we do not know what *is*, *will be* or *might be* happening, it is hard to answer that question. When an office is told that they will be moving premises, but are not being given information about where or when (perhaps because the management have not yet decided), it is difficult for the staff to make any decisions and plans of their own.

When someone says they *don't know what is going to happen* they are experiencing uncertainty about the future. Staff going through organisational change will often worry about what is ahead. They become troubled by potential problems, problems that they cannot predict. Faced with a future, particularly one that seems 'out of their control', many people will experience the 'anxiety of the unknown'. In these times, they tend to forget that the future is *usually* unknown; no-one can really predict with certainty what will happen. The further into the future we look, the less certain we can be. It is as if the further you seek, the more chaotic it appears. Normally, we don't think about what might happen, but if the concept of the future is brought into our awareness the problem then appears to be *knowing* that something might happen but not knowing what it is.

When faced with an uncertain future, some people go into a viciously circular argument: "If I knew what was going to happen, I could plan for it. I cannot plan because I don't know what will happen." Since this leaves them feeling 'out of the driving seat of their own car', what can they do to feel differently?

No matter the situation, there will always be a limited range of likely possible scenarios the future may present us with. It could be seen as a case of possibilities and probabilities. So consider:

1. Write down what *could* happen. What are the possible future alternatives or the likely consequences of the change?
2. Then take each alternative and plan how you would handle it. If x happens then I will do a, If y happens then I will do b etc.

Sometimes, the future uncertainty is about not knowing the result of an action or decision. When faced with uncertain consequences, some people do not act or decide as they feel it is not safe to do so. Until they know what will happen if they act, they will maintain the status quo. When this entails remaining passive and not speaking up, the results of this 'no action' can be devastating for an organisation. Issues and faults are not raised and may only be discovered when problems come to a head. An example of this would be 'groupthink' where people do not speak up because no-one else is speaking up.

Most projects and activities will carry risk. Things might go wrong, but this is no reason to avoid taking on the project. Being too risk averse would mean never getting out of bed. However, we *can* predict risks and then decide both how we might prevent specific risks and/or how we will deal with them if they happen. This is known as 'contingency planning' and is outlined further on in this chapter.

Uncertainty of Knowledge

For some people the problem is not having enough knowledge, information or data. They don't know the details, perhaps not having the experience, expertise and know-how. Here are some examples:

a) A project manager who is managing a technical project without full knowledge of the technicalities.

b) A manager whose people do a job they don't have the full knowledge of.

c) A member of staff who is new to the organisation and new to their job so is still unclear of their role.

d) A buyer who is unaware how much the item they are buying is worth or how much it costs the seller.

e) A consumer who doesn't know their rights. They don't know what is 'allowable' and what is unacceptable. They don't know what is 'normal' or if they are being 'wronged'.

On one level, the answer to all of these is 'find out'. Take time to prepare, investigate, seek out bodies of information. Make friends with specialists and talk to others who have dealt with these kinds of situations. Build a list of contacts. Keep track of what you are learning and write yourself some aide memoires and check-lists. Challenge people who say it cannot be done.

Another perspective is that you cannot be expected to know everything. This is why you have people around you. As a manager (or project manager) it is useful to learn some top level information about the technicalities. How long should things take? What are the consequences of mistakes or delays? What are the positive consequences if it goes well? What is the purpose of a particular technical activity... it is done in order to what?

<u>*Uncertainty of Overload*</u>

As is highlighted in Schwartz's "The Paradox of Choice" (2005), we live in a society of choice overload. How do you know which brand of toothpaste to choose at the supermarket from the twenty to thirty different types? How do you find the specific information you are looking for in a world of information overload? How do you know which is most correct or best?

For many people, information overload can lead to a paralysis similar to that of having no information at all. It is as if:

0 options is ignorance,
1 option is no option,
2 options is a dilemma,
3 to n options is a choice,

$n+1$ to $n+infinity$ options is overload (tending towards ignorance).

When faced with **option** overload you might follow these steps:

1) Determine your ultimate outcome. What do you want (e.g. to achieve)? Make sure this is positively stated (i.e. what you want as opposed to what you don't want).
2) Establish your success criteria: What would a good 'x' look/sound/feel like? How would you know it was good?
3) Establish the qualities/functions that will enable you to get what you want:
   - I want *a thing/product* that will do x, y, z.
   - I want *a process/activity/service* that will give me x, y, z.
4) Go to the place where previously there was overload and seek that which best fulfils your criteria.

When faced with **information** overload you might follow these steps:

1) Determine your ultimate outcome. What do you want (e.g. to achieve)? Make sure this is positively stated (i.e. what you want as opposed to what you don't want).
2) Consider the following questions:
   - What do I want to know?
   - What is the question I am asking?
   - What do I want to do with that information?
   - What kinds of words are my criteria for searching (i.e. 'key search terms')?
   - Who else might know (an answer or where to get an answer)?
3) Establish the qualities/functions that will enable you to get what you want:
   - I want *information* that will help me understand/do x, y, z.

By understanding your specific requirements, this will help you to focus and filter out redundant information. It will also help you to scan read for key terms.

Preventing Uncertainty

1) Contingency Planning

When faced with such things as change, projects, presentations, meetings, and interviews, many people feel nervous in delivering a good performance because they feel at the mercy of external factors. They don't know how things are going to go and so the whole thing feels like too much of a risk. These unknown external factors create a sense of uncertainty.

To prevent a great deal of uncertainty, it is helpful to have a set of back up plans, designed to resolve potential risks and issues that might occur. The idea of a plan B (and C, D, E etc.) is known as a contingency plan and is a sensible way of managing risk.

The following technique is called a 'contingency diagram'. It can help you see what might or could go wrong and so allow you to prevent potential problems and/or have a strategy for dealing with problems if they arise. The 'contingency diagram' is a user-friendly risk management tool that allows you to involve others in formulating your back up plans. Indeed, it is usually a valuable part of the process to get other's input as it gives a broader set of risks and solutions outside of your own experience. The diagram starts with identifying what could go wrong (i.e. risks) and then establishing some potential solutions.

The key benefits of the contingency diagram are:
- Helping to establishes risks that might otherwise have been missed, catering for the unforeseen.
- Increasing probability of success.
- Creating a more professional approach.
- Giving more confidence to the performer.
- Saving time in the long run by being proactive rather than reactive.
- Showing where the event/thing may need to be exited/terminated or postponed.

The main steps to creating a contingency diagram are:
a) Write down all the things that could go wrong (risks) with your event/thing.
b) For each risk, write down some ideas for:
  - preventing this risk from occurring,
  - preventing it from being a problem,
  - dealing with it if it happens,
  - dealing with the knock on consequences if it happens.
c) Incorporate the appropriate ideas into your preparation and plan of action.

The ideas and solutions from a contingency diagram should give you a list of the following types of things:

- Materials/equipment/tools resources needed,
- Actions to take/research that needs doing,
- Considerations/info/options that may need to be explored.

By creating a contingency diagram or list (complete with ideas and solutions) and then building these ideas into your preparation, you should find that your plan of action will be more robust and that your performance will be even more effective and confident.

2) Contracting

Have you ever been given (or taken on) a task, and then not known exactly what the task is, or how it needs to be done, or perhaps why it needs doing? How confident and motivated were you to do that task?

Uncertainty is often the immediate result of a communication break down. This in turn may generate, for example: misunderstandings, arguments, conflict, lack of clarity, work not done or doubled up, different agendas and positions, 'problem behaviours', poor performance or drop in performance, frustration, confusion, demotivation, procrastination. When we look at what happens when communication breaks down, there seems to be a rational element (i.e. information missing) and an emotional element (i.e. how people feel). Anger and frustration are sometimes described as *the gap between expectation and reality*. Hence, it benefits us to find a way to close that gap by managing the expectations.

One potential solution to the 'problem' of uncertainty is *contracting*, particularly in the context of communication. Contracting is about providing clarity, managing expectations, establishing boundaries/roles and 'agreeing agreements'. It is designed to counter assumptions and to provide a system or process of communication that works for all and prevents ambiguity.

According to Julie Hay (2007, p111): "Contracts may be written or verbal. Although the term 'contract' has a legal meaning, it is also customarily applied to any ways in which two or more parties come to an agreement." If you and the other party have the authority to make decisions, the contract lies between you and them. Often, however, there is a third party involved, e.g. your manager or the other party's manager. Sometimes there is a fourth, fifth (etc.) party involved. Whoever else has an input into the final decision or could throw a "spanner in the works" needs to be contracted with. This is why it is essential to ask early on in any business negotiation: "Will anyone else be involved in the decision making process?"

It is worth finding out if there are any other decision-makers in a contract and who they are. If possible, it is a good idea to contract with each of them directly or indirectly (e.g. through your manager). To contract effectively, go through any appropriate items in the 'Logical Levels of Contracting' (below), making sure everyone is clear about what is expected of them.

The Logical Levels of Contracting

When contracting it is helpful to raise and answer questions. The amount of questions (and which ones) will depend on the context you are in. When raising questions, a good place to start is the classic set of open questions: What, How, Who, When, Where, Why (and Which). Dilts' Logical Levels model, introduced in chapter 5 can be a useful framework to determine that everything important is covered, understood and agreed.

Level	Key Question	Example Question	Example
Spirit	Who for?	Who is this being done for?	Customer/Stakeholder/End User
Identity	Who?	Who has the decision making power to do it? Who is going to do it? Who will be liable?	Authority Responsibility/ownership Accountability
Beliefs & Values	Why?	Why does it need doing? How important is it compared to other tasks?	Reason Priority level
Capability	How?	How does it need to be done? To what standard? How many? How much?	Process/steps Quality/service levels Quantity Budget/Costings
Behaviour	What?	What outcome is required? What needs to be done?	Deliverable Action point
Environment	Where?	Where does it need to happen? Under what conditions should it happen?	Location Context/Situation
	When?	When can it be done? When does it need doing by? When will we review it?	Opportunity Deadline Milestones

Contracting Delegation

When delegating, there are other things you will want to do. Looking at where delegation goes wrong, it seems that nearly all 'problems of delegation' fall into one or more of the following:

- not enough (or too much) communication,
- problems not raised or handled well,
- people bring back something different to what was asked for.

In order to prevent these problems, it is essential to contract the levels of authority, responsibility and accountability.

- **Authority** means having 'decision power', being able to affect and change how things are done. When delegating, ask yourself: "What is the impact of the task/activity you are delegating?" (i.e. what would happen if it went wrong/what are the consequences?) and "What is the experience of this person for this task?" (i.e. their track record). For each question answer: high, medium or low. The 'Authority level' you give the person will then equate to their experience less the impact of the task:

Authority level = Experience of individual - Impact level of task.

This will help to determine:
a) How much communication and how often?
(Less authority = more communication and vice versa)
b) What happens if a problem arises?
(Less authority = more control and awareness from delegator and vice versa)
c) How much flexibility to alter/adapt the process?
(Less authority = less flexibility and vice versa)

- **Responsibility** means who owns the task and who is doing it. If you cannot give full authority then you will need to accept joint responsibility. The level of responsibility you give someone will need to be the same as the level of authority. If, as a manager, you are not giving full authority (e.g. because of the member of staff's low level of knowledge and experience for this area), then you cannot expect the person to be fully responsible for the task/decision. In this case, you are joint owners, both responsible and both involved in the actions and decisions that make the task/decision a success. When people are told they are responsible for a task but then not given authority to carry it out, this can be very demoralising. Project managers are often in this situation where they are responsible for a project but have to run decisions by stakeholders and therefore have a limited authority level. It is not uncommon for a project manager to be blamed for the downfall of a project that has been consistently interfered with by the stakeholders.

Responsibility level = Authority level

- Accountability means being liable and answerable, having the ability to give an account. Where does the 'buck stop' and who 'carries the can', as it were! Whoever is delegating a task remains accountable for that task. In the case of 'empowerment' however, the empowered person needs to be accountable.

The points made here about Authority and Responsibility are also true of empowerment. To manage the risk of empowerment, it first needs to be acknowledged that empowerment means 'freedom within boundaries'. Management needs to set and/or agree the boundaries with staff. Like delegation, the boundaries will again be informed by the impact of the task/decision and the person's experience for doing that particular task/making that kind of decision. If the impact is high and the experience is low, the boundaries will need to be tighter (i.e. low level of authority). If the impact is lower and the experience is high, the boundaries can be looser (i.e. a higher level of authority).

The key difference between delegation and empowerment will be in the *accountability* for the task (i.e. who is 'able to account' for it). If a manager delegates a task to an individual then the manager is still accountable for it. You can delegate authority and responsibility but accountability rests with you. However, if someone is being

229

empowered to do a task, it becomes theirs, perhaps part of their job, and hence they become accountable for that task.

Setting Boundaries and Ground Rules

Contracting is also apparent when setting ground rules. Meetings are an excellent example of where contracting can be used to agree a way of working together. Once upon a time, a meeting was a place where people would talk over each other and compete for 'airspace'. And so some classic meeting ground rules were introduced: no side conversations, adhere to the agenda, the meeting will start on time and good timekeeping in the meeting. After a few meetings, these behaviours shifted from being explicit to implied, usually becoming the 'unspoken' and/or 'unwritten' rules. Some of these rules became universal and embedded in to 'how things are done'; however they sometimes needed re-expressing if a group lapsed into old ways. New technologies can introduce new challenges of course; some meetings are now plagued by laptops, mobile phones and email checking.

Effective contracting will adapt to the situation, developing as new 'spanners are thrown in the works'. Where there is a ruffle in the procedure, a new ground rule can help to iron it out and smooth things over. This may initially seem like the start of a bureaucratic system of ground rules, however, most 'rules' will become the norm and it is no longer necessary to express them overtly. Only if a ground rule is being broken and it becomes an issue again will it need to be re-introduced. This means the contract is partly overt and partly covert. The overt part of the contract must reflect the current conditions to be effective and credible. In the next section of this chapter, we will address the point where new 'rules' add up to a whole system or subsystem and what can be done to prevent bureaucracy.

The beauty of contracting is forging agreements on how we work together. If everyone has been involved in the agreement, they are more likely to stick to it. People don't tend to reject their own ideas! As new people are introduced, the rest of the group will tend to verbally or non-verbally temper any new behaviours that work against the group contract.

3) Setting up Responsive Systems

Sometimes, communication and contracting is not enough to resolve or prevent issues. This is usually when the 'system' does not support such communication. If this is the case, it may be worth introducing new elements into the system in order for people to do what they need to do more easily.

Uncertainty at this level is usually a result of 'gaps and holes' in a system that become apparent when people find themselves unable to do something. This may then manifest in group procrastination, a broad range of outcomes, certain things being missed, not done or taking an inordinate length of time. In a group environment, these 'gaps and holes' will manifest in high emotion. If someone mentions a gap, the room lights up and the energy spikes (usually with anger or cynical humour). After the spike, there may be a lull as the group comes back to an experience of learned helplessness. It may help to joke about it but it doesn't solve the problem.

A 'responsive system' is a learning system. As new issues arise, so a new rule or set of steps is introduced to the system to enable people to have something to follow in a consistent manner. If misunderstandings are common in a particular area, problem-solve this and add the solution to the system. Other ways of creating a responsive system might be to introduce processes, check-lists, templates, success criteria and/or FAQs (frequently asked questions).

A team might get together and look at what kinds of obstacles (e.g. mistakes, changes and/or problems) are making them reactive and/or what pressures are causing the most amount of stress. Take the most time consuming/stressful issues and problem-solve them by introducing a new rule or set of steps.

The responsive system approach is an organic way of developing a system so that it meets the needs of the situation. However, if we continue to add rules and steps to the system, it may eventually become overly complex and cumbersome. A system that grows in this way may become slow, obstructive and bureaucratic. This is like many anti-virus software programs for the PC. When first introduced to a new PC, the computer can handle the processing. However, as the virus database grows and the software runs longer checks on the system, the perfectly good computer is brought to a grinding halt. What once served as protection now serves as the cause of a new level of problem.

The communications department of an organisation I worked with a few years ago had problems with staff within and outside the department being 'off brand' and 'off message' when sending communications (e.g. emails, letters, brochures, press releases) both in-house and to the outside world. So they introduced a simple guidebook for all users. As staff made off brand/message 'mistakes' that were not covered by the guidebook, a new piece was added to the guidebook. Eventually the guidebook became known as the 'brand bible' and it was considered 'law'. Staff were feeling so constrained, constricted and distrusted that very few communications were taking place. Then the floodgates opened and staff rebelled against the branding 'police'. The only way to restore order was to get rid of the 'brand bible' and start again with simplicity and trust.

There are at least two answers to the problem of a responsive system, and both of them require a system owner:

1) Grow organically and cut back regularly. As the system grows because of new rules and steps, it is important to review on a regular basis and seek simplicity. An unchecked system will become chaotic, so seek order. Notice where and how the system has grown. Check that the 'categories' are still relevant and balanced or whether they are becoming lopsided. If there is too much complexity in area of the system, you may need to recategorise and/or reduce certain areas. The answer here is to **grow organically and seek simplicity regularly**. For example, a simple website that is added to without reviewing will likely become complex and unwieldy in certain areas or there will be too much information on the homepage. This makes it progressively more difficult to find things. At this point, the website will need simplifying and re-ordering.

2) Treat a system as a net rather than a catch-all. Acknowledge that a policy (set of rules) or procedure (set of steps) in a system will not cover every possible situation. Design the simplest policy/procedure you can that will capture ninety to ninety five percent of situations. Then have a 'contingency' rule: if in doubt, contact the system owner.

A staff/employee handbook is a classic example of a responsive system. As problems arise and employment law changes, the handbook is updated.

There are times when we may need to go beyond the system for longer term solutions. This will probably involve some 'double loop learning' (see Chapter 4). Good processes and systems are fine, but if the product we make or the service we offer isn't needed or wanted, we will need to change what we offer. If we have great systems but people don't know they are there or where to look for them or how to use them, we need to train ('up-skill') the staff and shift perceptions.

Chapter 14

Managing Conflicting Positions and Disagreement

In This Chapter...

In this chapter you will explore the relationship between polarity, conflict and disagreement. You will gain a set of tools to help you prepare for negotiation and conflict resolution in order to find a win-win outcome in tough situations.

We will be exploring the following questions:
- What is win/win and is it really possible?
- What are the stages of a negotiation?
- What are the golden rules of negotiation?
- How do you resolve conflicting positions?

Conflict and Disagreement

It is said of some people that they could start an argument in an empty room. Usually, however, disagreement involves two or more parties. Since we are all unique, with our own history and perspective, it makes sense that we will have differing needs, views and opinions about things.

When two or more parties get together with a view to coming to an agreement, we could say that each person's 'position' is flexible. We are able to move towards one another until we reach a consensus. This is an opportunity for us to negotiate.

However, sometimes people get 'stuck' in positions and appear unable or unwilling to move. At this point, positioning becomes 'conflict' and things seem to be more difficult. Conflict might arise for any number of reasons. In a business environment, this could include: different goals, misunderstandings, competition for resources or a clash of personalities, values and/or beliefs. It may involve us being stuck in a position against someone else, or us being a third party helping the others to resolve their differences.

Conflict resolution is about moving out of our stuck position in order to explore the situation, or mediating other parties to move out of their positions. Whether we are in it or outside it, the aim is to understand more about the situation and needs of all concerned, with a view to finding an agreed solution that works for everyone.

One of the questions I am often asked (as a trainer of negotiation skills) is: "How can I negotiate if the other person is not prepared to move?" The answer is: "You don't, you use conflict resolution and influencing skills until you can negotiate." In order to help make this easier, the following should give you an idea of when to do what:

a) Negotiation
Negotiation is useful when people start in different positions but are prepared to move towards one another. This movement might be towards a compromise or to a win/win. You would use negotiation skills when:
- You and they have something to offer one another
- You and they can and want to trade/reach a deal
- You and they want to move towards an agreement and work together on a common goal

b) Conflict Resolution
You would use conflict resolution skills when:
- They are not prepared to move

236

- There is no immediate/obvious common ground
- There has been a conflict/fall out/bad feeling
- Things have gone wrong
- Things/people are 'difficult'

Approaches to Managing Conflicting Positions

As discussed in Chapter 11, the approaches to a negotiation or conflict resolution can be presented as a dialectic construct. This section looks at some of the approaches people take and the possible consequences of each. There are two key factors that will likely influence our approach:

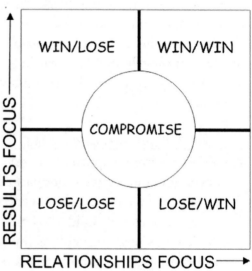

Relationships:
- How important is the relationship with the other party?
- Will we be dealing with them again in the future (short or long term)?

Results:
- How important is it to get a really good deal for us?

Approach 1. Lose/Lose (I lose, you lose):

This is rarely, if ever, an effective strategy as we don't get what we want, and it may adversely affect the relationship. It will usually lead to a lose/lose result. A lose/lose approach usually indicates a situation where an individual has lost faith in the negotiation or relationship. Alternatively, it might indicate someone who doesn't like negotiating and would rather avoid the whole process.

Approach 2. Lose/Win (I lose, you win):
Lose/win may be an effective short-term strategy in order to forge a relationship or to get a good deal in the long term (use a sprat to catch a mackerel, as it were!). However, we need to beware of using this strategy too much as it may set a precedent for the future. By starting with a 'soft approach', it can then be difficult to introduce the 'tougher' aspects at a later point, as we have already created an expectation for how we work. When selling, it can sometimes cheapen our product/idea, which means people won't pay more for it later. A lose/win approach usually leads to lose/win result. A lose/win approach might indicate a tendency to give things away, to give in too easily or to take the passive path of "please like me/I'm very nice".

Approach 3. Win/Lose (I win, you lose):
Although a common approach, win/lose is only really effective if we are never going to see the other party again. For example, going to a dealership to buy a car – we want to get the best deal we can. However, it does not build a relationship of trust. It can make all future dealings more difficult as the other party may end up using the same strategy. This turns into a competition of wills/egos and can lead to people taking positions and not moving. Taking a position and not moving usually indicates that we are no longer in a negotiation, we are in a conflict. A win/lose approach will usually lead to a win/lose or lose/lose result. Although designed to be the 'hard bargain' approach, win/lose tends to indicate a lack of confidence or fear of losing.

Approach 4. Compromise (Split the difference):
Compromise is an approach to take if we want a quick deal that seems fair to both sides. If we are only negotiating over one thing (e.g. price) and there are no other tradeables (see below), a compromise is likely to be the best option. Remember that the result of a compromise could fall into the areas of: win/win (both parties feel okay about the result), win/lose or lose/win (one party gets a little bit more than the other) or lose/lose (both parties feel as if they

have given things away, lost something and/or 'been compromised'). The Compromise approach might indicate an inexperienced/ uncomfortable negotiator, someone who is in a hurry or someone who is not prepared to explore alternatives and possibilities.

Approach 5. Win/Win (I win, you win):

Win/win is the best approach to take if we want to build and maintain long-term relationships with the other party and get what we need from the deals we do. It engenders a feeling of partnership and working together, and tends to involve going beyond the obvious into co-operative problem solving, creativity and action planning. Remember that win/win is a matter of perception; it is an area of possible outcomes as opposed to a specific single outcome. Although win/win often takes more time to reach than a compromise, it tends to indicate a desire for fair dealings.

Approach 6. Win/Win or No Deal

The 'win/win or no deal' approach is discussed fully in Stephen Covey's 'Seven Habits of Highly Effective People' (1994). It is a principled approach that sets a ground-rule for the way we do business with someone. It is best introduced up front by stating that when we work with others, we work to make sure that both parties get what they need and are happy with the deal. And if this is not possible, no deal will be agreed on. If the other party cannot agree to this, we do not do business with them. If they agree, we have a ground-rule to refer back to later (e.g. if the other party tries to play win/lose at your expense). As long as the 'win/win or no deal' approach is genuine, it indicates a negotiator who is assertive enough to be honest up front and who wishes to be fair and build a working relationship.

Is Win/Win Really Possible?

Sometimes, the concept of Win/Win is met with scepticism. Some regard it as an unrealistic Utopian ideal, or simply a bit of hopeful (or sometimes manipulative) jargon. So, what needs to happen for Win/Win to become a reality?

Achieving true Win/Win requires:
1) Good preparation - know our needs and theirs
2) 'Tradeables' – to take the negotiation wider
3) Time to explore alternatives, possibilities, new options and solutions
4) A step by step discover/reveal/discover/reveal etc. (See 'Discussion Phase' - below)
5) Movement from both sides
6) Trust – from communication and rapport building skills
7) Having a win/win or no deal philosophy
8) Having an environment, desire and ability to be creative

Whether we are negotiating or resolving conflict, in order to achieve a Win/Win outcome, it is useful to seek a common aim (and hence common ground) at the beginning. This may be that we both want to resolve the difference, or we both want to reach a deal. By starting with a common aim, we are already working together.

Directions of Thinking: 'Chunking up' and 'chunking down'

With regards to the type of thinking that resolves difference, it is perhaps helpful to understand the nature of what is known (in NLP terminology) as 'chunking up' and 'chunking down'. As discussed in Chapter 7, when we chunk up, we are seeking the bigger picture and becoming more generalised and abstract. Chunk up questions might include: "in order to what?", "for what purpose" and "what would you get by having that?". When we chunk down we are becoming more details oriented and specific. Chunk down questions might include: "what specifically do you want?" and "what is an example of that?"

When we chunk up, we will eventually find agreement and when we chunk down we will eventually find difference. For example, if we are discussing the purchase of a photocopier, the first issue may be: "do we need a photocopier?". If we chunk up first we can both agree that we need to copy things. If we chunked down first, we would probably have got into a discussion (and possible disagreement) about which brand and model of photocopier we might want. If we start with the big chunk agreement that we want to copy things, we can then chunk down slowly by asking: What kinds of things do we want to copy? How many things are we wanting to copy? If we get into disagreement, we chunk up again, e.g. "we want colour copying for what purpose?"

When people take positions on an issue or need, it is because they have chunked down too quickly. Each party believes they 'know the answer' to what is required and what specific outcome they want. When this is the case, in an ideal situation, both parties would be prepared to start by saying "I want X, in order to Y", thereby giving the chunk up of why they want what they want. If X is not immediately possible, then we can work at the level of Y. For example: "I want a pay rise in order improve my quality of life". If we cannot give this person a pay rise (specific but closed) then how else might we help them to improve their quality of life (more general and open)?

Negotiating Through Conflict

As an approach to negotiating, compromise could be considered 'fuzzy logic' as it works on a continuum and falls

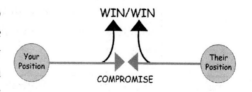

somewhere between the polarity of Win/Lose and Lose/Win. Compromise is about meeting somewhere in the middle and 'splitting the difference'. Win/win, on the other hand, is a dialectic approach, where we are seeking the best for both parties and transcending the original positions that have been taken. We treat one person's position as the 'thesis' and the other person's as the 'antithesis'. Then we seek a 'both/and' synthesis that gives both parties what they want and perhaps even more.

The Stages of a Negotiation: An Overview

An effective negotiation tends to follow a logical sequence. There may be movement back and forth along this sequence, but it can be detrimental to the process if any of the stages are missed out. The stages outlined below give a solid structure to any negotiation. It is important to be aware of where we are within the stages, as this will help us to keep track and to keep control. The following is a summary of the stages which are then explored in more detail.

Negotiation Stages	
0) Preparation	The preparation stage is essential. The bigger or more important the deal is to us, the more time we need to spend in preparation.
1) Discussion	The discussion stage is an opportunity to find out more about the other party and reveal a bit about ourselves. It is a time to ask questions and listen, to test any assumptions we may have made. This stage also serves the purpose of working on the relationship, building rapport and trust.
2) Testing	This stage is about testing for movement. What are they prepared to move on and roughly how much? What is most important to them? At this stage, we are asking vague and tentative questions and making tentative suggestions to weigh things up.
3) Trading	This stage is more definite. Figures are discussed, possible

	deals are put forward and are countered or accepted.
4) Agreement	This stage is where the deal is struck, where hands are shaken and then, when appropriate, contracts are drawn up.

There will usually be some 'to'ing and 'fro'ing between the *discussion, testing* and *trading* stages. Sometimes, you might need to take a time-out to go back to the *preparation* stage.

The Stages in More Detail

This next section provides a 'how to' guide to the key steps with some general hints and tips to make the negotiation process easier and more productive.

Preparation

It is recommended that you spend about a third of our preparation time on your case and two-thirds on the other party's. You will need to consider what questions you want to ask them, what questions they are likely to ask you and how you will answer those questions. At the end of your preparation, you need to check what assumptions you have made and you will need to test these assumptions in the discussion phase of the negotiation.

If you have only a short time to prepare for a negotiation, the following four items are the absolute essentials. Without these, you are in danger of losing a deal or a relationship. Even with quick preparation, **you need to consider these four items from the other party's perspective as well**.

1) Objective and Purpose
o   What is your overall goal?
o   Why are you negotiating in this particular situation?

2) Your WEB – *Deciding your range.*
o   What would be the Worst and the Best deal for you?
o   What do you Expect the deal to be?
During the negotiation, your "Best" should be your starting offer.

3) Your BUP: *Back-Up Plan*
If you enter a negotiation without a back-up plan (BUP) or a possible alternative in mind, you are stuck with whatever deal the other party wants. Without a BUP, you have less power to walk away from the deal. If you cannot walk away from a deal, your WEB is meaningless, as you may have to accept a worse deal than your worst!
o   What will you do if we cannot reach a deal?
o   What are your alternatives to reaching a deal with the other party at this time?

In terms of a back-up plan, here are some alternatives to a negotiated agreement:
- Alternative supplier/customer/ partnership
- Alternative time
- Alternative resources
- Alternative relationship e.g. changing from a supplier/customer relationship to a partnership – sharing responsibility
- Alternative tradeables
- Alternative area e.g. geographically or type of business
- Secondary goals: What are the benefits of achieving the deal/goals/objectives? Could these benefits be met another way?
- Alternative approach e.g. influence/persuasion, moving out of positions, problem solving.
- Alternative resolution e.g. mediation, arbitration, escalation, legal action.

4) 'Tradeables'

Tradeables' are the added extras you bring to a negotiation. They are sometimes known as concessions, sweeteners and optional features. When considering what 'tradeables' the other party might have to offer, list them into Essentials and Desirables.

o 'What are your 'tradeables'? Examples of 'tradeables' might include:

- Time (eg. offering your time, doing something more quickly, waiting for someone, bringing something forward)
- Reduction in cost, discount
- Percentage of a task
- Speed of service
- Training
- Levels of service/quality
- Skills/knowledge/experience/ expertise
- Information
- Movement/flexibility
- Resources (and/or the use of)
- Equipment (and/or the use of)
- Use of facilities
- Another service or product you/they might offer
- Guarantee/insurance/covering a risk
- Responsibility level (who is responsible for what)
- Consultancy
- Bonus for early completion/high quality

Discussion Stage

When negotiating, it is helpful to spend about 75% of your time in the discussion stage. This doesn't mean labouring the point, but being prepared to return to the discussion stage whenever you need to. Remember that a good negotiation will move back and forth between discussion, testing and trading. Take time to find out more about the other party's needs, what they are looking for, what interests them and what is important to them. Slow it down. This stage is not just a 'necessary formality', it is an opportunity to set the scene and the frame of working together.

At the start of the negotiation, establish what you are sitting down to discuss. This is the time to set an agenda outlining general topics that both parties want to cover. The agenda should only apply to the *discussion stage* however, as too much structure later on will tend to restrict free flow and creativity during the *testing* and *trading* stages.

AN EXAMPLE AGENDA
- Welcome
- Why are we here? (Overall common purpose e.g. to discuss/resolve/agree/explore.)
- Domestics including names and roles.
- Background info about:
    1. Your understanding of situation/history
    2. People and companies – what do you/they do?
- General areas/issues/problems/needs you want to discuss/agree on and they want to discuss/agree on. (E.g. the possibility of purchasing X.) Are all these areas in the limits of this negotiation?
- Discuss each area to narrow down what people want and/or are looking for.
    1. Avoid discussing what people are prepared to offer or are willing to pay to get what they want.
    2. Deflect any 'instant questions' like: How much are you looking to pay?
    3. Avoid tying anything to anything yet – you are looking to find out requirements – they can be matched up later on.
- Summarise
- Any other questions?

At this stage of the negotiation, take a step by step: discover a bit, reveal a bit, discover a bit, reveal a bit etc. If they are asking all the questions, they will be in control and you may end up revealing too much too soon. Having a step by step approach means staying in the driving seat whilst the other party feels comfortable with the process. It is okay to reveal what you want (i.e. your Best) at this point but it is more effective to express an interest as opposed to a definite 'got to have it'.

The discussion phase is also the time to test the assumptions you have made in your preparation and to ask the questions you want to ask. It is a time for listening and seeking to build rapport and trust. Many negotiations are 'make or break' as a result of how well this stage goes so use the *discussion stage* to get to know them a little better. Look for other areas of interest/common ground where you might help them and vice versa. If you can, find out more about why they want what they want. How do they use it? Where does it fit in? How often do they use it etc.?

In summary, before moving on from the *discussion stage* completely it is important that you have:
- Asked the questions you wanted to ask
- Found out what you needed to know
- Checked any assumptions you made in the planning stage
- Found out what they are looking for (probably their Best)
- Revealed some of what you are looking for (your Best)
- Summarised and checked understanding

Testing Stage

When entering the testing stage, you are looking at possibilities rather than looking to make any firm commitments. This allows you and the other party to explore options more freely, without feeling like you are going to get stuck with a bad deal. When you make a proposal, it is interesting to note their facial reactions as well as anything they might say. Most people reveal their pleasure or displeasure immediately with their facial expressions. If they are not happy with a proposal, explore why.

Find out what they are prepared to move on and what is non-negotiable. Start considering what might be traded against what. It is worth getting into the habit of using "if...then..." phrases (as in "if you give me X then I will give you Y"). However, at this stage, the language needs to be 'vague' and tentative; avoid talking in specific figures, instead cover more general areas. For example: "If you were to consider moving on the price, then we might look at making a number of purchases." If you wanted to be even more tentative you might ask instead: "If we were looking at a number of purchases, then would you consider moving on the price?"

Other examples of tentative language might include words and phrases like: possibly, perhaps, might, maybe, may, supposing, theoretically, what if, hypothetically, look at, think about, consider, possibility, potentially.

In summary, before moving on from the *testing stage* completely it is important that you have:
- Found out what they can/are prepared to move on
- Found out more about what they are looking for
- Summarised

Trading Stage

The trading stage is where you use "if... then..." statements, making sure you trade something that is valuable to you for something that is valuable for them. Trade something for something rather than simply giving things away. The best deal is based on trading what is cheap for them to give and valuable to you to receive in exchange for what is cheap for you to give and valuable for them to receive. Whilst the *testing stage* is non-committal, tentative and non-specific, the *trading stage* is time for definite offers with specific figures, for example: "If you move the price per item to £45, then we will buy 3 items."

Using the conditional language of 'if... then...' will help you negotiate because it:
- Helps to structure a trade, "if you give this, then I'll give that".
- Helps to create movement and works toward agreement, "if you move, then I'll move"
- Prevents you from giving things away without getting something back in return.
- Prevents either party from 'making demands', expecting something for nothing.

However...
- Avoid negative 'if' – 'then' statements (e.g. "If you do bad thing, then we will do bad thing") as this tends to spiral the negotiation into 'lose/lose'.

In summary, before moving on from the *trading stage* completely it is important that you have:
- Fully understood exactly what is being traded for what, the specific costs/figures and where appropriate how much things are really worth
- Summarised

Agreement Stage

When heading towards agreement, you need to test their readiness: "Where are we on that?" It is time to summarise and check understanding of the deal as it stands. If you want to move things along, you might ask: "What would need to happen now for you to agree to a deal?" If there are any final objections, go back and deal with them, for example: "If it weren't for this issue, would we have an agreement?"

In order to close, check their body language. Do they look happy and ready to finish? At this point, you need to be clear and show that you want to close: "So, do we have a deal?"

In summary, before moving on from the *agreement stage* completely it is important that you have:
o   Summarised and 'agreed to what you have agreed to'

The Golden Rules Of Negotiating

1) Always start with your Best (from the WEB).
Although this may seem obvious, people often say: "Okay, I've done my preparation, but what do I pitch as my starting offer?" After having worked out their WEB, they then go ahead and ask for their Expect, or something just below their Best. If you have worked out your WEB so that your Best is justifiable, then you can ask for it.

2) Avoid simply accepting their first offer (If you do, they may feel cheated!)
If you accept the other party's first offer than you are not negotiating, you are simply entering a transaction of buying or selling. More importantly, imagine the following scenarios:

> First scenario… you are selling your old car for £5000. Someone looks at the car and with a smile says: "I'll take it," and then hands you £5000. There may be a part of you now thinking: "I should have asked for more," and feeling disappointed despite the fact you got your Best (from you WEB).

> Second scenario… you are looking to buy a car that is on the market for £5000. You go in low (with your Best from the WEB) and offer £4200. The dealer immediately agrees to your offer. You will no doubt now be feeling stitched

up and wondering what is wrong with the car. Again you got your Best, but you come away disappointed.

Although you may want to be nice to the other party by accepting their first offer instead of negotiating, you will probably leave them feeling cheated and disappointed.

3) Avoid jumping in straight away with definite offers.
Jumping straight in misses the point of negotiation. You may well miss a good deal. Make sure you take enough time to discuss the needs and details of both sides, as it may lead you to a better "Win/Win" deal at the end.

4) Never give away something without getting something in return.
This is the classic rule of negotiating. If you give things away then you are not negotiating, you are simply giving things away! If you feel you have to give something for good will, then label it as something like a 'favour', so that you can use it later to call in that favour (remember however, that favours are not guarantees). Also, if you give things away, you may be cheapening your product or service, and you may be setting a precedent for the future, where the other party expect "freebies" from you. Giving things away can damage your credibility and value.

5) Summarise regularly.
Summarising is possibly the most effective behaviour in a negotiation because it:
- helps you maintain control of the negotiation.
- means you are clear about where you are and what you are doing.
- prevents going round in circles, getting lost and feelings of helplessness.
- can prevent frustration, irritation and the breaking of rapport and trust.
- can help shift a temporary deadlock.

Summarising can take the form of a complete overview or simply paraphrasing what the other party has just said. Assuming you are looking for a win/win outcome, a summary must be genuine and as accurate as you can make it. Summarise regularly throughout the negotiation and write down what is being traded.

6. Slow it down and take it wider than the initial proposals.
Take your time... avoid rushing. Trying to push forward too quickly can make you look inexperienced and may mean that you miss an opportunity. Slowing it down allows you to take control and stay on top of even the most complex negotiation. Bring in tradeables and look for alternative solutions to help achieve the Win/Win outcome. Ask questions and listen properly to the answers. Get creative and be prepared to explore possibilities and to do a bit of lateral thinking. As mentioned above, keep a track of proposals, needs and tradeables by writing them down.

Resolving Conflict

Sometimes a conflict is simply a polarity of positions where we both seem to want the opposite things or perhaps it might be a strategic difference of views. If both parties are prepared to explore options and possibilities then I recommend using some of the techniques in chapter 11, particularly the 'Dilemma Integration Technique'.

However, when a conflict has 'bedded in', there are now at least two layers to the problem. There is the original disagreement and wrapped around that is the second layer of the two parties not being prepared to discuss ways forward.

A position is a viewpoint or a personal frame of reference... "where I am now!" However, when people get 'stuck' in opposing positions, they are usually not prepared to move towards each other. There is usually an emotional element to it which can lead to problems like deadlock and loggerheads. Both parties may feel wronged in some way and so take the moral high-ground, becoming stubbornly entrenched in their positions.

As a general rule of thumb, you can tell that someone else is stuck in a position when they repeat the same point again and again. But here is the important bit: you know *you* are stuck in a position when you know you are right (and they are wrong)!

Conflict resolution comes into play when people have become stuck in opposing positions because of a conflict of, for example:
- emotions (e.g. hurts, upsets, unhappiness and dissatisfaction),
- beliefs (e.g. true/false, "that's not how it happened")
- values (e.g. right/wrong, "you're not like me"),
- needs (e.g. resources, "I wanted that"),

The aim of conflict resolution is to get both parties finding a solution that they can agree to and then work with. This involves moving from opposing positions to underlying needs and then to working *together* on a joint solution. As soon as both parties begin working together again, and have the feeling of

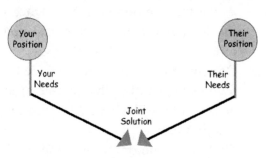

"we are on the same side," the issue has shifted from a conflict to a problem to solve.

The Process of Resolving Conflicts

The first part of the approach will be mainly to 'pull', to find out where the other party is at. If you try and 'push' your perspective on them, they will likely carry on pushing back or clamming up.

Key steps:
1) Consider your approach. What will your first line be? What will you say and how will you say it?
2) Seek to find immediate common aim. E.g. "I get that we both want to find a way forward here" or "I'd really like to find a way of working together, could we look at how that might happen?" or "Although we seem to have different opinions, I think we both want the organisation to be successful".
3) Acknowledge their position and that it is important to them. You do not have to agree with them at this point, simply acknowledge what they have been saying to you. This can take a degree of emotional maturity but it is a step towards resolution. Ask yourself which is more important to you here, finding resolution or being right!
4) Find out their situation and underlying needs. Ask questions and listen. Be prepared for them to throw 'stuff' at you. If there has been a difficult history, you may have to take some emotional downloading from the other party. And remember it is just that... emotion. Any offence you may take at what they say is your offence. If they call you names, you might say: "I didn't realise you felt so strongly."
5) Describe your situation and needs without blame. Own your own feelings rather than making the other party responsible for how you feel. Blame at this stage may take you both back to the beginning.
6) Find any common ground and work together to find a solution that meets needs. For example, a couple who go on holiday where one wants to do activities and the other wants to relax by the pool... the common aim of the holiday may be to recharge their batteries. If the common aim is taken into account, they can look for a mixture of things they could do together and separately that might help them do just that.

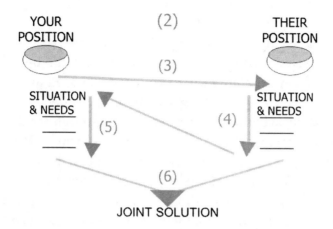

Responses and Reactions

Depending on the history of the situation, you may have to deal with attacks, accusations, blame, "hurtful" comments and/or sniping. When faced with attack it is tempting to react by attacking back, becoming defensive, giving up, arguing or go quiet. The problem with such reactive behaviours is highlighted by Robert Dilts (1999, p38): "Negative responses often serve to maintain and even escalate problematic behaviours, rather than extinguish them. Blame frequently produces a type of 'polarity response' which actually serves to stimulate rather than inhibit the unwanted behaviour."

Most of the time, the attack on you will not be about you. It may be who you represent, perhaps as a department or as an organisation. It may be that you represent a stereotype in the other person's 'map of the world'... you are X and so you fit in the category of Y. It is possible that you represent something in the other person that they find uncomfortable. Perhaps you are (or have been) behaving in a manner that 'pushes their buttons'. So, unless you have purposefully acted in a way to hurt the other person, it is likely that their attack is not actually about you personally. Obviously, if you have gone out of your way to hurt them, then feel free to take it personally! Then move on to find some resolution.

Sometimes you might be dealing with what you perceive to be a 'difficult person'. You strongest ally here will be empathy (combined with your ability to express what you need too). Here are some alternative ways of looking at a 'difficult person':

1. Consider what they must have gone through for them to be feeling this way and to behave in this fashion. If you have ever behaved that way, what caused you to do it?

2. A difficult person is a person in difficulty. This is linked to the first point but is a more helpful way of approaching a situation. It is likely that you are more likely to want to help a person in difficulty that a difficult person. But what if they were one and the same?

3. Separate the person from their behaviour. You can like a person but not like some of the things they do. You and the other person are more than just your behaviours. You use behaviours to get what you want in life. It is not who you are.

4. It is helpful to presuppose that 'every behaviour has a positive intention' (Dilts & Delozier 2000). This means that all behaviours are driven by a need and/or desire for something. It may only be 'positive' to the person who is doing the behaviour, not necessarily everyone else. However, if you can identify what is driving a behaviour, you can focus on helping the other person to achieve that in another way.

5. A difficult person is simply someone you haven't yet found the resources to deal with. You will experience less and less difficult people as you learn more and more strategies. They will still crop up from time to time, but certainly less often. We might say that a difficult person is someone who has taken us to the edge of our map (of familiarity) and so we feel 'all at sea' when trying to deal with them. As we grow our map by exploring new territory we tend to learn greater flexibility in dealing with the world.

In order to keep things moving on during the process of conflict resolution, here are some responses that can help (particularly if expressed with genuine empathy and desire to resolve the conflict):

- Tell me more about that
- So, would you like me to do more of/less of...?
- What is it that upsets you about...?
- What do you need from me/us/the situation?
- So does that mean you need...? (Turn problems into needs)
- So what would need to happen for you to feel okay about...?
- How might that help?
- If we could resolve this particular issue, are you happy with the overall solution?

The 'Rescue' Question

If faced with someone who really seems to be trying to 'win/lose' at your expense and nothing else seems to have worked, you might try what I call the 'rescue' question:

"If we can find a way forward that works for you and works for us, would you be prepared to look at how we could make that happen?"

This may seem like a long question (and you will find your own way of saying it), but it is designed to do a number of things. Firstly, it demonstrates that you know things are not balanced and hence it is a 'flag in the sand'. It is what is known as a 'meta-comment' as it takes you to the level of how you are communicating (process) as opposed to what you are discussing (content). Secondly, it appeals to fair play and is a way of seeking a joint win/win approach. Thirdly, it is a closed question, seeking a 'yes' or 'no' answer. If they answer 'yes' then you can bring the discussion back to what works for both of you and you can refer back to this agreement as a ground-rule if things become unbalanced again. If they answer 'no' then you have discovered why you are finding the situation less than easy. In this situation, I would ask: "why?" and see if there is a secondary level of conflict that needs resolving first. Perhaps they feel angry at something one of your colleagues has done but haven't told you that. If I wanted to continue, I might ask something like: "what would need to happen for us to work together on sorting this out now?" If this still isn't getting you anywhere, you may need to walk away to rethink your options.

A Note on Mediating

To be a mediator is to be objective and have no positional agenda in the conflict. The process of mediation is where a third party acts as a facilitator in helping the two conflicting parties in finding a solution together. The process is still the same as above, with both parties being given an equal amount of time to express their situation and needs. Equal time should also be spent with each of the parties before they come together. For further reading on mediation I would recommend the book Everyone Can Win by Cornelius & Faire (1994).

Chapter 15

Paradox Management as an Organisational Intervention

In This Chapter...

In this chapter you will explore the potential case for paradox management and how it might work as an organisational development tool. You will then be introduced to the challenging issue of measuring the RoI (return on investment) of organisational interventions and discover three methods of establishing the success of such interventions

We will be exploring the following questions:
- Is paradox management necessary?
- How might paradox management be applied as an organisational development tool?
- How might we measure the success of using paradox management in an organisational intervention?

The Case for Paradox Management

Dilemmas, tensions, double binds, conflict and vicious circles: each a potential cost to business, manifesting in the forms of stress, indecision and dissatisfaction in the workplace. In an environment where the pace and amount of work increases, there is likely to be increased pressure, conflicting priorities and dilemmas that need to be resolved quickly.

Today's management "find themselves pulled in more directions than ever before" (Stroh & Miller, 1994, p28), "spend much of their time living in the fields of perceived tensions" (Quinn, 1990, p3) and need to "make decisions in a fraction of the time previously devoted to similar decisions" (Harvey et al, 2004, p218). Added to this is the increased amount of information available, leading to information overload and heightened levels of ambiguity (eg. Schwartz 2005). In order to cope with ambiguity, managers and staff are forced to take some kind of position. As soon as there are positions, there will logically be counter-positions and hence polarities are created potentially leading to conflict and argument. These polarities and vicious circles can be summed up in one word: 'paradox'.

The challenges facing organisations and their management appears to be changing. McKenzie (1996) links these changes to paradox: "The more turbulent the times, the more complex the world and the more paradoxes there are" (p39).

Aside from the notion of 'conflict management', there is an apparent gap in the management 'toolkit' to help handle the growing trend of polarities, tensions and vicious circles. This research is intended to fill that gap with what the author calls 'paradox management', which as a discipline would sit alongside such activities as change, project, knowledge and performance management.

'Paradox management' would not replace more traditional approaches to organisational research and development; indeed, its role would be to complement it. In agreement with Bobko (1985), both the 'bipolar' (either/or logic) and 'nonbipolar' (beyond either/or) perspectives "need to be embraced by organisational science" (p107).

Paradox management appears to be a relatively new subject. Indeed, the term 'paradox management' is not even a recognised term. Although it crops up occasionally in the literature (eg. McKenzie 1996), this appears more for the sake of expression as opposed to the formulation of a new management discipline. Some literature refers to 'managing paradox' (eg. Price Waterhouse 1996) whilst other use the term 'paradoxical thinking' (eg. Fletcher & Olwyler 1997). There are references in the general literature to the paradoxes in organisations (eg. Peters & Waterman 1990, Senge 1993, Morgan 1998), but less regarding its management or resolution.

The lack of a cohesive discipline in paradox management is further confounded by a range of synonymic approaches, for example 'managing tensions' (Dodd & Favaro 2006), 'polarity management' (Johnson 1996) and 'integrative thinking' using the 'opposable mind' (Martin 2007).

Challenges for Paradox Management

Without paradox management, even when we have identified a paradox or tension (and we know that our problem is a paradox), as soon as we begin to talk about it we may still go round in circles. Most likely, this is because we are still applying our 'normal' problem solving logic to the situation and this is the kind of thinking that got us stuck in the paradox in the first place!

In addition, there is something rather compelling about tensions and paradoxes. We like to try and solve them by getting into the content of what happened, what people did and who said what to whom. If we are not mindful, we may get sucked into the story and become a part of the drama, trying to fix it from within. As we have seen, the skill of managing paradox is in staying at the level of process (rather than content). This allows us to stay 'outside' or 'beyond' the problem looking in with a bigger picture perspective.

Another factor that might keep us stuck in the problem is the potentially emotional nature of paradox. People sometimes know what they 'should' do, but they don't want to. They may feel resentful or anxious or angry or frustrated; any number of feelings may be distorting their vision and distracting them from their destination. As the listener, it is easy to get consumed by the emotional content and to sympathise to the point of being stuck in the hole with them. It's hard to throw someone a rope to freedom when you are stood next to them in the hole.

Can Paradox Be Managed?

If we are seeking to get unstuck from paradoxical problems, perhaps the questions we need to return to are: Can paradox *be* managed and/or resolved... and if so, how? To *resolve* a paradox would be to remove it. To *manage* a paradox would imply that although we may not be able to remove it, we *can* work with it more effectively.

As to the manageability of paradox, O'Neil (1996) and Farson (1996) argue that paradox is neither manageable nor resolvable and Handy (1994, pp12-13) takes a half way position in saying that paradox is manageable but not necessarily resolvable: "we cannot make them disappear, or solve them completely, or escape from them... paradox has to be accepted, coped with and made sense of."

From the literature on logics (e.g. Horn 1983) it appears as if O'Neil, Farson and Handy may be looking at paradox from a formal logic perspective. Whilst maintaining a limited 'either/or' frame of thinking they are perhaps right. Paradox does not respond well in an environment of formal logic style thinking. However, in a dialectic or trialectic frame (see chapters 11 and 12), paradox becomes both resolvable, manageable and also a drive for innovation. For example, O'Neil's (1996) 'paradox of success' suggests that success at work comes at the expense of home, relationships, family, personal interests etc. This is formal logic 'either/or' thinking, either success at work or success at home. A dialectic perspective would seek both/and, both success at work and at home, seeking a synthesis of the two, i.e. the best of both worlds. A trialectic logic approach might be to reframe *true success* to mean 'winning at work and at home', whereas success at work at the expense of home might actually be considered a 'failure'.

To apply the dialectic principle to the discussion of manageable versus not manageable, what if paradox is *both* manageable *and* not manageable? What if paradox has at least two forms and in one form it can be managed and in another form it cannot? Figure 15a (below) suggests that this 'can vs. can't' debate boils down to levels of abstraction. If paradox is viewed as conceptual and in the realms of potential, it cannot be resolved/managed as there is nothing specific to solve (e.g. in general terms, should leaders lead from the front or from the back?). However, if paradox is viewed as a manifest problem, i.e. it has a context, then it *can* be resolved/managed (e.g. in a specific situation, the leader of an organisation has a choice to lead from the front or the back or some combination of both depending on the skills and willingness of each individual department.)

Conceptual paradox is in the realms of potentiality and it is only when it becomes perceptual and manifests into somebody's 'personal reality' that it actually becomes a real problem (or 'paradoxical problem'). Figure 15a highlights the 'journey' of a paradox as it manifests into the real world. Hampden-Turner (1990) draws a parallel to the potential/manifest nature of a problem by differentiating between *pure* dilemmas (which

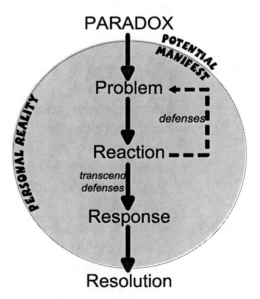

Figure 15a: Paradox as simultaneously potential and manifest

are philosophical and designed to be insoluble) and *practical dilemmas* (which exist in the real world). He suggests (p29) that: "Creating value consists of reconciling practical dilemmas."

The following table is a description and example of the stages outlined in figure 15a. Although the example given is not THE solution to the specified problem, it gives an idea of what might happen at each stage.

Stage	Description	Example
Potential Paradox	Here the paradox is conceptual, philosophical and unresolvable as there is nothing specific to resolve.	*There is always a potential tension placed on a manager between the needs of the organisation and the needs of the team. (See Buffer Zone model in Chapter 5.)*
Manifest Problem	A paradox becomes 'realised' and is now an active problem.	*At 11.00 one day, an individual tells their manager that they need to go for a dental check-up at 3.00 that afternoon so will need the afternoon off.*
Reaction	The affected person/people experience the problem and react either by implementing avoidance/defensive routines or by choosing to handle it.	*The manager is surprised by the request and knows that company policy says people should arrange such appointments in their own time or give a week's notice.*
Defences	Those involved dance around the issue and do not properly address it. This means that the original issue is still there and another layer	*The manager is unsure what to do and is angry at having been placed in this predicament when the member of staff already knows the policy. Not wanting to annoy*

	(e.g. avoidance, lie, sarcasm) is added to the problem.	*the person or have everyone going off to the dentist, the manager tells the person to pretend to be ill and not tell anyone the real reason they are going.*
Response	Analysing the problem and seeing the polarity/tension/paradox for what it really is. The problem is then managed, accepted, reframed or resolved. Or a new rule/system/policy (or change of rule/system/policy) is introduced.	*Manager perceives the polarity as: whether to let them go (hence setting a precedent for the future and for other staff to do the same) or not let them go (hence a grumpy member of staff who may then demoralise others). Manager checks there is cover for the afternoon, checks how the person will make up the time, lets them go but reminds them of the policy and sets a ground-rule for the future (i.e. next time will be 'no'). Manager then tells team of her decision, commenting how the person will catch up and resets the ground-rule for the team.*
Resolution	Checking the solution has worked and if necessary maintaining the new system. The new solution/system bypasses or resolves the problem, hence putting the paradox back out into the potential/conceptual.	*Manager keeps an eye on the situation and if anyone asks to take time off for appointments (assuming it is not an emergency), she makes a decision as to whether they will have to take leave, reschedule the appointment or catch up in some way. She finds that people rarely ask.*

I would recommend an excellent article on paradox in organisations by Lewis & Dehler (2000). They outline a process of 'Learning through Paradox' which works in a similar fashion to the stages outlined above. Lewis and Dehler's 'Learning though Paradox' approach involves a chain of: *Contradiction* (polarity and relatedness) to *Paralysis* (anxiety and defences) to *Management* (transcend through paradoxical thinking).

Paradox Management as an Organisational Development Tool

Paradox management as an activity would sit comfortably in the field of organisational development (OD). OD has been developing as an approach since at least 1960 (Huczynski & Buchanan 2001) and according to Beckhard (in Connor 1977) OD is "an effort (1) *planned*, (2) *organization-wide* and (3) *managed* from the top, to (4) increase *organisation effectiveness* and *health* through (5) planned *interventions* in the organization's "processes", using behavioural-science knowledge". In helping to understand, predict and resolve paradoxical problems in organisations, paradox management could not only help to 'oil the wheels' of an OD intervention, but possibly become an OD intervention unto itself.

Obviously, paradox management is useful as an OD intervention *only* if there *are* paradoxes to be managed and according to the literature it would seem that paradoxes *do* exist in organisations. Paradoxes are found in, for example: strategic alliances and partnerships (Clarke-Hill et al 2003), decision making (Janis 1982), success (O'Neil 1996), effectiveness in organisations (Cameron 1986), productivity of IT (Rei 2004), strategy (Thompson 1998), results versus development (Beer 2001), commitment management in call centres (Kinnie et al 2000), career management (Thite 2001), 360-degree feedback (Ghorpade 2000), organisational trust (Barnes 1981), change (Hopfl 1994), empowerment (Wikisier 1997), teamwork (Rabey 2003), project management (Bourne & Walker

2005), knowledge management (Jasimuddin et al 2005) and corporate social responsibility (Bakan 2004).

Critiques of OD interventions such as change management (eg. Alexander 1991) suggest that the key reasons that change fails is due to conflicting priorities and expectations, mismatches between perception and reality (e.g. real world problems and how long things really take), differences between current skills/ leadership style and the task in hand, and polarity in thinking styles between big picture and detail. OD itself is not always immune to paradox. If the role of OD is to empower an organisation (Huczynski & Buchanan 2001), the OD practitioner often walks a fine line between directing and empowering the organisation (Beeby & Simpson 1998). When it comes to the contradictions and polarities in organisation work, it could be argued that there is currently a gap in the OD field and perhaps paradox management could help to fill that gap.

Cummings & Worley (2004) suggest that organisational development programmes tend to follow seven stages: (1) scouting, when the client and consultant initially meet, (2) entry, where the consultant is officially called in, (3) diagnosis, information gathering, (4) planning, jointly establishing goals, (5) action, where intervention strategies are implemented, (6) stabilisation, where change is 'refreezed' and outcomes are assessed and (7) termination, where the consultant withdraws. It would be interesting to explore where paradox management might fit into these stages.

Table 15a suggests where paradox management might fit into Cummings & Worley's (2004) seven stages of organisational development:

Table 15a: Paradox Management as part of the process of OD

OD Stage	Paradox Management
1) Scouting	Whilst engaged in the initial discussion, the OD practitioner would keep an open mind as to the

	existing tensions.
2) Entry	The OD practitioner would contract (and set expectations, roles etc) with the client to avoid *creating* tensions between the practitioner and the organisation. An awareness of paradox management would also help the practitioner to explain the nature of tensions to the client.
3) Diagnosis	Part of investigation and diagnostic phases, understanding the underlying tensions that are perpetuating the problem(s). Interviews in particular might help to pick up on subtle cues and language pattern indicators.
4) Planning	Contingency planning with tensions in mind. Understanding how new plans might impact on other areas. A useful approach here would be to combine paradox management with the McKinsey 7S model (Waterman et al 1980). By combining the two concepts, it should become clearer where tensions lie and therefore what kind of intervention may help.
5) Action	If the OD programme hit a problem, it is feasible that paradox management might be a 'mini cycle' within that larger OD programme. Where problems/tensions have been identified that are preventing the OD programme from carrying on, a paradox management 'mini-cycle' might follow four key steps: • Identify presenting problem(s). • Investigate defences and underlying paradoxes/tensions/polarities. • Use paradox management techniques to provide goals, solutions and innovations. • Implement solutions (whilst maintaining systemic awareness of new tensions arising) by building paradox management solutions into the overall OD plan. If necessary, part of the solution may

	be training managers in the tools and skills of paradox management.
6) Stabilisation	An understanding of the dynamic nature of paradox may help here in creating virtuous circles of improvement instead of vicious cycles (and negative self fulfilling prophecies) that may damage the stability of the OD intervention.
7) Termination	Before disengaging, the practitioner and the client may need to establish whether the organisation has enough resources and knowledge to be empowered to resolve its own tensions in the future.

Regardless as to whether or not paradox management is a viable OD intervention in and of itself, it seems evident that an awareness and ability to manage paradox could aid the OD effort, for example in the areas of reframing, defences, use of metaphor, language indicators and a deeper understanding of the nature of organisational tensions.

Measuring the Immeasurable

For many interventions in an organisation, be it learning (e.g. a soft skills training course), change (e.g. rebranding), organisational development (e.g. a senior management team build) or a combination, the challenge sits in measuring the success of that intervention.

How do we know it has worked? How do we know it has had a positive impact on the bottom line (i.e. financial)? Those that are investing in the intervention will usually want some objective, scientific measurement of the return on investment (RoI). However, many interventions are notoriously difficult to measure. The results are often intangible and confounded (or aided) by other variables outside of the intervention. Perhaps, for example, a team build has been successful because of the 'management day out' or perhaps it has been successful because the previous boss has left and been replaced with someone more effective.

Paradox management as an organisational intervention (small or large scale) is no exception to the 'difficult to measure' problem. Through paradox management we may appear to help resolve an issue but can we guarantee that it was our doing and not because of something else?

Obviously, the notion of measuring an intervention implies measuring it *against* something else. The time to generate a 'success criteria' would be before the intervention takes place. What would success look, sound, feel like? How would we know we have been successful? What are some of the other possible variables that may help or hinder the intervention (or that might be responsible for the 'success' happening anyway, regardless of the intervention)?

Where there are clear objective means of measuring the outcome of an intervention, this is great. Sometimes we can easily measure in terms of financial savings or income generation. Or perhaps we might measure specific time savings of using a new system. The challenge is when we are measuring the performance or quality of an intervention. Ideally we would have something tangible (e.g. a template, a working example or a benchmark) that we can compare the result to. Amongst other things, quality can be measure in terms of specifications/features (number of), performance (does what is defined), finish (appearance – e.g. looks good, is mistake/tarnish free) and model/template (how close is the result to the template)?

In order to generate some form of benchmarking (and possibly to justify the intervention to management), here are three methods of 'measuring the intangibles':

1) Income Generation

First things first, some interventions will have tangible financial benefits. As a result of your help, perhaps there may be some profit making or cost cutting activities proposed or acted upon.

Secondly, you may want to look at the financial value of non-financial outcomes. Examples of non-financial outcomes might be: staff morale, time savings, lower stress levels, higher quality, new behaviours, customer satisfaction, stories, green/environmental benefits, fulfilling strategy, happiness, corporate social responsibility, publicity. In a given intervention, if you could put a price to any of these things, what would you estimate?

If you are struggling to put a financial value to the intervention or to the non-financial outcomes, ask the people who have been involved in the process (for example: "How has the process benefitted you personally, your team, your department your organisation? What financial benefits and savings would you estimate have resulted in the process and/or the benefits?").

Beyond *time* and *money* measures, other *methods* of measuring the benefits of an intervention include: scoring performance reviews (e.g. 360 degree appraisal), questionnaires and surveys (e.g. customer satisfaction survey), feedback forms (e.g. customer comments), interviews (e.g. structured/unstructured one to ones) and focus groups (e.g. staff forum groups).

2) Cost Prevention

Another approach to evaluating the value of an intervention is look at the potential cost of taking no action. What would happen if we made no changes to the current situation and left it as it is? By listing out the potential issues of taking no action, we might put a financial cost to each of those. If we can then demonstrate that the intervention is designed to address such issues (and hence the

271

related costs), we can make a financial business case. By establishing the evidence for resolving each of these issues we can then create a 'success criteria' for each issue. In this way we have something to measure against.

For example, if a tension or conflict is causing a team to work together ineffectively, we might ask: "what is the cost of poor team working?" With 'poor team working' as an example, although it is difficult to equate exact monetary figures, it is clear that this issue has a cost in terms of organisational time and money. If we can establish a rough cost to the consequences of *no intervention* and then put a change in place to improve team working, we can claim 'Cost Prevention' (or 'savings'). In the table below (15b), how much time is spent handling each 'cost'? How much does each 'cost' cost?

Table 15b: Costs and Consequences of Poor Team Working

General Cost	Examples	Cost Related Consequences	£s?
Conflict	• Personality clashes • Lack of co-operation • People do only their own job and don't cover others • Lack of communication	• Management time is taken up on having to handle 'people issues' which has an impact on manager's job getting done.	
Task mismanagement	• Tasks not being done (or duplicated) • Deadlines missed	• Impact on projects • Customer dissatisfaction	

'Demotivation'	• Absenteeism • Low morale • Stress	• Cost of sick leave • Impact on tasks (quality, productivity and efficiency) • Customer dissatisfaction due to lower standard of customer service.	
Staff turnover	• Staff leave due to poor / unpleasant working relationships	• Financial implications of having to recruit a new member of staff. • Loss of knowledge • Impact on reputation as employer of choice • Possible tribunals	

Of course, many of the consequences could be caused by other things; however it is clear that poor team work contributes to the negative consequences. If we can demonstrate that our intervention (e.g. facilitated team event) is designed to help counter the costs of poor team working, we can hence provide ROI in the form of cost prevention. In the example of team working (as with many interventions), it must be understood that the ROI for such an event may not be realised without management support. The manager of a team sits at a higher level of authority to the team itself and hence has the power to help and/or hinder the team's progress.

3) Business Contribution

This third approach involves talking to stakeholders and leading them along a 'reverse' path to showing where and how your intervention can add value to the organisation. We start with the big picture and drill down into further and further specifics until we reach something we can measure.

Business contribution is about demonstrating that your intervention will support the business in achieving its goals, vision and/or mission. Indeed we may be able to propose that our intervention will enhance the business in some very specific ways. The trick is to drill down to the specifics with the stakeholders.

Imagine that customer satisfaction levels are dropping in part of our organisation to the point where we are losing customers and hence losing business. We start with big picture by asking stakeholders: "What does the business need to stay in business?" Typical responses might include: Loyal customers/end users, good communications, a quality product/service, motivated staff, effective procedures and systems. Depending on the intervention we are aiming at, we would then zone in on one area. Of course, there may be tensions to resolve in a number of areas but let us explore just one here. For example, we might focus in on 'loyal customers' by asking: "What does the business need to attract and keep loyal customers?" Answers might include: good customer service and after sales care, effective marketing and authentic sales. We drill down again: "What does the business need to have good customer service and after sales care?" sample responses might be: polite staff, staff able to resolve conflicts, effective complaint handling, good listeners and effective problem solving. At this point, we are heading towards competencies. If we can demonstrate that our 'customer service workshop' is designed to improve staff competencies as outlined above and that those competencies might be scored (e.g. self scored by workshop delegates) before and after the course, we could then claim 'Business Contribution'.

In general terms, if you cannot measure the 'ends' of an intervention (i.e. the outcome/output), then you may need to measure the 'means'. This might be done by creating a competency framework or benchmarking framework as a way of demonstrating measurability of performance and behaviour. In this way we might show that as a result of the intervention, the organisation (or staff, system, product, service etc.) can now do x,y,z.

Appendix 1

The Paradox Management Process

To summarise the process of paradox management in a problem solving context:

1. **Identify impossible problem**
    o   What is the problem now?
    o   *How* is that a problem?
    o   What are the symptoms of the problem? (See chapter 3)
    o   What are the layers involved in the problem? (See chapter 4)
    o   What is known about the context and cause(s)? (Remember that if causes go outside of your control/influence, ask 'how does that affect me directly?' in order to work with what is actually within your control and influence.) (See chapter 5)

2. **Seek the polarity(ies) in the problem**
    o   What is this a problem between?
    o   What is the 'either/or'?
    o   What are the contradictions/conflicting positions?
    o   What are the opposite ends?

3. **Seek the positives of both ends of the polarity**
    o   What are the benefits/advantages of each end/side?
    o   What positives would you get by having side 'a' and what positives would you get by having side 'b'? If there is a third or fourth position, ask the same question.

4. **Decide approach, e.g.:**
   o Purposely maintain the paradox (hold it open) (See chapter 9)
   o Polarity management (follow and drive the flow) (See chapter 9)
   o Explore the polarity as a continuum (See chapter 10)
   o Integrate the positives of both ends (See chapter 11)
   o Reframe the situation (See chapter 12)

5. **Check the impact of the approach in the 'real world'**
   o When you have decided a potential way forward, consider any implications/ripple effects of implementing your idea.
   o How might your solution impact on you, others and/or the organisation in the short, medium and long term? The aim here is to prevent 'unintended consequences'.

6. **Action plan (with contingencies)**
   o Before putting a plan together, consider the following:
     ▪ What barriers you might face in implementing your solution?
     ▪ What could go wrong?
     ▪ How might other people resist your ideas?
   o For each response to the questions above, seek prevention and cure solutions:
     ▪ How might I prevent that from occurring?
     ▪ How might I prevent that from becoming an issue?
     ▪ How might I deal with it if it happens?
   o With these prevention and cure solutions, you can put a more robust action plan together. (See chapter 13)

7. **Take action and review**

Appendix 2

Principles of Paradox Management

There are a range of principles that have emerged through my research into paradoxical problems. Although they would probably be impossible to 'prove', they can be helpful as a mindset in the resolution of seemingly impossible problems.

1. **An unresolvable problem will be driven by a paradox**
    The reason 'impossible problems' are unresolvable is because they shift and reappear when you try to solve them. There is sometimes a sense of going round in circles or going backwards and forwards. Perhaps proposed solutions are rejected because there are problems with these solutions. When we explore an unresolvable problem from the perspective of paradox, we will usually see the two (or more) poles that the problem shifts around. Sometimes the problem is held in place by a higher level (e.g. a policy, procedure, manager prevents a member of staff from effectively carrying out their role as defined in their job description... the individual cannot succeed until something changes).

2. **A paradox is often the result of seeing something from a limited perspective/only one angle/without a context.**
    When we see something from a limited perspective, we may only see part of the complete picture. We are only seeing or hearing one side of the story. For example, if two people have fallen out and we listen to only one person's perspective, we will likely have a skewed version of events. We may find ourselves taking sides. This is where we get into the frame of either/or... either one party is correct/virtuous/innocent or the other party is. When we see the situation from a larger perspective and/or understand the context/history around the

situation, we may see that both sides have merit and we may even see how both sides can be correct/virtuous/innocent.

3. **The basis of paradox is polarity**
   A paradox will be contradiction between two (or occasionally more) things. Most paradoxes are the result of a duality of opposite counterparts which is the polarity of 'X or Y' (or 'X or not X'). (See chapter 1)

4. **The dynamic of paradox is polarity in action, manifesting in splits, loops and flips.**
   When we apply thought or action to a paradox, it will move into a dynamic state. As soon as we try to see it from one perspective, it will shift into another contradictory perspective. When we try and solve one end of the paradox, the other end will surface as the problem. This is the dynamic that takes us back and forth or round in circles.

5. **Both ends of a polarity will hold something valuable.**
   When exploring a polarity it is helpful to identify the advantages of both sides. Indeed, it is often our desire to explore the negatives of one (or both) sides that keeps us stuck in the paradox. When we can identify the positives of both sides we can (for example) seek to integrate the positives and create the best of both worlds.

6. **Well managed paradox leads to innovation. Mismanaged paradox leads to stress.**
   When a paradox is acknowledged and then solutions are welcomed and rewarded, an organisation will reap the benefits of innovation. However, where paradox is denied, buried and punished, the organisation will reap the consequences of ongoing tensions and stress.

References

Adams, S. (1996) *The Dilbert Principle* Boxtree

Alexander, L.D. (1991) "Strategy implementation: nature of the problem", in Hussey, D. (Ed), *International Review of Strategic Management*, John Wiley & Sons: NY, Vol. 2 No.1, pp.73-96.

Andreas, S. (2006) *Six Blind Elephants: Understanding Ourselves and Each Other - Volume II Fundamental Principles of Scope and Category* Real People Press

Argyris, C. (1986) "Reinforcing organizational defensive routines: An unintended human resource activity" *Human Resource Management*, Vol.25, No.4, Winter, pp541-555

Argyris, C. (1988) "Crafting a Theory of Practice: The Case of Organisational Paradoxes" in Quinn, R.E. & Cameron, K.S. (eds.) *Paradox and Transformation: Towards a Theory of Change in Organization and Management* Balinger. (pp 255-278)

Argyris, C. (1990) *Overcoming Organizational Defenses: Facilitating Organizational Learning* Allyn & Bacon: Simon & Schuster

Argyris, C. (1994) *On Organisational Learning* Blackwell Business

Bakan, J. (2004) *The Corporation: The Pathological Pursuit of Profit and Power* Constable: London

Bandler & Grinder (1975) *Structure of Magic* Science & Behaviour Books

Bandler, R. & Grinder, J. (1982) *Reframing: Neuro-Linguistic Programming and the Transformation of Meaning* Real People Press

Barnes, L. (1981) "Managing the paradox of organisational trust" *Harvard Business Review*, March-April, pp107-116

Bartunek, J.M. (1988) "The Dynamics of Personal and Organisational Reframing" in Quinn, R.E. & Cameron, K.S. (eds.) *Paradox and Transformation: Towards a Theory of Change in Organization and Management* Balinger.. (pp 137-162)

Bateson, G. (1978) "The birth of a matrix or double bind and epistemology" in Berger, M.M. (ed) *Beyond the Double Bind* Brunner/Mazel Publishers: New York. (pp 41-64)

Bateson, G. (1979*) Mind and Nature: A Necessary Unity* E.P. Dutton

Bateson, G. (2000) *Steps to an Ecology of Mind* University of Chicago Press

Bateson, G., Jackson, D.D., Haley, J. & Weakland, J. (1978) "Toward a theory of schizophrenia" in Berger, M.M. (ed) *Beyond the Double Bind* Brunner/Mazel Publishers: New York. (pp 5-27)

Beckhard, R. & Harris, R. (1987) *Organizational Transitions: Managing Complex Change.* Addison-Wesley

Beeby, M. & Simpson, P. (1998) "Barriers, boundaries and leaks in an organization development intervention" *Leadership & Organization Development Journal,* Vol.19 No.7, pp 353 - 361

Beer, M. (2001) "Embrace the drive for results-capability development paradox" *Organisational Dynamics,* Vol.29, No.4, pp.233-247.

Berg, D.N. & Smith, K.K. (1995) "Paradox and Groups" in Gillette, J. & McCollom, M (eds) *Groups in Context: A New Perspective on Group Dynamics* University Press of America (pp106-132)

Berger, M.M. (1978) *Beyond the Double Bind* Brunner/Mazel Publishers: New York.

Blake, R.R. & Mouton, J.S. (1966) *The Managerial Grid* Gulf Publishing Company: Houston, Texas

Blake, R.R. & Mouton, J.S. (1981) *The New Managerial Grid* Gulf Publishing Company: Houston, Texas

Blake, R.R. & Mouton, J.S. (1985) *The Managerial Grid III* Gulf Publishing Company

Blanchard, K. & Zigarmi, P. & D. (1994) *Leadership and The One Minute Manager* Harper Collins

Bobko, P. (1985) "Removing assumptions of bipolarity: Towards variation and circularity" *Academy of Management,* Vol.10, No.1, pp99-108

Bolman, L.G. & Deal, T.E. (2003) *Reframing Organisations: Artistry, Choice, and Leadership* Jossey Bass

Bourne, L. & Walker, D.H.T. (2005) "The paradox of project control" *Team Performance Management,* Vol.11, No.5/6, pp.157-178.

Buenger, V. & Daft, R. (1988) "The Puzzling Paradox of Just-In-Time Manufacturing" in Quinn, R.E. & Cameron, K.S. (eds.) *Paradox and Transformation: Towards a Theory of Change in Organization and Management* Balinger. (pp 195-203)

Cameron, K.S. (1986) "Effectiveness as paradox: Consensus and conflict in conceptions of organizational effectiveness" *Management Science*, Vol.32, No.5, pp 539- 553.

Cannon, T. (1996) *Welcome to the Revolution: Managing Paradox in the 21st Century* Pitman Publishing

Carini, G., Livingstone, L. & Palich, L. (1995) "Trialectics: A questionable logic for organi zation change research" *Academy of Management Review*, Vol.20, No.3, pp 503-509

Caswell, H. (1983) "Trialectics, Cybernetics and Zedah's theory of state" in Horn, R.E. (Ed) *Trialectics: Toward a Practical Logic of Unity* Information Resources, Inc.: Lexington, MA (pp 157-190)

Cheal, J. (2007) "Who is' 'I? Who is 'me'?" *Rapport*, Issue 8.

Cialdini, R. (1993) *Influence: The Psychology of Persuasion* Quill: New York

Clarke-Hill, C., Li, H. & Davies, B. (2003) "The paradox of co-operation and competition in strategic alliances: Towards a multi-paradigm approach" *Management Research News*, Vol.26, No.1, pp1-20

Claxton, G. (1998) *Hare Brain, Tortoise Mind* Fourth Estate: London

Clegg, S.R. (ed.) *Management and Organisational Paradoxes* John Benjamins Publishing Company

Clemmer, J. (1992) *Firing On All Cylinders* Business One Irwin

Connor, P.E. (1977) "A Critical Inquiry into Some Assumptions and Values Characterizing OD", *Academy of Management Review*,Vol.2, No. 4, pp 635-644.

Cornelius, H. & Faire, S. (1994). *Everyone Can Win: How to Resolve Conflict.* Simon & Schuster

Covey, S. (1994) *Seven Habits of Highly Effective People* Simon & Schuster

Cummings, T.G. & Worley, C.G. (2004) *Organisation Development and Change* International Thomson Computer Press

D'Andrade, P. & Johnson, D. (1983) "Dialectics and Trialectics: A comparison of two analyses of change" in Horn, R.E. (Ed)

Trialectics: Toward a Practical Logic of Unity Information Resources, Inc.: Lexington, MA (pp 79-119)

Dell'Olio, A. (1983) "Trialectics within the conversation of contemporary philosophy" in Horn, R.E. (Ed) *Trialectics: Toward a Practical Logic of Unity* Information Resources, Inc.: Lexington, MA (pp 121-140)

Dilts, R. (1990) *Changing Belief Systems with NLP* Meta Publications

Dilts, R. (1999) *Sleight of Mouth* Meta Publications

Dilts, R. & DeLozier, J. (2000) *Encyclopedia of Systemic Neuro-Linguistic Programming and NLP New Coding N-Z* NLP University Press

Dilts, R. & Grinder, J. & Bandler, R. & DeLozier, J. (1980) *Neuro-linguistic Programming: Volume I: The Study of the Structure of Subjective Experience* Meta Publications

Dilts, R. & Smith, S. (1999) *Dealing with Double Binds* Genesis II (Video)

Dodd, D. & Favaro, K. (2006) "Managing the right tension" *Harvard Business Review*, Vol.84, No.12, pp62-74

Eisenhardt, K. & Westcott, B. (1988) "Paradoxical Demands and the Creation of Excellence" in Quinn, R.E. & Cameron, K.S. (eds.) *Paradox and Transformation: Towards a Theory of Change in Organization and Management* Balinger.. (pp 169-193)

Evans, V. & Green, M. (2007) *Cognitive Linguistics: An Introduction* Edinburgh University Press

Farson, R. (1996) *Management of The Absurd: Paradoxes in Leadership* Touchstone: New York

Fine, C. (2007) *A Mind of Its Own* Icon Books

Fletcher, J. & Olwyler, K. (1997) *Paradoxical Thinking: How to Profit from Your Contradictions* Berrett-Koehler Publishers: San Francisco

Ford, J. & Backoff, R. (1988) "Organisational Change in and out of Dualities and Paradox" in Quinn, R.E. & Cameron, K.S. (eds.) *Paradox and Transformation: Towards a Theory of Change in Organization and Management* Balinger.. (pp 81-121)

Ford, J.D. & Ford, L.W. (1994) "Logics of identity, contradiction and attraction in change" *Academy of Management Review*, Vol.19, No.4, pp756-785.

Gadamer, H. (1976) *Hegel's Dialectic: Five Hermeneutical Studies* Yale University Press: New Haven & London (Translated by Smith, P.C.)

Gilbert, P. (1993) *Counselling for Depression* Sage

Gillette, J. & McCollom, M (eds) (1995) *Groups in Context: A New Perspective on Group Dynamics* University Press of America

Ghorpade, J. (2000) "Managing five paradoxes of 360-degree feedback" *Academy of Management Executive*, Vol.14, No.1, pp.140-150

Gottman, J.M. (1999) *The Seven Principles for Making Marriage Work* Three Rivers Press

Gottman, J.M. (2007) *Why Marriages Succeed or Fail* Bloomsbury

Hall, L.M. (2001) *NLP: Going Meta* NSP

Hall, L.M. & Bodenhamer, B.G. (2002) *Mind Lines: Lines for Changing Minds* ISNS

Hall, L.M. (2007) *Unleashed!* NSP

Hampden-Turner, C. (1990) *Charting the Corporate Mind: From Dilemma to Strategy* Blackwell

Handy. C. (1994) *The Age of Paradox* Harvard Business School Press (published in the UK as *The Empty Raincoat* Random House)

Harvey, J. (1996) *The Abilene Paradox and Other Meditations on Management* Jossey Bass: Wiley

Harvey, M., Novicevic, M.M., Buckley, M.R. & Halbesleben, J.R.B. (2004) "The Abilene Paradox after thirty years: A global perspective" *Organizational Dynamics*, Vol.33, No.2, pp215-226.

Hatch, M.J. & Ehrlich, S.B. (1993) "Spontaneous humour as an indicator of paradox and ambiguity in organizations" *Organization Studies*, Vol.14, No.4, pp505-526.

Hay, J. (2007) *Reflective Practice and Supervision for Coaches* Open University Press

Hay, J. (2009) *Working It Out At Work 2nd Ed* Sherwood

Hayes, J. (1991) "Expectations regarding the controllability of outcomes in organisations: Implications for management and organisational development" *Journal of Organisational Change Management,* Vol.4, No.2 , pp48-63.

Hofstadter, D. (1980) *Godel, Escher, Bach: An Eternal Golden Braid* Penguin Books: London

Holmes, B. (2011) "Total Reboot" *New Scientist,* no 2805, 26th March

Hopfl, H. (1994) "The paradoxical gravity of planned organisational change" *Journal of Organisational Change Management,* Vol.7, No.5, pp.20-31.

Horn, R.E. (1983) *Trialectics: Toward a Practical Logic of Unity* Information Resources, Inc.: Lexington, MA

Huczynski, A. & Buchanan, D. (2001) *Organisational Behaviour: An Introductory Text 4th ed.* Financial Times: Prentice Hall

Hughes, P. & Brecht, G. (1978) *Vicious Circles and Infinity: An anthology of Paradoxes* Penguin Books: London

Hussey, D. (Ed) (1991) *International Review of Strategic Management,* John Wiley & Sons: NY, Vol. 2 No.1

Ichazo, O. (1982) *Between Metaphysics and Protoanalysis* Arica Institute Press

James, T. & Woodsmall, W. (1988) *Time Line Therapy and The Basis of Personality* Meta Publishing

Janis, I. (1982) *Groupthink* Houghton Mifflin

Jasimuddin, S.M., Klein, J.H. & Connell, C. (2005) "The paradox of using tacit and explicit knowledge: Strategies to face dilemmas" *Management Decision,* Vol.43, No.1, pp.102-112.

Johnson, B. (1996) *Polarity Management: Identifying and Managing Unsolvable Problems* HRD Press Inc: MA

Kahler, T. (1975) "Drivers—The Key to the Process Script" *Transactional Analysis Journal,* 5:3

Kimberly, J.R. & Quinn, R.E. (1984) *Managing Organisational Transitions* Richard D. Irwin Inc.: Illinois

Kinnie, N., Hutchinson, S. & Purcell, J. (2000) "'Fun and surveillance': the paradox of high commitment management in call centres" *International Journal of Human Resource Management,* Vol.11, No.5, pp.967-985.

Koestler, A. (1964) *The Act of Creation* Hutchinson

Koestler, A. (1978) *Janus: A Summing Up* Hutchinson: London

Korzybski (1958) *Science and Sanity* Inst of Semantics

Kosko, B. (1993) *Fuzzy Thinking: The New Science of Fuzzy Logic* Hyperion: New York

Kostere & Malatesta (1990) *Maps, Models and the Structure of Reality: NLP Technology in Psychotherapy* Metamorphous Press

Kotter, J. (1996) *Leading Change* Harvard Business Press

Lakoff, G. & Johnson, M. (1999) *Philosophy in the Flesh* Basic Books

Langer, E. (1989) *Mindfulness* Merloyd Lawrence

Lewis, M. (2000) "Exploring Paradox: Toward a More Comprehensive Guide." *Academy of Management Review* Vol.25, No.4, pp 760-776

Lewis, M. & Dehler, G. (2000) "Learning Through Paradox: A Pedagogical Strategy for Exploring Contradictions and Complexity" *Journal of Management Education*, Vol. 24, No 6, pp 708-725

McKenzie, J. (1996) *Paradox - The Next Strategic Dimension: Using Conflict to Re-energize Your Business* McGraw-Hill

Marsh, S. & Macalpine, M. (1999) "The search for reconciling insights: a 'really useful' tool for managing paradox" *Journal of Management Development*, Vol.1, No.8, pp642-651.

Martin, R. (2007) *The Opposable Mind* Harvard Business School Press

Maslow, A. (1954). *Motivation and Personality*. New York: Harper

Merton, R.K. (1996) *On Social Structure and Science* University of Chicago Press

Milgram, S. (1997). *Obedience to Authority*. Pinter & Martin

Morgan, G. (1998) *Images of Organisation* Berrett-Koehler Publishers: San Francisco

Naisbit, J. (1986) *Global Paradox: The Bigger the World Economy, the More Powerful its Smallest Players* Nicholas Brearley Publishing Ltd

Nalebuff, B.J. & Brandenburger, A.M. (2002). *Co-opetition*. Profile Books

O'Brien (1997) *Positive Management: Assertiveness for managers* Nicholas Brealey Publishing: London

O'Connor, J. & McDermott (1997) *The Art of Systems Thinking* Thorsons

O'Neil, J. (1996) *The Paradox of Success: When Winning at Work Means Losing at Life* McGraw Hill

Pascale, R. T. (1990) *Managing on the Edge: How the smartest companies use conflict to stay ahead* Simon and Schuster

Peter, L.J. & Hull, R. (1969) *The Peter Principle* Publisher Unknown

Peters, T. (1989) *Thriving on Chaos – A Handbook for a Management Revolution* Pan Books

Peters, T (1992) *Liberation Management: Necessary Disorganization for the Nanosecond Nineties* Macmillan: London

Peters, T. & Waterman, R. (1990) *In Search of Excellence: Lessons from America's Best Run Companies* Harper & Row

Poole, M.S. & Van de Ven, A.H. (1989) "Using paradox to build management and organisational theories" *Academy of Management Review*, Vol.14, No.4, pp562-578.

Price Waterhouse (1996) *The Paradox Principles: How High Performance Companies Manage Chaos, Complexity, and Contradiction to Achieve Superior Results* Irwin: Chicago

Quinn, R.E. (1990) *Beyond Rational Management* Jossey-Bass

Quinn, R.E. & Cameron, K.S. (1988) *Paradox and Transformation: Towards a Theory of Change in Organization and Management* Balinger.

Quinn, R.E. & Cameron, K.S. (1988b) "Paradox and Transformation: A Framework for Viewing Organisation and Management" in Quinn, R.E. & Cameron, K.S. (eds.) *Paradox and Transformation: Towards a Theory of Change in Organization and Management* Balinger. (pp 289-308)

Quinn, R.E. & Kimberly, J.R (1984) "Paradox, planning and perseverance: Guidelines for managerial practice" in Kimberly, J.R. & Quinn, R.E. (eds) *Managing Organisational Transitions* Richard D. Irwin Inc.: Illinois

Rabey, G. (2003) "The paradox of teamwork" *Industry and Commercial Training*, Vol.35, No.4, pp.158-162.

Rei, C.M. (2004) "Causal evidence on the 'productivity paradox' and implications for managers" *International Journal of Productivity and Performance Management*, Vol.53, No.2, pp129-142.

Rhodes, C. (2002) "Politics and popular culture – Organisational carnival in the Springfield nuclear power plant" in Clegg, S.R. (ed.) *Management and Organisational Paradoxes* John Benjamins Publishing Company (pp 119-137)

Rowe, D. (1987) "Depression: The way out of your prison" Routledge & Kegan Paul

Russell, B. (1954) *History of Western Philosophy*

Schneider, K.J. (1990) *The Paradoxical Self: Towards an understanding of our contradictory nature* Insight Books

Schwartz, B. (2005) *The Paradox of Choice* Harper Perennial

Seligman, M.E.P. (1998) *Learned Optimism* Free Press

Senge, P. (1993) *The Fifth Discipline* Century Business.

Senior, B. (2002) *Organisational Change* FT: Prentice Hall

Shapiro, L. (2011) *Embodied Cognition (New Problems of Philosophy)* Routledge

Siporin, M. & Gummer, B. (1988) "Lessons from Family Therapy: The Potential of Paradoxical Interventions in Organisations" in Quinn, R.E. & Cameron, K.S. (eds.) *Paradox and Transformation: Towards a Theory of Change in Organization and Management* Balinger. (pp 205-227)

Smith, K.K. (1984) "Rabbits, lynxes, and organisational transitions" in Kimberly, J.R. & Quinn, R.E. (eds) *Managing Organisational Transitions* Richard D. Irwin Inc.: Illinois

Smith, K. & Berg, D. (1987) *Paradoxes of Group Life: Understanding Conflict, Paralysis and Movement in Group Dynamics* Jossey-Bass: San Francisco: London

Stroh, P. & Miller, W.W. (1994) "Learning to thrive on paradox" *Training & Development*, September, pp28-39.

Thite, M. (2001) "Help us but help yourself: the paradox of contemporary career management" *Career Development International*, Vol.6, No.6, pp.312-317.

Thompson, J.L. (1998) "Competence and strategic paradox" *Management Decision*, Vol.36, No.4, pp.274-284.

Van de Ven, A. & Poole, M.S. (1988) "Paradoxical Requirements for a Theory of Organizational Change" in Quinn, R.E. & Cameron,

K.S. (eds.) *Paradox and Transformation: Towards a Theory of Change in Organization and Management* Balinger. (pp 19-63)

Vince, R. & Broussine, M. (1996) "Paradox, defense and attachment: Accessing and working with emotions and relations underlying organizational change" *Organizational Studies* Vol.17, No.1, pp1-21

Voorhees, B.H. (1983) "Trialectics and rational theory construction: A theory of theory" in Horn, R.E. (Ed) *Trialectics: Toward a Practical Logic of Unity* Information Resources, Inc.: Lexington, MA (pp 47-77)

Wagner, J.A. (1978) "The organisational double bind: Toward an understanding of rationality and its complement" *Academy of Management Review*, October, pp786-795.

Walsh, K. (2003) "Understanding and learning from organisational failure" *Qual Saf Health Care* 2003;12:81-82

Warn, J. (2001) "Overcoming learned helplessness" Australian Defence Force Journal, http://www.defence.gov.au/adc/cdclms/Overcoming%20Learned%20Helplessness.doc. (Accessed 05.05.11)

Watzlawick, P. (1993) *The Situation is Hopeless But Not Serious* Norton: New York

Watzlawick, P., Beavin, J.H. & Jackson, D.D. (1967) *Pragmatics of Human Communication: A study of interactional patterns, pathologies and paradoxes* W.W. Norton & Company: New York

Watzlawick, P., Weakland, J. & Fisch, R. (1974) *Change: Principles of problem formation and problem resolution* W.W. Norton & Company: New York

Whitehead, A. & Russell, B. (1970) *Principia Mathematica* Cambridge

Wickisier, E.L. (1997) "The paradox of empowerment – a case study" *Empowerment in Organisations*, Vol.5, No.4, pp.213-219.

About the Author and
The GWiz Learning Partnership

Joe Cheal is a partner in the GWiz Learning Partnership. He has been involved in the field of management and organisational development since 1993. In focusing his training, coaching and consultancy experience within the business environment, he has worked with a broad range of organisational cultures, helping thousands of people revolutionise the way they work with others.

He holds an MSc in Organisational Development and Neuro Linguistic Technologies (his MSc dissertation was an exploration into 'social paradox'), a degree in Philosophy and Psychology and diplomas in Coaching and Psychotherapy.

Joe is an NLP Master Trainer who enjoys learning new things... by exploring diverse fields of science, philosophy and psychology and then integrating these 'learnings'. *Solving Impossible Problems* is based on his MSc research along with nearly 20 years as a consultant. He is the creator and editor of the ANLP Journal: Acuity.

He is a regular speaker at conferences and groups.

He can be contacted at: joe@gwiztraining.com.

The GWiz Learning Partnership

The GWiz Learning Partnership is a consultancy that specialises in inspiring the natural potential of organisations, leadership, management and individuals through OD, L&D and Executive Coaching.

We work with clients from a broad range of sectors and aim to work in partnership with our clients, enhancing the profile of leadership, learning and development in our client's organisation.

Since 1993 we have experience of working with thousands of people from many organisations including:

Aeroflex, Amnesty International, ARA (Aircraft Research Association), Astra Zeneca & AstraTech, Balfour Beatty, Bedford Borough Council, Central Bedfordshire, Beds Health, Beds Magistrates Courts Committee, Bio-Products Laboratories (BPL), Birdlife and Plantlife, British Gas, BT, Calderdale Council, Cambridge City Council, Cambridge University Press, Camelot, Cellnet, Central Bedfordshire, Cranfield University, Dixons Stores Group International, Emmaus Village Carlton, GSK, Herts Magistrates Courts Committee, Hertsmere Borough Council, Inland Revenue, Langley Search & Selection, Lockheed Martin, London Borough of Camden, Luton Borough Council, NewhamCouncil, North Herts District Council, OAG, Olympic Blinds, RSPB, Sainsbury's, Serco, Shepherd Stubbs Recruitment, Staverton Park Conference Centre, The Assessment Network, Tesco, Welwyn Hatfield Borough Council, Willmott Dixon, The Wine Society.

The GWiz Learning Partnership offers a range of consultancy services including:
- Change management, OD and L&D consultancy
- Courses
- Executive coaching and skills coaching
- Facilitation
- Team development
- Myers Briggs profiling and Emotional Intelligence testing
- ILM accredited qualifications
- Qualifications in NLP
- GWizzlers ('bite-size' sessions)

Our courses and topics include:

LEADERSHIP DEVELOPMENT
Change Management
Coaching Performance
Coaching Skills for Managers
The Complete Leader: Inspirational & Practical
Delegate!
Feedback for Effectiveness
Leadership in Action
Making Meetings Work
Management Development Programme
Managing Home-Workers
Managing People Successfully
Mentoring 1: Becoming a Mentor
Mentoring 2: Developing Further Mentor Skills
Motivate!
Project Leadership
The Supportive Manager
Team Building and Development

RESULTS AND RELATIONSHIPS
Advanced Customer Care
Assertiveness: Clarity and Focus
Building Partnerships
Communication
Conflict Resolution
Customer Care
Dealing with Aggression
Dealing with Difficult People
Handling Conflict in Meetings
Influence and Persuasion
Listening Completely
Magic of Mediation
Negotiation Skills
Rapport
Understanding Personalities

IN FRONT OF THE AUDIENCE
Advanced Presentation Skills
The Essential Presenter
Persuasive Presentations
Train the Trainer

PERSONAL IMPACT
Career & Profile Development
Coping with Change
Dealing With Pressure
Innovation: Getting Creative
Lift Off: Personal Development
Making Your Life Work 4U: Confidence
Managing Your Performance
Networking Skills
Personal Power
Self Awareness & Personal Development
Staying Positively Happy
Stress Management
Time Management

EXECUTIVE DEVELOPMENT
Advanced Negotiation Skills
Becoming a Mentor
Beyond Selling
Business Hypnotix
Executive Leadership in Action
Making NLP Work
Managing Tensions
Organisational Development
Organisational Politics
Storytelling in Business
Strategic Change Management
Troubleshooting: Problem Resolution
Working with Transactional Analysis

HR SKILLS FOR MANAGERS
Appraisal
Capability & Disciplinary
Controlling Absence
Dealing with Poor Performance
Introduction to Counselling
Managing Difficult People
Recruitment Selection & Interviewing
Tackling Bullying & Harassment

CPD FOR HR PROFESSIONALS
Building Working Partnerships
Influencing the Organisation
Raising the Profile of HR

293

Next Steps: Training in Neuro-linguistic Programming (NLP)

NLP (Neuro-linguistic Programming) could be described as the psychology of excellence and the science of change. Through understanding more about how the mind/brain works (neuro) and how language affects us (linguistic), a practitioner is able to initiate and sustain change (programming) on a personal, interpersonal and organisational level.

NLP was designed originally to model excellence. By establishing exactly how someone achieves something, excellence can be modelled, taught to someone else and repeated again and again. From this starting point, over the last thirty years, an array of processes, concepts and techniques have been developed to enable you to:

- become more resourceful in managing attitudes, thoughts, emotions, behaviours and beliefs
- relate to others easily and effortlessly,
- understand how language and its use has a direct impact on your state, your brain and your success in communicating with others.

In addition to all this, as a GWiz NLP practitioner, you will learn techniques designed to help you develop your own skills and help others develop theirs. The principles will be introduced conversationally and with activities throughout the course allowing you to learn on many levels consciously and unconsciously.

As NLP Master Trainers we offer the complete three levels of certified NLP courses throughout the year:

- NLP Practitioner
- NLP Master Practitioner
- NLP Trainer

If you are interested in personal and professional development and would like to more about NLP, have a look at our website: www.gwiztraining.com or contact us: info@gwiztraining.com.

Lightning Source UK Ltd.
Milton Keynes UK
UKOW050726280512

193417UK00001B/1/P